Praise for Robe

Life's harshest stings have a way of bringing out the best and the worst in all of us. To share the "best" with the world is one thing. If that's all one shares then the rest of us are tempted to extol a hero, a saint, even a martyr yet always wondering about the "rest of the story."

In Rob's account we come face-to-face with the whole package: the good, the bad, the ugly. That's what makes Rob's story so compelling. For the past several years and during the return of his leukemia, I have been struck by Rob's honesty in the face of great pain, disappointment, hope, and fear.

Pain has a way of stripping off the superficial, easy answers. But what is so striking in this book is that through the anxiety, pressures, and tears, the roots of Rob's faith have sunk deeper into the soil of God's sovereignty and grace. Such discoveries are what Rob lays before us in great vulnerability, transparency, and—yes—with his characteristic humor.

Rob's gut-level honesty is a gift to all readers, but especially to those who are called to care for anyone who faces extreme and prolonged health crises. For the medical team, the family and friends, the spiritual advisors: you will come away after reading this book with more tools to help yet others who seek understanding in the crucible of their suffering.

— *Scott Owsley*
Executive Pastor
Hillside Evangelical Free Church
San Jose, California

"But I Was in Such a Good Mood This Morning!"

TO DONNA —
ITS AN HONOR TO SIGN THIS COPY
OF MY MEMOIR FOR YOU. TAMI &
GORDON ARE DEAR FRIENDS — TWO
OF MY CHEERLEADERS WHEN I WAS
BATTLING CANCER AND A PATIENT
AT THE CITY OF HOPE (CLASS OF '89)
I HOPE YOU FIND THIS READ TO
BE HELPFUL AND ENCOURAGING —
PERHAPS YOU WILL ALSO GET
A LAUGH OR TWO FROM IT.
ALL THE BEST!
ROB

"But I Was in Such a Good Mood This Morning!"

Facing cancer and other harsh
realities in my life

A MEMOIR

Robert Henslin

Post-Traumatic Press

SAN JOSE, CALIFORNIA

Published in the United States by Post Traumatic Press and Createspace, an Amazon.com company. First Edition.

Book cover and interior design by Robert Henslin

ISBN 978-0-615-55649-9 (pbk.)

Printed in the United States of America.

"But I Was in Such a Good Mood This Morning!" is available at:

https://www.createspace.com/3702885
http://www.amazon.com

Dedication

To Lauren and Kristen, for being the best daughters a
dad could ever wish for. You are miracles, and I thank God
for both of you every day.

Thank You

To Michele, for February 11, 1989, and the twenty-two
years and one month that followed.

Contents

Preface

On February 11th, 1989 I had the honor of marrying Michele, my best friend and the woman I believed was my perfect match. Seven months later, our world was rocked by three words:

Acute Lymphoblastic Leukemia.

Following several years of living with cancer in what felt like constant tumult, our life returned to something more closely resembling "normal." Nearly two decades passed cancer free. In that span of time we laughed and smiled and enjoyed good times, but we also wrestled with doubts, fears, and each other.

Along this path we were confronted with seemingly hopeless circumstances. At the same time, we experienced God's faithfulness and love, his grace and forgiveness, his presence in the midst of trials, and his miracles.

My odyssey began in 1989. It is by no means a completed journey.

Rather, it is an ongoing, daily exercise of seeking to die to self and choosing to live joyfully in spite of circumstances.

My memoir is not neat and clean. There are no ribbons tied around it at the end, and no beautiful bow on top of the box. It is merely an attempt to present a snapshot of experiences along what has been and continues to be a most challenging life path.

For those of you facing cancer or other life challenges and for those who love and care for you, it is my hope that within these pages, you find connection, empathy, encouragement, information, and even a laugh and smile or two that you can take with you and draw upon to find strength as you walk your path.

Rob
September 2011

Acknowledgements

It is only because of the encouragement, friendship, love and support of the following people that this memoir became a reality. It's been said that one should never hike alone. As I ventured out on this hike, this first foray into creative writing and a memoir, the following amazing people helped me in my journey. They saw me through the good times and bad.

Their encouragement was rooted in the steps they took with me, as we walked and sometimes climbed together. In some cases, our hikes were long and date back nearly thirty years. For others, our walk was brief, but our time together drew us close. Where years did not bind us together, what we experienced did.

I am thankful to you all, beyond what I will ever be able to fully express. This work is not my work. It is *our* work, and my hope is that our work will reach others and make a difference in their lives.

Thank you:

Mom – for banging on the gates of Heaven and expecting an answer.

Gordon – for thirty-plus years of friendship and still going strong. Hey man, you okay?

Forrest – for your friendship, teaching, and example at a critical time in my life.

Dr. Steve – for your quiet confidence and for giving me some straight answers.

Dr. Nade – for always taking time to visit and have some laughs.

Dr. Robert F. – for teaching me five simple words.

Dr. Robert N. – for your confidence and positive attitude.

RN Farrah – for your jokes and your smile on one of the hardest days of my life.

RN Anne (who always wore pearls) – for the compassion and smile I clung to for forty-eight days.

George – for all the laps you took with me and our great conversations.

Dr. Wes – for your time and your friendship. You're a jewel! Time to rearrange that living room!

Tracy – for your kindness, friendship, positive spirit, and marketing voodoo!

Dave – for always showing me the upside.

Dawna – for your vulnerability and our wonderful conversations.

Lou – for knowing me really well for a long time, and in spite of that, still calling me your brother from another mother. Love you man.

Penny – for opening your home and your heart and for being a great wife to that guy you live with.

Bethany – You had first eyes on. Thank you for pumping me up!

Roberta – for your friendship and love. We hike our long trail together.

Janice – for our wonderful late night (or was it early morning?) instant messages. You're a good friend, Mrs. Wiggins.

Peggy – for many years of friendship, and we still have never met face to face! The cap is helping my drive but not yet my putts.

Rich – for taking time to skim but then diving in. You were right. I've been bitten, and there's no stopping now. Thank you for your kind and inspiring words.

Michael – for your selflessness, and the incredible gift of life you gave me.

"Trials, temptations, disappointments-all these are helps instead of hindrances, if one uses them rightly. They not only test the fiber of character but strengthen it. Every conquering of temptation represents a new fund of moral energy. Every trial endured and weathered in the right spirit makes a soul nobler and stronger than it was before."

—James Buckham

Home Sweet Home

We were led through a seemingly endless maze of institutional-green corridors. The staff greeted us with smiles as my wife Michele and I approached the nurse's station on Wing Six. The clerk from the hospitals' admissions department ended our journey at a reception counter of sorts, where several nurses were engaged in conversation.

I'm sure I had a "deer in the headlights" look on my face. I had just come from a hospital. Now I was deep in the bowels of a cancer treatment center. I couldn't hide. Those folks had my number. I was a cancer patient.

The Admitting clerk introduced us and wished us well as she turned to leave.

Yes, you have a nice day as well. I thought.

One nurse emerged from behind a desk.

"Hi Mr. Henslin. Let's get you settled in."

"Settled in." Was that even possible?

She led us almost to the end of the unit, passing several closed doors on each side of the hallway, until she came to one door and stopped. *What was going on behind all those other doors,* I wondered.

Most likely, a whole lot things I didn't want to know about, and sights I could probably go a lifetime without seeing. The nurse pulled on the brushed aluminum handle and held the door open.

"Here we are," she said, as if welcoming us to our suite at some luxury resort. I wished that were the case. Her cheerfulness made me mad. *Don't be so darn happy I'm here! I don't want to be here. I'm not supposed to be here.*

We entered a small but comfortable-looking room. It was clean and bright, bathed in a blue white glow from the overhead fluorescent light panel. The air smelled fresh—too fresh—like our arrival was fast on the heels of someone who had scrubbed that room up one side and down the other.

Who had been here before me, I wondered. *What happened to them after they were "settled in"?*

A light brown, three-drawer dresser flanked the left side of the bed. A padded vinyl chair sat near the corner of the room. Two large windows converged in that corner, and offered a view of an expansive lawn, and a flower garden that ran the length of the unit.

The nurse left us alone to settle in. "I'll be back in a few minutes with some supplies for you, and we'll need to get some blood drawn as well."

Yes, I suppose "we" will need to do that.

When the door closed behind her, Michele and I couldn't hear a sound. It felt like we had been placed in an isolation chamber; our apprehension was visible to one another.

A small bathroom and shower was just off the main room. Tall banks of brown storage cabinets lined the wall by the room's entry door. I set my Duffel bag on the chair next to the bed. Michele leaned against the wall by the bathroom door. We stared at each other.

The quiet of the moment offered no solace. We both knew we were in for the ride of our lives. Michele fixed her gaze on me from across the room.

"Well, okay, here we are," she said nervously.

That room would be my home sweet home for the duration of my inpatient stay at the City of Hope. I had no idea how long my stay would be, or if I would even walk out of the place alive when they had finished with me.

I hoped with everything in me I would be out of there quickly without too many scars.

2

My Best Friend, And the Best Wife a Guy Could Ask For

Michele and I had only been married for six months before I showed the first signs of having a serious illness. I'd met Michele in the fall of 1982, at Azusa Pacific University. It was a small Christian liberal arts university nestled against the foothills of the San Gabriel Mountains in Azusa, California.

I transferred there after two years at Pasadena City College to pursue a Religion major, and Michele was a freshman in the School of Nursing. Our particular programs were such that it was like being swallowed up by a black hole. We enrolled, moved into our campus housing, and didn't see each other again.

Neither one of us really "existed" on a day-to-day basis. We were essentially holed up in our rooms for the vast majority of the time, writing, researching and otherwise trying to stay ahead of the curve, or working off campus to log required lab hours.

Occasionally you could catch a glimpse of Michele running to class in the early morning hours with a spoonful of peanut butter in her mouth. I could frequently be seen exiting the library at closing time with an overwhelmed look on my face and a trail of Greek flash cards in my wake.

A few years later we emerged from the black hole of our studies wearing caps and gowns, not exactly sure what had transpired or how long we had been gone from the "real" world.

Though our studies did suck us into that black hole of near non-existence, Michele and I became good friends, and we had some fun over the years at Azusa Pacific. She set me up with her roommate on "Get Your Roommate a Date" night.

We made midnight road trips to Foster's doughnuts with eighteen other friends crammed into my 1970 Ford Econoline 200 van. It sported a thick shag rug, orange vinyl-padded bench seat and an eight-track and cassette-tape player in the dash. Good times.

It wasn't until we had both graduated that we reconnected, and our friendship grew into something very special.

My roommate, Dalton, and I frequented a Denny's restaurant a few miles from our apartment. He was an undergrad at Azusa Pacific. I was in the first year of my graduate program.

Motivated in part by a fear we would both fall asleep at our desks if we tried to study at our apartment, we spent late evenings at Denny's, typically a few nights each week. It broke up the routine and got us out of our four walls.

We slammed down coffee and studied long into the night. We always had a good time, but for the most part had our heads in the books, highlighting and taking notes like two crazy men.

There were usually other study groups from Azusa Pacific and the local community college scattered throughout the restaurant as well.

On one such night in the fall of 1986, Michele and her roommate, Sandi, a former classmate from nursing school, came in for some pie. They sat down in the booth right next to ours. I didn't see them come in. I hadn't seen Michele since graduating from Azusa Pacific a year prior. Within just a few moments, I recognized her laugh.

I thought, *That's Michele. Oh my gosh.* I was startled and pleasantly surprised. I turned around in our booth and leaned over into theirs. "Hey, can you gals keep it down? We're trying to get some work done." Michele was caught off guard and really surprised.

The conversation came easily as we spent time catching up with one another. We filled our corner of the restaurant with laughter that night.

I've often marveled at the circumstances that brought us together. It was only because the Carrow's restaurant in Azusa had locked up their pie cabinet in compliance with a local alcohol ordinance. It was not just the drinks that stopped flowing at 10:00 p.m. at Carrow's, but any dessert items containing alcohol as well. Last call for pie!

So the gals decided to head to the Denny's in Glendora, just across the city line, and we were brought back together again.

By early 1987, we were dating and really hit it off. I knew within two weeks I was falling for her in a big way. I felt totally comfortable when I was with her. Our conversation and laughter always came easily.

There were many nights where I returned home after spending the evening with Michele and entered my apartment with my head spinning as I realized my life was changing.

I had not been looking for a relationship, but one blossomed out of nowhere with her. I found it difficult to concentrate on my studies. My thoughts often wandered to Michele and our deepening relationship.

I looked forward to our talks and spending time with her. After dating for nearly two years, I was deeply in love with her. Using diamonds that belonged to my grandmothers, I designed an engagement ring for Michele and had a local jeweler create it.

On August 6, 1988, Michele and I were out for the evening. After dinner, we drove to the La Canada Country Club, and parked the car so we had a breathtaking view of the lights of the Los Angeles Basin.

We talked about life and our relationship and where we were heading as a couple. I had carried the ring with me for a couple weeks, waiting for the right time to propose.

That moment felt like the perfect moment. I handed the small jewelry box to Michele. I told her I loved her very much, and I asked her to be my wife. With a smile extending from ear to ear, she accepted and made me the happiest guy on the planet.

We met with Pastor Steve on several occasions for pre-marital counseling. Our times together were always filled with straight talk about the joys and challenges of marriage and lots of laughs as well.

On our wedding day, just before he led us in the exchange of our vows, Pastor Steve looked at Michele with a big smile.

"I don't know if you realize it Michele, but you are the perfect match for this guy."

My family members and many of my friends had told me the same thing in private conversations, but it resonated more deeply with me when Pastor Steve proclaimed it from the front of the church. I was beaming and felt so honored Michele wanted to be my wife.

We looked at each other with big grins on our faces. Our family members and friends enjoyed a good laugh when Steve made his remark. He was right. We were a good fit. She was my best friend, and the best wife a guy could ever ask for.

She was amazing. I was blessed.

We honeymooned in Yosemite National Park in the heart of California's Sierra Nevada mountain range. It was the middle of winter, and there wasn't much of a crowd. We felt like we had the run of the place.

Yosemite in winter was one of the most beautiful places on the planet. Granite walls rose thousands of feet straight up from the valley floor, bathed in bright, golden sunlight, and capped with a thick crust of snow. Towering evergreens, dusted with snow, populated the valley floor like a vast army keeping watch over sacred ground.

A drive through the valley was a ballet of light and shade. Filtered shafts of sunlight danced with rock, earth, and water. The soft, flowing sounds of the icy Merced River provided an audible reminder that the valley floor was alive with life underneath its crisp, blue-white blanket.

We spent several days hiking, cross-country skiing, and enjoying the unique silence created by the blanket of fresh snow. There were times when we never saw anyone else on the trails and only heard the sounds of the river or the nearly frozen flow of a distant waterfall.

When we returned home, we settled into our apartment in Azusa and began our new life together. We enjoyed lots of evenings out, Saturday road trips, movie nights, and just hanging out. We were plugged-in at a local church. Michele worked in oncology at a local hospital. I put my graduate studies on hold and worked for Focus on the Family, a local non-profit organization.

Life was good. We laughed, a lot.

3

A Little Vacation

Several months down the road, we took a mini-vacation to Vancouver and Victoria in British Columbia. We met up with my brother who lived in Seattle, Washington at the time. From there, the three of us rode a hydrofoil to Victoria, and we connected with some friends of mine who had made plans to meet us there.

The five of us took in the sites for a couple days; the old world architecture, the many fine restaurants and shops, and Butchart Gardens, a lush, fifty-five acre estate virtually covered in floral displays of all varieties—a photographer's paradise. The sights and smells were intoxicating. We soaked up the late summer sunshine and blue skies like it was the first time we had seen such beauty.

Later in the week, Michele and I had a couple days to tour Vancouver on our own. One of my favorite memories from that part of the trip was watching the city lights shimmer across the water of the Burrard Inlet. We enjoyed the view over an incredible salmon dinner at Forester's in the Gastown district.

Low light, linen on the table, fresh bread, warm smiles, and good conversation. Perfect. It was a wonderful night. A day later we headed home feeling refreshed with a camera full of memories.

We could never have imagined at the time that cancer was wreaking havoc on my body. It would only be a matter of weeks until the beast would begin to reveal itself.

To this day, twenty years since my original diagnosis, it's painful to look at photos from that trip. I doubt I could ever visit Vancouver or Victoria again without a lump in my throat, feeling a profound sense of loss and sadness over what might have been; what should have been.

What I thought was to be the plan for our life together was not to be.

4

Uh Oh…

I developed a chest cold shortly after our return home from Washington. It got bad enough I contacted my primary care physician, Dr. Joe. He was a good man—a young doctor, building his practice. He was upbeat and enthusiastic about medicine and people, and confident in his abilities. I had every confidence in him, too.

He diagnosed my condition as Pleurisy, an inflammation of the lining of the pleural cavity surrounding the lungs. A course of antibiotics was prescribed, but they were ineffective; whatever had sunk its' claws into me wasn't letting go.

In light of red flags he saw in my blood labs, Dr. Joe referred me to Dr. Myron, a very sharp liver specialist at Huntington Hospital in Pasadena. Dr. Joe kept tabs on my case and watched in dismay as my physical condition worsened, and the plot thickened.

I felt like I had a lingering, awful case of bronchitis. I was away from work, serving on a jury in a Superior court case. My illness got so bad I was excused from jury service—and I really did want to serve.

My absence from work because of civic duties turned into a medical leave. Blood was drawn each week for analysis. My wake-sleep cycle inverted. I was up all night, unable to sleep, and wiped out during the day. My bones ached.

When I could sleep at night, I experienced "night sweats" that soaked my tee shirts and required several changes. *What kind of strange world was I spiraling into?*

My appetite was practically non-existent, which historically had never been a problem. I felt more exhausted with the passing of each day. Michele and I began to flip out, as the signs and symptoms indicated something much more serious than a chest cold. It was way beyond anything I could have fabricated to dodge public service as a juror.

5

The Neon Banana

I knew I was in real trouble the morning I woke up with bright yellow skin, from stem to stern. It pretty much happened overnight and was very unsettling. I remember waking up early in the morning when the first rays of sunlight filtered through our drapes.

There was enough light in the room that I could see the strange color of my hands and arms.

I bolted for the bathroom. When I looked in the mirror, my skin was bright yellow as were the whites of my eyes. I looked like a visitor from a distant galaxy.

Michele took a photo of me in that condition that I hope we've lost. Whatever my problem, it had infiltrated my liver and caused severe Jaundice, a yellowish discoloration of the whites of the eyes, skin, and mucous membranes, caused by the accumulation of bile salts.

Just great. Bile salts. What's happening to me?

Over the years, I've learned a lot about my liver and jaundice, and all sorts of other things I could have gone a lifetime without knowing.

Jaundice ranged from a slight yellow tinge on the low end of the spectrum to an intense yellow at the other end (read: neon banana). When it was that bad, it meant the liver essentially called its own "Code Blue."

The jaundice was very intense, covered every inch of my body, scared small children, and allowed me to function as a human glow stick when the lights were out. On a "1 to 10" scale, my jaundice was a "12." Michele had never seen jaundice so intense. I was a neon banana.

On October 6, 1989, after nearly two months of testing, poking, labs, X-rays, and other forms of invasive analysis, I received the call from Dr. Myron I had been dreading. "Something is killing your blood Robert," he said. I will never forget those words. Panic washed over me when I heard them.

I stood alone in my apartment and gripped the phone tightly as the doctor rattled off the latest lab values, and commented about the downward-spiraling trend he had tracked over the previous several weeks.

"I want to admit you to the hospital as soon as possible—today. I'm very concerned, Robert. I think you have some type of blood disorder. We will need to do more testing to determine exactly what is going on."

I don't remember much about our conversation, except that my responses to him were scattered. We hung up after a few moments.

I stood in the middle of my living room, frozen. My eyes traced patterns on our beige carpeting. I heard the little girl who lived in the apartment next door crying, and her Mom, with her fiery red hair and short fuse snapping at her to stop whining and go to her room.

It was at that moment, with my neighbor yelling, and faint bubbling sounds coming the aquarium that sat on a counter in our hallway that I was hit with the full impact of what was happening to me.

Up to that point, I had gone about the business of doctor visits, examinations, medications—all of it—without thinking too much about what was at stake.

But I was just twenty-six years old. My life, my career, and my new marriage were just taking flight. I couldn't believe it might all come to an end. I was too young for this to be happening to me.

After a few moments, I called Michele to break the news to her. It was one of the hardest phone calls I've ever had to make.

I think she knew such a call was imminent.

I was broken up before the third ring. When Michele answered, I could hardly get a word out of my mouth. There were several moments of searching silence. We cried. I heard her heave a few quiet sighs.

Images of our wedding, honeymoon, and our brief vacation ran through my head. I wondered if that was it.

How many more memories would we make in the future?

How bad were things going to get?

We just got married, I thought. *This is not what's supposed to happen— not to us.*

When I hung up the phone, I wanted to throw it across the room. I wanted to curl up into a ball on the floor; anything but calmly, rationally process the news I had just received.

Something is killing your blood, Robert. *Oh, okay. I guess I'll make a sandwich and watch TV.*

6

And So, It Begins…

I spent a week at Huntington Hospital, where I had been born twenty-six years earlier. Lots of visitors streamed through my room that week, including Dr. Joe. When he came to see me, he was really down. He sat at the foot of my bed and stared out the window at the Pasadena nightscape.

"I can't believe this is happening to you," he said. Doc shook his head back and forth in disbelief as he stared down at the linoleum floor. He continued. "I wish I could do something for you Rob. This is so frustrating."

I hadn't ever seen that side of a doctor—the frustrated human being behind the white coat. It was good to have Dr. Joe hang out with me that evening. We talked for a long time about the way things were and what loomed on the horizon.

Even in the midst of his frustration over not having caught my problem early on, Dr. Joe was a real source of encouragement. I will always remember his taking time to be with me.

7

The Necessary Evil

Perhaps it is just the way my warped brain works, I'm really not sure. But in my experience, it seemed every good thing, every amazing blessing, every pleasure in life more often than not came with strings attached. There was always some kind of necessary evil that was part of the package.

That seemed to be even more the case in the medical realm. A highly effective therapy was available to treat problem X, but it grew fur on your tongue, turned your skin into tree bark, and caused insatiable cravings for bacon-flavored ice cream.

The Bone Marrow Aspiration and Biopsy or "BMA" was one of those good things with a downside. It was instrumental in the diagnosis and treatment of leukemias, lymphomas, and other conditions as well. It afforded my doctors a unique look at the functioning of the blood "factory" deep inside the larger bones of my body. That was the wonderful part.

Wouldn't it be cool if that were the end of the story? Of course, it's not.

The downside to the BMA, the "string" attached to it, was that it was one of the strangest, most awkward of procedures. Depending on many factors, including who was performing it, how I was positioned on the treatment table, and perhaps even the phase of the Moon at the time, it could be incredibly painful. There was no way to get around it with anesthesia—or bribes.

There was "Yin and Yang," and then there was "Yin and *Youch!*

Are You *Kidding* Me?" The BMA procedure pretty much embodied the latter. The first time it was performed, it took everything in me to keep from coming out of my skin.

Bone marrow produced several blood products essential for normal functioning. Red cells carried oxygen, and they helped expel carbon dioxide and toxins upon exhalation. White cells were essential for a strong immune system to keep the body resistant to infection. Platelets helped blood to clot so one didn't "bleed out."

The BMA extracted samples of the bone marrow so the quality and quantity of each of those blood products could be analyzed. It was a necessary evil. In my case, it was performed quite frequently.

Like Root Canal's more evil twin brother, it was nasty. Like many medical procedures, it involved a needle and assurances from the doctor everything would be just fine.

Cool. Keep telling me that, because right now I'm not buying it.

The preferred site locations were the hip or the section of bone located just above the buttocks. A doctor at Huntington Hospital (Dr. Funkendoodle or Dr. Frankenstein or something like that) first introduced me to the procedure during my weeklong stay.

He used the words "needle" and "bone" in the same sentence. I thought, *That can't be good.* When doc performed the first BMA, I quickly realized two important truths.

First, he did not have "the touch." Second, "the touch" played a critical role in my having a good day or not. He was quite an arrogant chap with whom I struggled to connect.

Like the legend of Bigfoot, I had heard of the existence of such doctors but had never personally encountered one. When I did, it was just my dumb luck he had a big needle stuck into me like a thermometer on a pork roast. Dr. Frankenstein is the only doctor with whom I never hit it off. There was no exchange of Christmas cards between us.

He was all business. I suppose under the circumstances that was probably a good thing. A carload of circus clowns at that time would not have been much help.

I was on my stomach, staring at the pale white wall behind my bed, unable to see what was happening. Dr. Frankenstein didn't say much, which heightened the tension.

The area to be probed was scrubbed clean, and sterile paper drapes were placed around the site, revealing only a small portion of my lower back. Overhead panels and a fluorescent fixture above the head of my bed brightly lighted the room. The air was filled with the smell of Betadine, an iodine-based topical antiseptic. It was brownish in color and cold against the skin, with a distinct "metallic medical" smell.

I always knew something bad was about to happen when I smelled Betadine.

There was a pinprick as numbing medication, and I'm almost positive shards of broken glass were injected into my lower back. I winced a little. A second pinprick after just a moment injected more medicine down to the bone.

Those initial steps were tolerable; essentially they were a couple of shots into fat and muscle, followed by a warm, slightly burning sensation as the medicine saturated the tissue.

Okay, this isn't so bad. I can do this.

I didn't feel the insertion of the needle until it was forced into the bone. "Force" is a word I hate to associate with medical procedures. It's a word better suited to describe military strength, gravity, or a great evening out (we were forced to order dessert, because it was included in the price of the meal).

The local anesthetic numbed that tissue, and I felt no discomfort up to that point. But when doc hit the bone, the needle was forced through the outer layers to reach the chewy center. That step is where I had the toughest time.

"Where did these come from?"

"Oh, those. Those are your eyeballs. You should be able to put them back in when we're done."

"Oh, okay. I guess I'll just cradle them here on this pillow for now."

The needle punctured the marrow space, which is essentially a closed system, a vacuum if you will. Dr. Frankenstein, still not saying much, drew back on the syringe attached to the needle, and aspirated several CCs of the thick blood from inside the bone.

Jeez doc! Do you have some pent up anger we should discuss?

It was an intense, dark pain that caused me to wonder if my eyeballs might be sucked right back into my skull. Any thoughts of maintaining a calm, cool, and collected demeanor at that point were gone.

How much cash do I need to come up with to end this? I thought. *Everyone has his price.*

The second part of the procedure was to biopsy the spongy bone marrow. After I recoiled from the pain of the aspiration, I reinserted my eyeballs back into my face, and Dr. Frankenstein began his quest for the core sample.

There was repeated downward pressure on my back as he pushed a different instrument in to (try) to extract a portion of bone. But he wasn't able to get one—not the first, second or third time he tried. And each time he went in for the kill, his manipulations sent "electric" shooters down my leg.

Did I mention Dr. Frankenstein lacked the touch?

Very quickly I was at my wit's end. It was a surprisingly short trip.

Without any cash on hand, I told doc he had one more shot to nail it, and then we would need to conclude our special time together.

Michele, who had stayed in the room to watch the procedure and lend moral support, finally had to leave when the doctor couldn't hit pay dirt after three tries.

I cannot recall if he was able to get the sample or not, but at some point he finished and left my room. I rolled over with a big bandage on my back side and decompressed for a while. I wondered how many more of those procedures I would have to endure.

When a friend of mine asked what the BMA felt like, I tried to think of the most fitting description. What came to mind harkens back to my childhood, and a vacuum cleaner that saw a lot of action in our house over the years.

My Dad called it "Sputnik," I suppose because its' round, ball-like shape resembled the famous Russian satellite. It was eighteen inches in diameter, "putty" colored with a bright red "Hoover" brand logo emblazoned across its face.

It was built to withstand a nuclear holocaust, sat very low to the ground on small rubber feet, and weighed as much as our car. A large hose was connected to the top of the round canister. When that sucker was turned on, Lord help you if you weren't ready. It could suck you back in time, but your rugs and floors would be left absolutely spotless.

The sensation of the bone marrow aspiration was like the feeling of placing my hand over the end of that powerful vacuum cleaner hose and then trying to pull it away. When I was a little kid, pulling it away did not always come easily.

We never had to call the paramedics. I never went back in time, but on a couple occasions, I had to enlist help to shut the machine off, so I could focus my energies on wrestling my fingers back from the mouth of the beast.

When I had my hand over the end of the hose, the suction increased, and the vacuum's motor wound up like it was about to explode. When I pulled my hand away, the pressure subsided. That's what the aspiration felt like, except it took place in my low back, with Frankenstein breathing down my neck.

As the procedure was performed many times over the years, I found a spot on the wall on which to focus and "burn a hole" with my eyes to ride out the pain.

Thinking happy thoughts didn't cut it.

On numerous occasions, the doctors who performed the BMA told me I had a very high pain tolerance. I guess that is a good thing. I had heard stories of patients who had to be completely sedated as the small amount of numbing medication was ineffective. If I focused on a spot on the wall, I could ride out the pain without screaming.

To date, I've had something on the order of sixty BMAs performed. They were much easier to deal with when I knew "what was coming next." Surprises, when someone had a needle stuck in my back, were very undesirable.

8

Welcome to the City of Hope

A fter more testing, lab work, X-rays and ultrasounds, I was transferred from Huntington Hospital to the City of Hope National Medical Center in Duarte, California. It was just a ten-minute drive from our apartment in Azusa.

I was discharged from Huntington on a sunny, weekday morning. The commuter traffic that always put the freeway into gridlock had passed. Michele and I took a quiet, pensive, and rather quick drive to the place I would call home for at least several weeks.

In our relationship, we were always comfortable with silence. It was never an awkward thing to just enjoy each other's company. But on that occasion, things were different. We could have cut the tense silence with a knife.

After the brief trip down the freeway, we exited in the city of Duarte, and made our way just a few blocks to the hospital's main entrance. Lush rose gardens and open patio spaces lined the main road leading to the patient drop-off area and parking lots.

Groups of employees were taking their morning break. Many were smoking. In my mind, that seemed akin to an accused man trashing the judge's car on his way into court.

I was struck by the irony of the scene, and wondered how many of those employees, when their break was over, would return to their work with patients suffering from lung cancer, and other smoking-related diseases. It was quite a stark introduction to the place. It seems we do have the freedom to make choices in this life, good and bad.

I am a graphic designer by trade. I enjoy and appreciate the arts—drawing, painting, sculpture, and photography. Outside City of Hope's main entrance, visitors were greeted by a large fountain and tall bronze sculpture of a man and woman holding a child high into the air.

Having lived in southern California all my life, I was familiar with City of Hope, and had seen their logo, based on that bronze sculpture many times in print ads and other media. For whatever reason, as Michele and I walked past it on our way to the main entrance, the hope of a vibrant life it portrayed really struck me.

For the first time in my life I experienced any type of emotional connection with a work of art. The water flowing from the fountain beneath the statue sounded like it came from a lush, garden oasis, where things lived and thrived; a good headspace to get into. Over the weeks that followed, I spent a lot of time outside, sitting by that fountain, drinking in the sights and sounds.

I desperately wanted that vibrant life.

Once I was allowed some time to "settle in" as the nurse had suggested, more extensive lab tests were performed. After enduring an emotional roller coaster of multiple errant diagnoses over the previous two months, including Pleurisy, Hepatitis A, Mononucleosis with Hepatitis, Epstein-Barr, Aplastic Anemia and Lymphoma, I learned what my problem was: Acute Lymphoblastic Leukemia (A.L.L.).

It was a disease of the white blood cells, where malignant, immature cells overproduced within the bone marrow. That type of leukemia typically struck young children but also a small percentage of adults as well.

9

Wrestling with God

It was my first night on the unit. The phone rang. "You're supposed to be here." I could hear the sadness in Michele's voice. She called from the apartment after the short drive home from the hospital. We both struggled for a few minutes to get a handle on things. Long moments of silence burned over the phone line. I was desperate to fix the problem and make the pain go away.

When I hung up the phone, I rolled over in my bed, and stared at a photo of the two of us in Vancouver I taped to the side of the dresser. I just stared at it for a while and thought about all the fun we had on that trip. I thought about how much I loved Michele. I felt helpless.

I didn't want to die.

Though she moved 400 miles south to pursue her nursing degree at Azusa Pacific, Michele's heart and her family, and most of her closest friends were up north in the San Francisco Bay Area. It was extremely tough on her not to have that support system nearby as my illness worsened.

She felt isolated and cut-off, and at times very much alone. The thought of Michele alone at home with her thoughts, frustrated, separated from her family, and contemplating an uncertain future tore me up.

Our world had been turned upside down. In seven months we went from being newlyweds with all the hope in the world for a bright future to a young couple wondering how much more time we would have together. We knew the experience had already changed us as individuals.

There wasn't a darn thing I could do about it.

It was at that moment, as I stared at the photo, for the first time in my life the reality of my faith was tested.

Seventeen years as a Christian—the growth, knowledge, service, study, and what I thought was belief—went right into the trashcan like spoiled leftovers.

Was my faith real or not?

What I had to do at that moment, like the character "Job" in the Old Testament, was stand in the ashes of what I had known, and what had been familiar, and choose to believe—or not—that God was indeed who he said he was, in spite of my circumstances. But I questioned myself, and God.

Though my situation was dire, did God have me in his grip?

Would he allow a burden on me greater than I could handle?

Would he really give me the strength to persevere if I trusted him?

I didn't know what the future held. *Did I really believe God held the future in his hands?*

Would He provide "the peace that passes all understanding" in the midst of the struggle as his word promised? I chose to believe. But that night was a spiritual wrestling match that made Olympic competition look like child's play.

10

Crash Landing

As if my coping skills hadn't been stretched enough at that point, on the first night of my inpatient stay at City of Hope, I was introduced to the world of blood transfusions—and blood reactions.

I was running out of red blood cells and platelets, and kind of falling apart at the seams, much like the scarecrow in *The Wizard of Oz*, after the flying monkeys had finished with him. I'll never forget the image of the poor scarecrow in that classic movie, his limbs torn from his body, and his hay stuffing strewn about the clearing in the middle of that dark forest. The monkeys did a number on him. I felt the same.

I was given a transfusion around 1:00 a.m. About halfway through the drip, I had tunnel vision, ringing in my ears, and dizziness. I knew I was going south, but I had no idea why. I hit the bedside "panic button" as I watched my hands, arms, and legs swell up almost instantly, which the nurses referred to as "Elephant Skin."

Is that a medical term?

The ringing in my ears worsened, and the tunnel vision got pretty extreme. It was like looking down a long, dark pipe. The nurse gave me a shot of Benadryl. Within a half hour, I was feeling a little better. The elephant skin went away just as fast as it came on. Weirdest thing I had ever seen.

The tunnel vision resolved itself as did the ringing in my ears. I did get a little sick and was light-headed, but I was relieved things hadn't gotten any more out of control. When the scene calmed down a bit, a nurse asked me to use the bathroom to provide a "specimen" for laboratory analysis. She motioned toward the bathroom door, without offering to help me complete that mission and stay in bed in such a weakened condition.

You know what's coming.

I followed her orders—like a dope—and made my way across the room. I stood up slowly and pushed my IV pole around the foot of the bed, into the bathroom.

After fulfilling her request I took a few moments to ponder my current state of affairs, posed like Rodan's "Thinker." I stood up, washed my hands, took a couple steps out of the bathroom, and promptly passed out.

I was 270 pounds of dead weight, and all of it headed for a crash landing. I was a big guy. For most of my life I'd shopped at big and tall stores, from fifth or sixth grade on.

Growing up in southern California, I shopped for clothes in downtown Los Angeles, where a lot of the local professional athletes shopped. I frequently found myself picking through racks of shirts and pants with players from the NFL's Los Angeles Rams. Those guys were big and buff. I was just big.

I woke up a few seconds later after I slammed into the wall on the other side of the room. Good morning everyone!

There was no time to drop the landing gear.

Needless to say, it was not the first impression I wanted to leave with folks on my first night on the unit.

When I crashed into the wall—and a chair and some kind of small table on the way down as I recall—I bent the huge needle stuck in my arm, tore out my IV line, and scared my neighbors half to death.

A "crash team" arrived at my door within a few seconds. They were wild-eyed and had the "zapper paddles" in hand, thinking I had collapsed from a heart attack.

When Michele heard the story she was livid and wanted to pummel the nurse who forced me out of bed. I don't know why I reacted to that transfusion, but I was relieved nothing more came of it than the rude awakening I gave my neighbors.

The next day I was the joke—or at least the talk—of Wing Six. Sue, one of my nurses and a good friend and former classmate of Michele's from the nursing program at Azusa Pacific, gave me a hard time.

"Hey Crash, heard you had a rough first night!"

"Yeah, laugh it up Sue."

That night is still a fond memory of sorts. I'm happy it's a single memory of a one-time event. I learned an important lesson that night. When you are light-headed, and someone asks you to get out of bed and walk to the restroom, refuse, and request the bedside collection option instead. That plastic bottle will save you a world of hurt, and no one will get pummeled.

11

Buddy Holly and Burning Flesh

Though twenty years have passed, I still have vivid memories from the first time I was treated for Leukemia, some difficult to deal with, but many of them are still hilarious in my mind. Recalling the events surrounding the insertion of my central line still gives me a chuckle.

A surgical procedure was required to insert a Hickman central line catheter, affectionately named after its inventor, Dr. Hickman. The catheter would be inserted into a large vein near my heart, and the toxic chemotherapy would be infused quickly through it and into my body to reduce the potential for tissue damage and other complications. *Swell.*

The surgeon who would perform the operation dropped by my room the night before my date with destiny. When he first walked in, he looked like he hadn't slept in weeks. Turns out it was just the shape of his eyelids, but it freaked me out. I had visions of the guy slumped over me snoring in the middle of my surgery.

The next morning I was moved to a pre-surgery prep area. A nurse shaved my chest with an old paint scraper. Her work seemed far more extensive, in my humble opinion, than I thought was required to create a clear surgical field. *Let's just go for the full body wax. How big a slice is doc going to make,* I thought. *We're not going to remove a lung.*

After a few minutes I was wheeled into a large operating room wearing a tee shirt and neon green swim trunks—stylin'. Had there been a power failure, and we were left in the dark, I could have led everyone to safety wearing those things. I thought I was dressed for success, but on short order was told to "lose the laundry." The preferred dress code for surgery: birthday suit only, chest hair optional. *Who knew?*

I was flat on my back. A long, tightly rolled towel was positioned under me along the length of my spine. The surface of my chest extended tight and smooth. It was a blank canvas on which the surgeon would create his masterpiece. Nurses covered me in sterile drapes, and scrubbed what would be the site of the incision in the upper left section of my chest with Betadine.

Ah, that familiar smell.

The anesthesiologist inserted a cannula in my nose, and started the flow of oxygen and his happy vapor concoction to send me into pain-free nirvana. I heard the hiss of the oxygen as the doc initiated the flow. A sterile drape supported by a metal frame was positioned a few inches above my head.

I would be awake during the surgery, unable to see anything beyond the warm green glow of the drape, but fully aware of what was happening. I was able to talk with the docs, and if needed alert them of any "discomfort."

The sounds of doctors and nurses setting up equipment and preparing the operating room, and instruments being placed on metal trays were replaced by none other than Buddy Holly singing "That'll Be the Day." Apparently doc was fond of music from the 50s. I sang along in my head as we got underway.

"Are you ready to go Robert?" asked the surgeon.

I gave him a "thumbs up" from under my drape. "Dive in whenever you're ready doc."

After some preliminary poking around on my chest, he fired up a cauterizing scalpel and, as Buddy whaled out "Peggy Sue," made his first incision.

Unlike a traditional scalpel, where an incision was made and blood loss controlled with suction and blotting with sterile gauze, the cauterizing scalpel allowed incisions to be made and surrounding blood vessels to be closed off simultaneously, which significantly reduced the amount of blood loss at the site.

It seemed innocent enough.

I sang along with Buddy and stared at the underside of the green drape that floated inches above my face, counting the stitches along the seams. After just a few moments, I realized not only could I hear the unsettling sizzling sound of the cauterization, but also smelled burning flesh.

It only took a moment for me to realize I was the one burning.

For just a second I thought perhaps that was the way it was supposed to be. I just needed to ride it out.

Keep singing!

It was my first surgical procedure. I had no clue what to expect. They amped up the dose of happy vapors, but a few moments later I felt what medical professionals referred to as "serious discomfort." At that moment I abandoned my tentative singing, lost count of the stitches, and called out to the doc.

"Hey doc? I can feel that, and I think I might be on fire!"

"Robert, you're not on fire, but I'm concerned you can feel the incisions."

I shared his concern. He quietly said something to the anesthesiologist, but I couldn't make it out, what with Buddy whaling away in the background. Within just a few seconds I couldn't feel a thing. In fact, I felt wonderful.

Too wonderful.

I thought, What's all the fuss about? It's a beautiful day, the room is full of good friends and conversation, and who doesn't like Buddy Holly?

At some point during the surgery I dozed off. The next thing I knew after resolving the burning flesh issue with doc, there was a nurse leaning over me in the recovery room tapping my hand, telling me to wake up. About the only thing I remembered at that time, was calling out to the doctor when the pain became intolerable.

Through that experience, I learned the importance of speaking up and making some noise if I felt like something wasn't right. During the surgery, it was painfully obvious that something was terribly wrong.

But there were other situations over the course of my treatment—conversations with my doctors or nurses, or discussions about a prescribed medication—where I had to be an advocate for myself.

Though I trusted my doctors and the many others who held my life in their hands, I didn't just blindly submit to their wishes if my gut told me otherwise.

12

The Fight for Life, Right Next Door

The nurse tapped my hand. "You're all done Robert," she said. She told me I was in the Recovery room. I felt really out of it, and not quite dialed in to reality, but rather quickly became aware of a flurry of activity that erupted out of nowhere around a man on the gurney next to mine. I mumbled to the nurse, "What happened to that man? Is he okay?"

She leaned down very close to my ear and whispered.

"His heart stopped and they called a Code Blue."

"Oh no. Is he going to be all right?"

"You should just relax and rest, and pretty soon we'll have you out of here."

Right. I'll just chill out here. You kids run along and knock yourselves out trying to save that chap's life. I'll just stay here and watch the life and death struggle play out before my eyes.

It was unnerving.

Within mere moments, there were so many doctors and nurses and bottles and tubes around that fellow I couldn't see him or his gurney. As all of that played out just a few feet from me, I slowly became more awake and alert.

My nurse told me I needed to rest in the recovery area for an hour, so they could be sure I was stable, and there were no problems with the central line catheter.

With all the doctors working on that man, and no curtain pulled between our gurneys to allow for any level of privacy, it was a long ride, like a scene from some reality TV show.

Eventually I was rolled back to my room. As I left, the team was still working hard on the man whose heart had stopped. I've always wondered how things turned out for him—an unknown that shall forever remain so, I suppose.

For me, someone right next-door, or in a bed just a few feet from mine, having a really bad day is what made my hospitalization so unsettling. It wasn't so much I had problem X that needed to be treated, but along with that strain, in the room right next to mine, there might be a guy my age with the same problem, not responding to treatment, and slowly slipping away. *Why was I doing okay and he wasn't?*

I often marveled at how my doctors, nurses, medical assistants, and other staff dealt with such a wide range of patient situations; they were a special breed. I wished I could maintain my focus, and deal with the constant tumult and uncertainty like they did.

Though I tried to keep mental blinders on and focus on my illness and my situation, I was constantly exposed to the struggle of others, like the man on the gurney next to me in the Recovery room.

My stay in the hospital was not just my stay, in my room. I was a stranger in a strange land. My whole world had changed. Nothing was a known entity.

Coming to terms with that reality was not an easy task. I tried to keep a simple truth in the forefront of my mind: though I was enveloped in a world unknown to me, I was not alone. God was there with me, and cared deeply about my situation. I believed that about half the time. I'm a slow learner.

13

The Honest Truth and My Marching Orders

He entered my room on a Saturday morning, wearing a flannel shirt and blue jeans. With a big grin on his face, he approached my bedside. "I hear you're looking for some straight answers."

"Yes I am doc. I'm feeling kind of lost."

"All right. What's on your mind, Robert?"

"What isn't, doc?"

Dr. Steve was the director of the Bone Marrow Transplant unit at the City of Hope. He played an integral role in my being accepted for treatment. With my diagnosis confirmed, my central line in place, and a couple days of residency under my belt, I was highly motivated to begin treatment.

Let's get on with it. What would Michele and I need to do in order to battle the beast that had dug its fangs into me, and our fledgling marriage?

I wanted someone to give me the straight dope, to show me the lay of the land in terms of what I faced. Dr. Steve was that man. Behind the scruffy mustache and beard was a very caring, intelligent, thoughtful guy, with a great sense of humor. He listened intently—both ears.

When he spoke, he did so with an infectious confidence.

We had an hour-long conversation on that Saturday morning. Doc gave me some perspective I could hang my hat on. Until that meeting, I felt like the only guy in the room who didn't know the big secret everyone was whispering about.

I was very vulnerable, and felt "out of touch," especially given the context and what was at stake—my life, hanging in the balance.

Help me make sense of this.

The news from Dr. Steve was not fabulous by any measure. The road he described was a long one; month-long cycles of infused chemotherapy alternating with month-long steroid therapy, frequent bone marrow aspirations, a series of six lumbar punctures, a ten-day course of brain radiation to get the party started, and miscellaneous other tests and procedures along the way.

"You have to think of the road ahead as your job," he said.

"My job. Okay."

I was restless in my bed, fingers tapping the top of the dresser next to me.

"You'll come here in the morning and will pretty much be here all day. You'll head home, sleep it off as best you can, and come back for more the next day."

"How long will I be on the job, doc?"

"You'll do that for about a year. Think you can do it?"

"Not now, but I'll get there. I have to, right?"

All of the tasks, tests and procedures Dr. Steve described were part of a well-honed, time-tested treatment protocol. There was a possibility it could lead to a happy outcome of survivability. But the odds were not in my favor the leukemia would remain in remission forever. Doc made that quite clear.

It was much more likely it would return, and that was just something Michele and I had to come to terms with. We had to focus as best we could on taking things one day at a time, with the knowledge the cancer monkey would always be asleep on our backs.

For how long? We didn't know when it might wake up again.

Following my first meeting with Dr. Steve, I saw him frequently in the corridors of the hospital. He always stopped, shook my hand, and offered some words of encouragement. It was clear he loved his job, and the opportunity he had to make a life-changing difference in people's lives.

What a good way to go through this life.

I spent a lot of time—too much time—in my room, fueled by a fear of fully acknowledging my condition and engaging in the treatment process. I was still trying to hide. I hoped each day I would wake up to find it was all just a horrible nightmare.

A quick note about taking things one day at a time: that was not a character trait I was blessed with at birth. My prayer: "Lord, teach me to be patient—*right now!*"

The patience I prayed for did not come easily. I just wanted to feel better—to feel any degree of "normal" again. I wanted to fill in the holes, and clean up some of my "tattered edges" as life went on as usual for those around me. I didn't want to be a cancer patient.

14

Opinion Overload

I wasn't prepared for how others reacted to my medical condition or the "advice" they would give in such a difficult time. At one point early on in my hospital stay, Michele told me several people had urged her to get out of the marriage; break it off cleanly. She didn't need that mess in her life and could do better.

I was blown away when she told me about those conversations. But Michele hung in with me. I wanted to be that kind of support for her, but I struggled to know how best to do that at the time. We were a team and did our best to face the unknown as such.

Just days into my stay at City of Hope, there was a knock on my door. I called out to whomever was on the other side to come in. A man about my age entered the room and greeted me with a warm smile. "Hi Robert. You don't know me, but I'm a friend of a friend," he said.

He told me he attended the same church as a colleague of mine at Focus on the Family. I welcomed him to my little slice of paradise and invited him to sit down.

He pulled his chair up close to my bedside—perhaps a little too close. I was a bit startled by his assertiveness.

I asked him why he had come to see me.

"Well, Robert, I believe I have a word for you, from the Lord."

When he uttered those words, I knew I was in for an interesting conversation.

"Really," I questioned.

"Yes," he responded, and leaned in closer to me.

"After I heard of your condition and your present struggle, I felt like I needed to come see you and speak this message to you."

"What message do you have for me," I asked.

The man looked down at the blanket on my bed and then drew his head up and looked me straight in the eyes. I wondered what on earth he was going to say to me, and I had a bad feeling I wasn't going to like the guy much in the next thirty seconds.

"I believe with all my heart that the reason you are suffering now is because you have unconfessed sin in your life and God is causing you to suffer so you will restore your relationship with him."

I had been at City of Hope for just a few days. I had spent the last two months trying to figure out what was eating me alive, from the inside out. I had come to God in prayer on numerous occasions, asking for understanding and healing and hope.

I had confessed my sins and had made it quite clear to God that if he was trying to get my attention he had done it. I was in no mood for this guy to drop a judgment bomb on me, but that's what he did.

He didn't know me from Adam, yet he claimed to have a message from God—for me. In any other situation, I would have gone after him and challenged him to provide some Scriptural basis for his position.

But given that I was facing the fight of my life, and not in any shape for a theological debate, I dug deep—very deep—and simply thanked the man for taking time to come and see me, and for praying for my healing. I told him I could not have any further conversation with him and asked him to leave.

It took everything in me to keep from jumping out of my bed, pinning him against the wall, and asking him if he had **any clue** what I was going through or the foggiest notion of how much my heart and mind had been in torment since learning my diagnosis.

The man was a bit stunned at my restrained, simple response. He hesitated at bit, like he was pondering for just a moment the wisdom of uttering another word. He wisely chose not to, wished me well and left.

Later that evening, I told Michele about my conversation with that fellow. Michele was really stunned.

I was still pretty hot about the encounter, even late that evening. But given what I faced in the days to come, I had to shake it off and focus on the tasks at hand. I told myself—out loud on several occasions to—"Let it go."

Put your blinders on, Rob, and keep your eyes on the prize. If you want to get out of this place alive, pick your mental battles and fight hard.

15

Shooting the Juice

When I was admitted to City of Hope, I was told if they could get me into remission, they would do it within six weeks; they did it in five. The chemo treatment was brutal and bowled me over like shoppers working a half-price sale at Walmart.

I will never forget the night we started, and I met my nurse, Rodrigo. He was a soft-spoken guy, just a few years older than me. When he was young, he came to California from Mexico, and found work picking fruit.

It was believed years of exposure to toxic pesticides in the agricultural fields led to his acquiring Aplastic Anemia, a disorder in which his body did not manufacture enough new blood cells.

Rodrigo received a bone marrow transplant at City of Hope. He decided to become a nurse, and returned to City of Hope to help others dealing with blood cancers. What a story.

His empathy was a silent bond between us.

Rodrigo entered my room gowned up like an invader from Space, ready to "shoot the juice." He addressed me through his mask and plastic face shield in a muffled tone. "Well Robert, are you ready to begin?"

"I guess as ready as I can be."

He gave me an approving nod. Before he administered the chemotherapy, there was a cocktail of three pre-meds that had to be injected into my central line. The chemo was always given at night, and Rodrigo usually got to my room around 11:00 p.m. I watched

"The Tonight Show with Johnny Carson" as Rodrigo prepared the meds and connected the syringes to my catheter.

As he pushed the first of the three drugs, Rodrigo warned me of things to come. "As I give you these meds, you might feel a warm flush, or your head may feel very heavy, or you may notice visual changes, but those should pass within just a little while. You won't feel the chemo when I push it."

Even before he had finished talking, I noticed as long as I stared at the TV mounted high above the cabinets opposite my bed, it appeared to slowly "drip" down the wall, all the way to the floor.

If I looked away for a moment, and then back at the TV, it was back where it belonged. But if I stared, the dripping began again. It was a full-blown hallucination.

I described my vision to Rodrigo. "Rodrigo, I think I can liquefy inanimate objects."

He laughed and shook his head.

"Those are the pre-meds Robert. Your special powers are medication-induced. It will probably be like that each night you receive your chemo."

In that strange world of unknowns, I found at least one thing I could count on, and plan for—mind-tripping on my pre-meds. *Ah, the joy of routine!*

16

The Ultimate Cheerleader

A s my illness progressed, my Mom was on the phone or writing letters to family and friends across the country with the latest updates and prayer requests. She was the consummate prayer warrior and encourager. When she learned of a need, she banged on the gates of Heaven and expected an answer. She believed the promises of God—more than I ever did.

She rallied the troops.

Because of her efforts, churches and individuals across the country prayed for Michele and me, and kept us in their thoughts. A church in the middle of Kansas led by our former pastor and good friend of our family prayed for us every Sunday morning—for several years. Literally thousands of folks we didn't know stepped up and banged on the gates along with my Mom.

When I was very young our family owned just one car, and Dad drove it to work each day. Mom did not work, and was home when my brother and I left for school and when we returned. She found great joy in hearing about our day, seeing the artwork or other projects we created, and always encouraged my brother and me to develop our creative abilities.

She was an incredible artist. Her watercolor paintings used to blow me away. As the years went by, Mom developed a dry brush style of painting that gave an almost photorealistic quality to her subject matter. She loved the ocean, so her art table was always filled with paintings of sea foam washing up on wet sand, seashells, or waves crashing against a rocky coastal outcropping.

I learned an important lesson from my Mom: if God blessed you with talents and abilities, you must use them; exercise them, and bless others with them. Mom was blessed with tremendous artistic ability, and gave many of her pieces away as gifts.

Even now, with Mom in her late-eighties, and her health declining, I still see glimpses of the woman who raised my brother and me, the woman of simple faith, with a wonderful sense of humor, and a love of life.

17

The Tough Guy Hangs Tough

My Dad had a very strong personality. He had a certain presence about him. I didn't best him at arm wrestling until I was in my mid-teens. In his professional life he had been a private investigator, and for nearly fifty years represented legendary insurance company Lloyd's of London, in malpractice lawsuits.

If you were a doctor accused of some type of negligence or other wrongdoing, you wanted my Dad on your side. He never lost a case.

He was ultimately happiest when he worked for himself rather than for the law firms he was associated with. I believe he passed that entrepreneurial "gene" on to me. If given the choice of punching a clock working for someone else or calling my own shots and working for myself, I much prefer the latter.

In his younger years, he was the consummate outdoorsman: horseman, fisherman, hunter, trap and skeet shooter. He enjoyed it all, and did his best to pass on his passion for those things to my brother and me.

I have fond and vivid memories from my childhood of the times Dad would load up the guns and take my brother and me to a shooting range just a half hour or so from our home. We always went to the range on Saturdays. The night before, we spent a lot of time cleaning the guns and loading our field box with supplies.

Those Friday evening sessions with Dad were special times. He collected antique firearms and loved to share the story about each of the pieces in his collection. Some dated back to the Civil War. They were incredible; cap and ball, octagonal barrels, full of nicks and scratches; battle scars from their years of service. They oozed history.

We cleaned all of them, from the smaller caliber handguns to the shotguns and hunting rifles. Every weapon was kept in immaculate condition.

When Saturday came, we usually left for the shooting range just after lunch. My brother and I helped Dad load the guns into the trunk of our car. We usually brought a couple .22 caliber rifles for target practice, but we also loaded one of Dad's beautiful, long-barreled shotguns.

Our time usually started on the rifle range, where we shot at targets 50 and 100 yards away. As a young boy, it was always a thrill to check our targets during the range breaks and find a tight cluster of bullet holes near the bull's eye.

Before we left the range at the end of our practice, Dad always pulled the shotgun from the trunk of the car and walked with us to the trap and skeet area. I remember the first time I watched him take his position with nine other shooters, and fire the .12 gauge when it was his turn in the trap line.

A small wooden shed concealed a machine that flung "clay pigeons," small, light ceramic disks shot into the air and away from the shooting line to simulate a duck or other foul flushed from a field. Dad only had a split second to get a bead on the clay pigeon and fire. If he hit it dead-on, the small disk shattered into a thousand pieces.

One round of trap afforded twenty-five chances to nail those clay pigeons. My brother and I used to stand in an area to the side of the trap line and watched in amazement as Dad usually nailed eighteen of them and made it look effortless.

When he was ready to shoot, he drew the gun in close, aimed at the wooden shed and called out, "Pull." That sent the clay pigeon flying and Dad had a bead on it in nothing flat.

He usually paid for two rounds, and usually bagged 23 out of 25 on his second round. My brother and I were amazed. I always looked forward to watching Dad work his magic on the trap line.

On a weekend afternoon, following my graduation from High School, Dad called me into the den in our home. It was in that room where a large, mahogany gun cabinet displayed many of his rifles and shotguns. A single drawer was built in below the gun stand. My Dad gestured to me and pointed to the drawer.

"Open it," he said with a twinkle in his eye.

I grasped the large knob, and pulled open the sturdy drawer. There was a beautifully finished wooden box, perhaps a foot deep and eighteen inches across. It had a latch on the front, with a small lock. I had never seen that box before. I looked up at my Dad.

"What's this?"

"This is your graduation gift. Your grandfather made this box to hold what's inside."

I never knew either of my grandfathers. The man who made the box, and the gun cabinet in which it was stored was my Mom's Dad. He was a master with wood.

I unlocked the box and opened it up. Inside were two Smith & Wesson revolvers: a .38 "special" and an identical, equally weighted .22. Each had six-inch barrels and checkered wooden grip stocks. They were absolutely beautiful.

Dad bought them decades prior. I had cleaned those guns on several occasions when I was a young boy, but never fired them. But I had never seen them displayed in that custom-made, felt-lined, wooden box. I was blown away.

"Dad, I don't know what to say. Thank you so much."

"Congratulations on your hard work in school, son. I know you will treasure these pieces for the rest of your life."

Dad was right about that. That matched set of revolvers is my most prized possession. When my daughters were old enough, I taught them how to shoot using those guns, along with the same .22 caliber rifle my Dad used to teach me. Both my girls are crack shots and both have fired shotguns as well. Dad would be so proud of them.

Dad was raised in the German Lutheran church. When it came to matters of faith, he didn't express much outwardly, and his church attendance was usually limited to Easter and Christmas services, which he felt were significant events that should be honored.

Though he didn't attend church with the rest of the family, he was fascinated with Biblical "end times" prophecy, and loved to watch the "doomsayers" as he called them on Sunday morning TV.

As my condition worsened, seemingly with the passing of each day, my Mom continued bangin' on the gates and trusting in God as the great physician.

But Dad spiraled into a deep despair, unable to believe what was happening; frustrated with recurring thoughts he might actually out-live his own son. He leaned heavily on Mom just to cope with each day's developments.

It was the first time I saw my Dad, the horseman and hunter, the man who could handle a .12 gauge shotgun with the best of them—the tough guy—broken, vulnerable, and feeling utterly helpless. It hurt so bad to see him that way, but Dad hung in there and did his best to take things as they came, one day at a time. I'm so proud of him for that.

Watching him go through that ordeal, I gained some insight into the true nature of my Dad's toughness. It wasn't about the guns or the horses or the hunting. It was about toughing out the hard times and not caving in.

Mom and Dad lived in San Marino, in the home where they raised my brother and me. It was just twenty-five minutes or so from our place in Azusa. They did whatever they could to help while I was in the hospital. They ran errands, brought us meals, and were simply there to support us. They loved my wife Michele to the bone; she was the daughter they never had.

At a time when we felt like we were walking a tightrope a mile high, the support Mom and Dad provided was like a safety net. It was such a comfort as we headed further into the unknown world of cancer treatment.

18

Matters of Faith

Our family attended the First Baptist Church in Alhambra, California. My Mom, brother, and I made the short trip across town each Sunday in our lemon yellow, 1966 Chevy Impala. Mom attended the church service while my brother and I went to our Sunday school classes.

My earliest memories of those times date back to 1968. I was six years old, and full of energy with a short attention span. The teachers taught lessons about God's love, Moses, Noah, Job, and about Jesus dying on the cross for our sins. They engaged us with filmstrips (remember those?), coloring sheets, craft projects, and puppet shows to reinforce the weekly lesson.

I looked forward to going to Sunday school!

After church, like we needed to be spun up any more, we usually walked up the street to the Winchell's doughnut shop to sample their line of delicious, nutrient-rich, heart-healthy snacks. Doughnuts and coffee flowed from a walk-up window.

The grown-ups gathered on the sidewalk in front of the shop. My brother and I played with the other kids and rode out our respective sugar buzzes in the parking lot nearby. I think our parents knew full well how much time was needed for us to come down from our highs before they disbanded and collected their kids for the ride home.

I can still hear my Mom talking with some of her friends, and enjoying a cup of coffee. "The time? Oh, we're fine. My two had buttermilk bars, so we've got a good half hour to chat."

When I was nine years old the guys in my Sunday school class went to Green Oaks Boys Ranch near Vista, California for a weekend camping trip. The camp was part of the ministry of the Union Rescue Mission in Los Angeles, an organization that helped men on "Skid Row" recover from addictions, learn skills to reenter the workforce, and develop a vibrant faith in God.

At camp, we slept in bunkhouses, hiked the rolling hills, played Capture the Flag at night, and rode horses on the maze of trails that covered the property. One night, following songs, skits, and an explanation of the Gospel message, I made a "campfire" decision to invite Christ into my heart to be my Lord and Savior.

I became a Christian, but nothing really changed as far as I knew.

"In order to have a better life." That was my answer when I was interviewed the next morning by one of the camp directors. He asked me why I made the decision to invite Jesus into my heart. I told him about the story I heard at the campfire the night before.

It was a story of a shepherd who was looking for a little lamb that had wandered away from the flock. The shepherd looked everywhere but couldn't find the lamb. But he never stopped looking for it. Eventually, he found it and brought it back to the flock.

The man who told the story described God as being just like that good shepherd, who cared deeply for his lost lamb. I asked Jesus into my heart because I wanted him to watch over me like the shepherd in the story, and so I would have a better life. The interview was aired on the Union Rescue Mission's AM radio program a week later.

"To have a better life" was the extent of my knowledge of the faith. I was still just a kid with lots of energy who wanted to get outside, ride his bike, play football, and blow up his G.I Joe.

In high school, my faith was reenergized when a new youth pastor came onboard at our church. There was excitement in the air about growing the youth group. We all became good friends, grew in our faith, and worked to be a force for good in our community, and not just a bunch of self-absorbed teenagers.

It was a critical period of growth and maturing. I learned, among other things, I probably wasn't setting the best example on those occasions when I peeled out of the church parking lot in my Dad's 1970 Pontiac Bonneville. It had the V8 455.

I'm sorry. There was just something about that car. It was made of steel; a lead sled.

Like a lot of church youth groups we met on Wednesday nights, and also like a lot of church groups, we played volleyball before doing anything else.

What is it about churches and volleyball?

We held bake sales, car washes, bike-a-thons, and other events to raise money for outreach projects and summer camping trips. We took frequent trips to an orphanage in Tijuana, Mexico, where we worked on repair projects, delivered bulk items like beans and rice (and toilet paper).

We spent time getting to know the large group of kids living there. They had essentially been discarded by their parents and the community at large and faced a very uncertain future. Those were great years, and I felt my personal relationship with the Lord growing as my faith was put into practical action.

My college years at Azusa Pacific were a real challenge. I was a religion major in a program that had me deep into the Biblical text, studying the history of the Old and New Testament worlds, the views and positions of conservative and liberal theologians on a variety of issues, wrestling with the concept of God's "call" on my life to full-time, vocational ministry, and serving on the staff of a local church for practical application of my coursework.

The culmination of that work was the development of a personal philosophy of ministry. It was a monster document, an attempt to crystallize the theological foundations of what I believed. That was half the paper. The second half detailed my plan for implementing that philosophy into a practical, cohesive ministry to bring children to a saving knowledge of Jesus Christ. My vision was to create environments, in a church setting, or through camping programs and the like, where kids could have an opportunity to hear the Gospel and be encouraged in their faith.

I defended my philosophy of ministry orally before a panel of my professors, and the pastor under whom I worked for my lab hours, and completed my college experience with a stronger sense of who I was as a Christian, and where God had me headed.

I really enjoyed working with children, and felt like I was on a path towards some type of youth ministry.

After graduation, I enrolled at Talbot Theological Seminary on the Biola University campus in La Mirada, California to pursue a Master's degree in Christian Education. I wanted to develop curriculum for Sunday schools, camp programs, and the like. If possible, I hoped to dovetail that with my training and experience in art production and graphic design.

The course work was challenging and intense—Old and New Testament history, Biblical interpretation, practical theology, soteriology, demonology, angelology—more "ologies" than you could shake a stick at, along with practical course work in youth leadership, curriculum development, and educational administration.

Once again, my faith was challenged and strengthened, and my practical knowledge base expanded.

I had a head full of knowledge, and a willing, seeking heart. I thought I had a rock solid faith. But all the education, all the deep theological introspection—none of it prepared me for a spiritual challenge that shook me to my core.

Just six months after my twenty-sixth birthday, I was flat on my back at the City of Hope, facing a long road of treatment for blood cancer. I had been a Christian for seventeen years, and I never expected my life to take such a turn.

19

The Six-week Run

After a week on the wing at City of Hope, I guess I "settled in." I looked forward to morning visits either from our good friend Sandi, who often stopped by after her night shift at Huntington Hospital, or Dr. Bruce, a former professor, mentor, and good friend from Azusa Pacific.

When I was an undergrad, he kicked my backside; taught me how to be a student, to research, and write, ask hard questions about my faith, wrestle with the notion of who Jesus was, and how faith in him played out in the real world.

Dr. Bruce stopped by on his way to the university and shared updates on my condition with his students. I know they prayed for me as well.

My parents usually arrived for their visit by noon. There was often a steady stream of folks who came by throughout the day. I looked forward to seeing familiar faces. In the evenings things quieted down, and Michele, with few exceptions, came by for a visit after work.

I cherished those times when it was just the two of us. She was my rock, and a daily reminder to me why I had to fight hard and beat my cancer.

Everyone who visited my room during those six weeks knew the situation, well aware of the cloud of uncertainty that hung overhead. But quite often, my room was filled with laughter, good conversation, and real joy. Unbeknownst to me, one of our friends strung a banner across the outside of my door that read, "The Party's in Here!"

One day, Margo, one of my favorite nurses who worked the day shift, came into the room with a big smile on her face. "I never know what to expect when I come in here. There always seems to be something going on."

She was right. I suppose filling that room with laughter was one way we battled the darkness. There may be no better way to kick cancer in the butt than laughing directly in its face.

When the four walls felt like they were creeping in on me, I ventured outside the unit to take in some fresh air. The City of Hope was located very near the foothills of the San Gabriel Mountains, a massive range of decomposed granite that spanned the length of the San Gabriel valley, and rose to elevations in excess of 10,000 feet in the backcountry.

Though the Los Angeles basin was famous for its smog, during the fall and winter months much of it blew out of that area, and the view of the mountains was beautiful.

Like a movie I wanted to watch on the big screen before it was released on DVD, I wanted to soak up that beauty, driven by a new-found desire to not take the simple things for granted.

I was deliberate about getting outside, because everything in me wanted to climb into bed and pull the covers over my head. I couldn't let my circumstances get the best of me.

20

Big Love

Friends from work stopped by frequently to visit. It was so cool to be able to keep in touch with them. Focus on the Family was a non-profit organization dedicated to strengthening families nationally and abroad, with a wide range of print, broadcast and film resources.

At the time of my illness, the organization employed several hundred people at their campus in Pomona. I worked in the art department within the Communications Division, on magazine and book publishing projects, and direct mail marketing programs.

Our department was filled with special people who liked to laugh and have a good time. We really put out the work volume and got the job done. I had no idea while Michele and I were in the midst of our medical struggles that a couple of those great friends essentially "passed the hat" and collected donations.

The funds collected were matched dollar for dollar through the organization's Employee Benevolence Fund, a reserve of cash set aside to help employees dealing with unexpected, hardship situations.

One morning, the senior vice president of our division entered my room with a smile on his face. He was an unexpected and welcome surprise. He said, "Everyone misses you and wants you back as soon as possible. We also know you and Michele have bills to pay, so we took up a little collection."

With that, he handed me an envelope with a check for nearly $2000 dollars. I, being an emotionless rock, promptly lost it, blown away by the thoughtfulness of those special friends.

I couldn't stop crying. I had only limited contact with some of those coworkers. They saw a need and went for it. And that wasn't an isolated event.

Our VP made several visits when I was at City of Hope. Each time he handed me another envelope with a check. I also learned Focus hosted a blood drive with the American Red Cross on my behalf. Ninety pints of blood were credited to my account. Later, I learned the blood drive set a new record for the most donations ever from a one-day event.

Additionally, employees I didn't know and departments I had never worked with at Focus held bake sales and other fundraisers in my honor. Moreover, checks from Focus continued to arrive, usually coinciding with big bills for insurance deductibles.

Beyond the support from Focus, we received cashier's checks from folks who wanted to remain anonymous, and note cards with checks or cash tucked inside.

People just bombed us with love.

Our savings had been wiped out in record time due to insurance deductibles at the onset of my illness. On a very practical level, those gifts of love helped us keep our heads above water.

21

The Newfound Faith of My Father

The acts of ministry by my coworkers and our friends not only impacted Michele and me, but they had a profound impact on my Dad as well. He had always held a certain disdain for the contemporary Christian church. He saw little more than a blend of hypocrisy and hucksterism from many of those in prominent church leadership positions.

His position was based in large part on the televangelists with the bad hairpieces he watched on TV. From his perspective, their "ministry" was more about amassing as much cash as possible for themselves and their empires. Perhaps there was some validity to that.

But when Dad witnessed what Focus and our friends had done for Michele and me, it changed him.

For the first time, he saw Christians walk the walk, and not just spew the talk.

Over the six weeks at City of Hope, I watched my Dad transform from a quiet, overwhelmed, concerned father, into a real encourager. He was a man on a mission with a growing faith in God.

He visited other patients on the wing, and afterward told me about the people he met, what they were dealing with, and about his conversations with them. He enjoyed the opportunity to do something positive rather than sit around and worry about me.

As the weeks progressed, Dad witnessed more and more evidence of God's faithfulness to provide for our needs, and keep us in his care. If we received some bad news about lab values or test results, it was my Dad who spoke up. "Well, all we can do is pray."

Powerful stuff. Watching my Dad's transformation taught me not to write someone off as a lost cause. I'm sure plenty of folks have written me off that way from time to time.

The best move I can make is to strive to not think that way about others. I pray God will give me the strength to do it.

22

Spinal Taps and Earthquakes

On October 17, 1989 I had a mid-afternoon appointment for the first of six lumbar punctures, or "spinal taps." Like a bone marrow aspiration, it was an uncomfortable procedure, wherein a needle *(it was always some kind of needle)* was inserted between the spinal vertebrae, and spinal fluid extracted for analysis.

The procedure was performed under Fluoroscopy, which was essentially a live X-ray. It was fascinating to watch the monitor mounted on the wall above my head.

With every breath I watched my lungs expand and contract, my internal organs and spine move, and saw the precise spot where the doctor had inserted the needle.

In my case, Methotrexate chemotherapy was injected into the spinal sack. The sack encompassed the length of the spinal cord and brain, and was a known hiding place for the immature, cancerous cells.

On one level, the procedure was amazing to take in. Then there was the moment where an occasional twinge of what felt like an electrical charge shot down my leg.

It was at those times that my fascination with medical technology went right out the window. I realized they were performing the procedure on me.

Uh, doc, I think you just set my leg on fire!

But that was as bad as it ever got; an occasional twinge that got my attention, and a few needles bent due to tense back muscles. Overall, smooth sailing.

It was made very clear to me following the procedure, that under no circumstances was I to raise my head or sit up, for at least several hours. Depending on how much fluid was extracted, the imbalance of fluid in the spinal sack could trigger a migraine-like headache if I made such a move.

I was returned to my room a little after 6:00 p.m. Within a few moments my room phone rang. It was my brother, calling from his place in Seattle. He had just spent several days hanging out with me at the City of Hope, and attending a friend's wedding in the Bay Area.

He was pretty freaked out. "Hey Rob, do you have your TV on?"

"No, man. I just got back to my room after the spinal tap."

"Get your TV on. You have to see this."

A major earthquake had struck the San Francisco Bay Area at 5:04 p.m. Since my in-laws and several friends lived there, I wanted to sit up and watch the news.

I decided to inch the head of my bed up a little at a time to try and get an angle on the TV. I watched the news in disbelief, as images of the destruction flashed across the screen.

In a matter of seconds, the quake had killed sixty-three people and injured another 3,757. *Jeez!* Life is so fragile, and circumstances can change, literally in an instant.

Reality check for Rob. Sixty-three people wouldn't be coming home to their loved ones. Sixty-three families were forever changed. You had to tough out an uncomfortable medical procedure. Keep things in perspective.

23

Sanity in a Four-Hour Dose

I became frustrated with the whole of my life being consumed with "medical." Three weeks into my six-week stay, I hit the wall. I was going stir-crazy. I remember talking about it with Dr. Nade, the oncologist assigned to my case.

She was a really special lady, an expert with my type of leukemia. Originally from Thailand, she laughed easily and called me "Big Bob." In spite of her frenetic schedule, she always made time for some conversation.

She would plop down in the chair in my room and tell me about her day, share funny things her kids had said, and recount the fun vacations she and her family had taken. We talked a lot about her years living in Thailand. She wanted to know the details about my life as well. We became good friends.

On the day I told her I was contemplating tunneling out of my room, she told me it would be possible to get a four-hour pass to leave the City of Hope campus and spend some time at home with Michele. I was allowed to do this on a couple occasions. It was a precious gift.

To be home for just a few hours, from 6 to 10 p.m., doing normal things like making dinner, paying the bills, and being with Michele in our apartment was such a relief in the midst of the storm; a much needed sanity break. I vowed then I would never complain again about having to pay the bills.

I struggled to find that place, that balance point where the cancer was part of my life but not the whole of my life. I didn't want my illness to define me.

Rob: Leukemia. Prognosis: Poor.

I suppose that is the struggle for all of us dealing with cancer or other life challenges. I never found the balance point. Leukemia and the treatment regimen to kill it off and get healthy were all-consuming.

In the early days of my treatment, the times away from City of Hope on those four-hour passes were as close as I came to achieving any sort of balance between my life and my disease.

24

My Low Microbial Life

I was discharged from City of Hope shortly before Thanksgiving. Walking back into our apartment, I felt a sense of relief and a certain degree of accomplishment for enduring the initial Induction phase of chemotherapy. I was in remission; there was no trace of leukemic cells in my blood. Physically I felt pretty good.

My immune system was very suppressed, not quite non-existent, so I wore a mask when I left the apartment and had to be hyper-mindful of infection risks. We had to get rid of all our houseplants because of the possibility of mold spores in the potting soil.

One evening, members of our Bible study group came by to "adopt" our plants. It was pretty funny, as everything from small tabletop flowers and potted plants to our large Ficus tree, staple of 1980's apartment décor, went right out the door like clearance items at the local nursery.

Not only did the plants have to go, but dietary restrictions were put in place as well in order to keep me safe from bacteria. If Michele cooked a meal, I could partake, but I couldn't have any leftovers the next day. Beyond that, anything else I ate had to be pre-packaged, processed, and otherwise free of contamination.

We called it the "vending machine diet."

If the item could be found hanging in a vending machine, it was safe to eat. Michele was very creative at finding solutions that allowed some level of "normal" when it came to putting together a quick meal. She found the smallest cans of tuna available on the market (made from very small tuna) and bulk quantities of restaurant-style packets of mayonnaise, mustard, and pickle relish.

With all of that mixed together and spread between two crackers, we pulled off a fairly respectable tuna sandwich hors d'oeuvre. Waffles? No sweat! We popped a couple frozen waffles into the toaster and squeezed the "genuine" maple syrup from the little pouches. *Yum.*

We embraced the vending machine or "low microbial" diet for six weeks—six of the most creative culinary weeks of our young marriage.

As my lab values improved, I was given the green light to resume a more normal diet. Because of the effects of chemotherapy, there were plenty of days when even the thought of food was enough to trigger bad nausea. But if anyone else in the apartment complex needed relish, mustard, mayo, or maple syrup, we had them covered.

Thoughts about what loomed on the horizon occupied my mind during those first few days at home. A ten-day course of brain radiation would precede the outpatient chemotherapy.

Leukemic cells sometimes found their way into the brain. The radiation therapy damaged the genetic makeup of those cells so if they were present, they could not reproduce and wreak havoc in my head. It was part of the standard protocol for treating my type of leukemia.

I had many questions about the treatment. *How would it affect me? Would it be a walk in the park or would I end up sacrificing my soul to the Devil when all was said and done?* It was a lot to consider.

I tried not to allow those thoughts to completely dominate every waking hour. The holidays were fast approaching, so I did my best to focus on the good times that lay ahead.

25

The Best Thanksgiving Ever—And the Calm Before the Storm

When I was a kid, the Thanksgiving and Christmas holidays were always a good time. On Thanksgiving Day, we often traveled an hour or so south from our place in San Marino to my Aunt Jo and Uncle Bob's home in Whittier.

Uncle Bob married into the Capra family, a large Italian family with a famous son, Frank, who directed such notable films as *Lady for a Day, Mr. Smith Goes to Washington,* and the Christmas holiday classic *It's a Wonderful Life.*

It was always a raucous gathering, with cousins, extended family, and friends overflowing the place. Their house was filled with the smells of great Italian cooking—lasagna, spaghetti, and (giant) meatballs.

There was usually even a turkey on the table… somewhere.

Several tables were strung together and spanned the length of the family room. If you wanted a dinner roll, someone would eventually toss you one. It was always a loud, warm and fun time with lots of laughs.

Though we did not gather with my cousins as we had when I was young, Thanksgiving of 1989 was an event for Michele and me that rivaled those wonderful family gatherings.

Our apartment was filled with family, laughter, and love—three of the best things a home can ever be filled with.

Michele's family—her Mom and Dad, older sister, and two younger brothers made the trip south from the Bay Area. My parents and brother joined in, and our place was full to the brim. The traditional smells of turkey, stuffing, gravy, cranberries, and a bunch of killer desserts, including a "Chocolate Decadence" cake my sister-in-law made, that to this day I'm not over, enveloped our apartment.

The conversation and laughter was like a fresh spring breeze after a long winter spent indoors.

We gathered around several tables, configured in a "T" that, like the gatherings at my aunt and uncle's house, spanned the length of our living room. We were packed in pretty tightly, but no one seemed to care.

It was a wonderful life that day.

The gathering was the first time our parents and extended families were together since the wedding. It was a great opportunity for everyone to get to know each other a little better. I will always appreciate my in-law family members making the 400-mile trek to be with us. They were really tremendous people, full of grace and confidence in God.

Michele and I talked often about that weekend being one of the best Thanksgivings ever, but it was also the calm before the storm. The Monday that followed brought the first of ten consecutive days of brain radiation. Thanksgiving weekend was the last chance to feel good, drink in quality time with my family, sport a full head of hair, and feast on a great meal for quite a while.

I knew in the not-to-distant future, I would probably be as sick as a dog, so I tried to savor every minute.

26

Off to Work

I woke up Monday morning following the Thanksgiving holiday with my spirits at rock bottom. I was in no way motivated to begin the outpatient program. I secluded myself in our apartment with my thoughts for several hours before Michele and I headed out for my mid-morning appointment at City of Hope.

On the drive to the hospital, we recounted the events of Thanksgiving Day and talked about this and that, but both our heads chased other thoughts.

How bad was this going to be?

Was I going to be worth anything at the end of the day?

Was our marriage going to be worth anything at the end of my treatment?

We entered the City of Hope campus and made our familiar trek past the beautiful rose garden that lined the main driveway. Yellowing leaves on several trees provided a subtle reminder of the change of seasons.

Michele dropped me off outside the main entrance, and offered words of encouragement to pump me up before she headed for work. After saying our goodbyes, I turned and glanced up at the sculpture outside the hospital entrance. I thought, *Oh man, here we go.*

It was time to fight for that vibrant life.

I made my way to the Radiology department, a couple levels below ground. The elevator ride felt like a surreal descent into the great unknown. I was going down into that dark place where all the nasty stuff happened; the stuff no one wanted to talk about. My mind made a bigger deal of the radiation treatment than it needed to, but that was where my head was on that first day.

I was greeted by one of the two friendly radiology techs that led me through Radiation Simulation prior to Thanksgiving. Her warm smile was a welcome sight in what felt like a very cold and sterile environment—a vibe I didn't tap into during the simulation.

During that two-hour session, I learned all the ins and outs of the treatment. One side of my brain would be zapped with a minute of radiation. The giant machine would then swing overhead in a 180-degree arc to treat the other side.

The technician escorted me down the hall to the treatment room where the banks of long, florescent light panels cast an eerie glow. The large radiation machine sat idle, quietly humming in standby mode, like a lion waiting to pounce on its next meal.

I was positioned on the metal table. The techs buzzed around me. They taped my head down, positioned lead shields to protect my face, and eventually covered me up with a couple warm blankets. It was not quite the "good book and cup of hot coffee" scenario I would have preferred on that cool fall day but that's the way it was.

Ballgame time.

The techs explained as they had during simulation what to expect. After I gave them a "thumbs-up", they ran for cover into their control room and fired up the machine. As it spun up, a loud buzz filled the room. I prayed a quick prayer. *Okay Lord, this is the next step in the path. Please keep me safe and strong.*

After the first minute of treatment concluded, the machine rotated over my head in a 180-degree arc, and returned to idle mode as I had been told it would.

What I had not been told about was the rather pungent "industrial disaster" smell that quickly filled the room. *Was it from the machine's hydraulics? Did one of the techs burn popcorn in the microwave oven? Did someone leave an old pair of gym shoes in the treatment room?* I didn't have a clue.

All I knew in that moment was that what I smelled was the worst odor known to man. It was far worse even than the smell of my own burning flesh when my central line was inserted. I had to fight hard to maintain any level of cool and keep my breakfast down.

"Oh, yeah that smell," one of the techs responded when I asked about the source of the odor. "We really don't know what specifically causes it, but lots of patients complain it makes them sick."

Ya think?

How comforting. Lying flat on my back with my head taped down to the table, and with a basic understanding of the laws of gravity that was not the best news to hear.

As the machine locked into position for the second minute of fun, I considered my options should the nausea morph into something beyond a funny feeling. Oh sure, I had a "panic button" to push if anything happened, but in my head I knew there was no way hitting that button would stop any physical reaction to the smell from playing out—fully.

I kept the silly button by my side as instructed in an effort to play by the rules and follow protocol.

I thank the Lord nothing nasty happened that day. On a very positive note, all my thinking and over-thinking made the second minute just fly by. That was one of the times I think God looked down from Heaven and thought, *"My son died for this guy's sins. He is a believer, and I love him, but he's also a piece of work. Come on Rob, hang in there."*

I wish I could report that over the nine days that followed the treatments went about the same as day one; that I was a tough guy who ate fear for breakfast and washed it down with a tall, frosty glass of "Is that all you've got?" But such was not the case.

Each day I was dropped off, walked by that beautiful fountain outside the main entrance, and headed straight for the restroom to do more than just rest. The mere thought and anticipation of that smell was enough to make me sick. I accepted that reality.

Sometimes I had a lump in my throat before I even walked through the main entrance. I smiled at folks as we passed in the corridor, but I didn't dare open my mouth. It would not have been a pleasant exchange.

One day I talked with my Uncle Bob who called to see how Michele and I were doing. He was a combat veteran of the Korean War. Later in his life, he had fought and won his battle against stomach cancer.

He was a tough guy, but to both my surprise and relief, he confirmed having the same response every time he went to the hospital for his outpatient treatments. "There was just something about the smell of the place that hit me like a ton of bricks every time I walked in," he said. "I had to go be sick first, and then the rest of the day I was fine."

27

Little Chart of Horrors

When I began my outpatient treatments, I spent considerable time each day waiting to be called for examinations, procedures, and finally my chemo infusion. On occasion I was given my chart and asked to sit tight with it until the Dungeon Master called me back to the chemo waiting room. I often had it with me for hours until my name was called, or someone from the Medical Records department came to retrieve it.

There were some days early on in that phase of treatment when I still felt pretty good, and I spent considerable time reviewing its contents. I'll always remember the first time I noticed a comment at the bottom of a doctor's report where my prognosis was categorized as "Poor." It was a bit of a reality check to say the least.

My heart sank the first time I read those words. As much as I tried to deny the fact that I was a cancer patient, seeing those words on an official hospital form hammered that reality home rather abruptly.

I struggled with the stark reality of my condition. My doctors were doing the best they could and rallying to fight hard against my disease, but the truth was my situation did not look good at all.

In hindsight, it might have been better if I had not seen all the gory details in my little chart of horrors, as the knowledge of my sorry state was a mental and emotional "speed bump" I negotiated each day.

I spent time in the research library on the hospital campus and poured over volumes of material about cancer. I determined to learn all I could about my type of leukemia and my "poor" prognosis. The time was fast approaching when I wouldn't give a rip about anything but getting through each day, and being thankful for each morning that I woke up and was still alive.

Looking back, I think the time spent in all those medical journals and textbooks really helped me keep my head on tight. I had a file full of articles titled, *"Leukemia: Everything You Never Wanted to Know."*

When the bad times came, I felt like I had been hit by a freight train and was lost in a fog over what was happening to my body. When that happened I often recalled something I'd read about the nausea or the depression or the effects of Prednisone, and it provided perspective to help me through the bad reactions.

Other times, Michele was the source of the information and reassurances I needed. She was working in oncology at the time, and then came home to her chemo-fried husband, which was a tremendous strain on her.

God bless her for hanging in with me during that horrible time. She did her best to provide good information I could lean on and better cope with my circumstances.

The more I knew about the treatments, the more I was able to cope with the treatments without panicking. I wasn't as fearful or anxious as I might have been if I had been blindsided by the unexpected and terrible side-effects. Knowledge gave me power to cope.

28

The Watering Hole

I learned very quickly during my first month of treatment the chemo waiting room was essentially a "watering hole," where patients gathered, laughed together, and sometimes cried together.

Bald men who didn't care about their sudden hair loss and bald women who did filled the room each day. Some wore snowcaps, others wigs, baseball caps, or bandanas.

We compared notes about our reactions to medications and how our treatments were going. We talked about our families, what we did for a living, and our hopes for a return to health.

Some passed around photos of their children and grandchildren; others read the paper and commented on the latest headlines.

Sometimes the room was quiet with only occasional chatter as bad days were a common thread. On any given day, the room could be filled with lots of folks, sick or just sick and tired, who had little or no interest in conversation.

There were plenty of days when I felt sorry for myself. I sat and listened as folks described their own struggles with medication side effects or the aftermath of some invasive procedure they had endured. Those times were a wake up call for me.

Suck it up, Rob.

The reality was and is to this day that my situation could always be worse. There was always someone who had been through much more, who was far worse off, and wouldn't be fazed a bit by my tough time. If others could get through it, so could I. That was a tough pill to swallow but a valuable lesson. I re-learned it almost every day.

29

Small World

Over the first two months of outpatient treatment, I got to know a fellow named Ron. He was a really cool guy, perhaps in his early sixties at the time. He had a rare and incurable form of lymphoma.

Ron spent years at the City of Hope. Many experimental treatment protocols were tested on him, and his doctors worked tirelessly to find something that would help. He was a journeyman cancer patient.

He was always in a good mood, and he had a nutty sense of humor that put a smile on my face. I never knew what he was going to say next.

We met up quite frequently in the chemo waiting room as our appointments coincided. We became good friends, but I only knew him by his first name.

One day—and I have no clue why—I took a hard look at him from across the room and thought, *He looks so familiar, like I've known him for years. How is that possible? I've only known the guy for a month or so.*

I asked Ron, "What's your last name?"

"Smith, why?"

"Because it just dawned on me you look an awful lot like a guy named Ron I worked with at a non-profit organization called Focus on the Family."

A huge grin came over his face.

"Ron is my son!"

It was the neatest moment, a reminder that it truly is a small world.

"Your son is a good friend of mine. We worked together almost every day, and we had a ball," I said.

"That's pretty cool, Rob. It's a small world, isn't it?"

"You bet it is. Ron was one of the folks that took up the collection for my wife and me when this cancer odyssey first began."

Ron Sr. was really excited to learn of my connection with his son. From that point on our friendship grew deeper. One day when we met in the main lobby, I asked Ron how things were going. His response was a real surprise.

"You know what Rob, today I'm telling my doctor that I've had enough of being a lab rat."

I was stunned.

"They're never going to figure me out, and I'm at the point in life now where I would rather move to Utah and ride horses for as long as I can before I die, rather than spend another day here on some new experimental drug."

The whole notion of choosing to be "done" and walking away from treatment was completely foreign to me. I was fighting for my life every day I came to City of Hope. When Ron shared what he did, I was blown away. We talked for a few more minutes about his decision.

He had already purchased the property in Utah. It was a done deal.

When he described how his life would be for however long he had left on the planet, he was very animated. I believe he was sincerely happy and content with his decision. The man had peace in his life, perhaps for the first time in a long while.

It was an exchange I have never quite been able to fully process. Perhaps that's what God intended. Perhaps not everything in this life is supposed to have a nice big bow wrapped around it in the end—Ron rides off into the sunset, cured.

Ron was riding off uncertain of the outcome. Perhaps having a big hole in the middle of our circumstances is so we may realize that our life isn't perfect, neat, or clean. Stuff just happens that we cannot change or control. Perhaps those holes in our life are there to drive us to a deeper understanding of our tenuous human condition, and our need to thank God for every day we're given.

Ultimately I'm dependent on him and not myself to find peace, especially in the midst of dire circumstances. Twenty years since my original diagnosis I still wrestle with that notion.

Now some holes are bigger, and the edges are even more tattered. But I hope I've made some progress in understanding the need for those holes, and the tattered edges that never seem to get trimmed up.

The impatient part of me wants to fill in the holes, and clean up those edges once and for all, and declare victory. It's not an easy path—not for me. But on those rare days when I actually have some perspective and the capacity for rational thought, I realize each new day quietly presents itself as another opportunity to make strides.

I try to forge ahead in solidarity with family members and friends who are in the midst of their own struggles and finding their way through—holes and all. Perhaps that is how it is supposed to be.

30

Sick as a Dog

By mid-December of 1989 the chemo treatments took their toll. I spent a lot of time being sick and sleeping. I lost twenty-five pounds in one week.

There were times when I was doubled over, heaving, and would not have been at all surprised to see all of my internal organs followed by my teeth, tongue and eyeballs drop into my bucket, like a $1,000 payoff from a Vegas slot machine. *Three buckets. We have a winner!*

On Michele's birthday, Sandi came over, and my parents came out as well to throw Michele a little party. I was super sick and spent most of the evening asleep in our bedroom. When I woke up, I heard the muffled sounds of conversation on the other side of the bedroom door.

I was happy and sad at the same time, hearing Michele's laugh—the same laugh I recognized that night at Denny's. This time, the circumstances were far different.

I'd connected with Sandi a few days prior to Michele's birthday to see if she could pick up a gift I could give Michele. She made it happen. Sandi picked out a really pretty blouse and skirt. When Michele opened that gift, she had a big smile on her face. I think it made her very happy. I'll always remember Sandi's act of love. She was the best.

At one point that night, I came out to visit but was back in bed within just a few minutes. I wanted so much to be part of the celebration, to give Michele a special night that was just about her, but it just wasn't in the cards.

31

Our Plastic Christmas

Because of my suppressed immune system, I was not to spend any quality time with live plants. A real Christmas tree was out of the question. We opted for what my good buddy Gordon referred to as "pseudofloraplastifolia."

He brought us just such a tree; a genuine artificial Christmas tree that had been part of his own family's collection of holiday decorations. It was great—the ultimate work around.

Not only did Michele and I embrace the mystery and intrigue of pseudofloraplastifolia, but my mother-in-law did as well. When she came down to our place for a visit a few days after Christmas, she caught the vision, and bought an artificial tree on sale at a local department store, and hauled it to their home a few days later.

Growing up, we always had a real Christmas tree. I used to love the way our house filled with a strong scent of pine.

Christmas of 1989 was my first Christmas as a married man, and I had looked forward to filling the apartment with that familiar pine scent. But it didn't play out that way.

I decided that ripple in my plans wasn't going to cause me to loose sight of what really mattered: family and friends. Ultimately, that was what the holiday was about. It really didn't matter what kind of tree we had in our apartment, or if we had a tree at all. It would have been far worse to have a real tree and an empty house on Christmas Day.

32

Earning My "Wired" Merit Badge

In the carefree days of my youth, I never drank or did any drugs. There were several dark years where I was addicted to Pepsi, but nothing more hardcore beyond that. I was a boy scout. Literally. Though I have memories of a few of our scout leaders falling off their camp chairs, drunk on our weekend trips (*we all knew there was more than just poker going on in the big tent*), I have no personal history with alcohol.

Okay, there was a dark period when I was three years old. I indulged in a few swigs of my Dad's Miller High Life beer when he took a break from yard work on the weekends. I've seen those incriminating photos of my infrequent and brief benders, but that's as nasty as I got, two feet tall and bulletproof.

Early in 1990 I began my first thirty-day steroid treatment. For the first time in my life I experienced the effects of intense drug use. Different from Anabolic steroids used by some athletes to build muscle mass, Corticosteroids were used to treat many illnesses, including leukemias, lymphoma, arthritis, and asthma as well.

My treatment protocol was a thirty-day cycle of infused chemo followed by thirty days of steroids, in a daily dosage powerful enough to drop a water buffalo in its tracks.

At first, the doctors prescribed Decadron. After riding that lightning for a few days, horns grew out of my forehead. I declared myself the lord of all I surveyed and tried to convince Michele a unicorn would make a great pet. She quickly contacted the docs and inquired about stepping things down a bit to a more "friendly," perhaps less demonic steroid I could actually tolerate.

The answer: Prednisone. *What a delight.*

Steroid therapy affected the function of the adrenal glands. The adrenal glands did not like to be messed with, and they absolutely hated surprises. At 125 milligrams per day, it didn't take long at all for the adrenals to get really hacked off, and the side effects manifested themselves.

I was wired, acutely aware of every fleck of dust floating in the air in front of me, and the spider crawling on the wall across the room. If the phone rang, I shot out of my seat like a rocket. I was moody and emotional (even more emotional than I usually am, which is bad enough) and hungry all the time.

The Prednisone caused a false sense of hunger and messed with my head. Some days I was in control. Other days, I would have eaten the legs off our kitchen table if given the chance.

On those nights I enjoyed a delightful, home-cooked meal with Michele. Two hours later, I walked to the "Chicken and Ribs" just a half block from our apartment and enjoyed a second, delightful, home-cooked meal.

The back of my neck and my face swelled up, something medical professionals referred to as "buffalo hump" and "moon face." They sounded like code names Navy Seals might use in a covert operation.

If I watched TV and just tried to maintain my sanity, the shows were all very intense and in brilliant living color. The NBC peacock never looked so good.

I was high as a kite.

One night I had a sensation come over me, where I felt like my tongue had swelled up inside my mouth. My fingers and hands felt like they had ballooned up and looked like gigantic "Mickey Mouse" hands but without the white gloves.

On a positive note, thirty days on steroids was thirty days I wasn't sick all the time with a bucket in hand, and my abdominal slot machine paying off big every fifteen minutes. But Steroids presented unique challenges. Given the choice between being sick or being wired like an addict, I preferred the latter.

Chemotherapy wiped me out. I slept all the time and was unable to even carry on a conversation. Steroids strung me out, but otherwise I felt good physically. It was like I was part of some bizarre game show.

Welcome back to "Pick Your Poison." We're in the lightening round, and Rob, it's time for your decision. Which of the two horrible options presented did you choose—and how much did you wager?

33

A Year on the Job

The alternating cycles of chemo and steroids lasted just over a year. It was indeed the rough road Dr. Steve had described, but to my relief, except for an infection at the site of my central line, there weren't too many surprises or complications along the way.

On a couple of occasions during steroid cycles, Michele and I made weekend trips north to visit her family and friends. In February of 1990, we spent a weekend in Santa Barbara to celebrate our one-year wedding anniversary. My recollections of that weekend are both pleasant, and upsetting.

We certainly had fun. We toured the Mission grounds, took in the beauty of the botanic gardens, shopped on State Street, bought a killer rocking chair from the Eddie Bauer Home Store, and enjoyed some delicious meals on the waterfront. But the weekend was also peppered with petty arguments and miscommunications.

We butted heads over stupid stuff: where to park the car, what side of the street to begin our shopping, whether or not to order an appetizer before dinner. Ridiculous. I believe those interactions were fueled by mutual frustration over our situation, and the role changes that had taken place between us.

At the onset of my illness, I became a patient and Michele became a caregiver. Neither Michele or I wanted to assume those roles. We just wanted to be husband and wife. A year later, as I completed the intense treatment regimen, those roles shifted once again.

It was rough going. But God kept us in his grip. We were two very frustrated individuals, but did our best to get through each day, each month. I believe it is only the grace of God that kept us moving forward, and committed to each other; committed to emerging on the other side of our mess, still intact as a couple.

34

Regaining My Focus

After graduating from Azusa Pacific University in 1985, I taught art classes at a private school in Pasadena and did freelance graphic design work on the side. At the same time, I began my graduate studies to further my theological training. I knew I wanted to combine my love of the graphic arts with ministry.

During that time, I had an opportunity to work as a freelancer in the art department at Focus on the Family, and out of that relationship, was offered a full-time position.

My job in the art department at Focus was the perfect fit. It allowed me to contribute my design and production skills to a wonderful cause—a ministry to families. My relationship with Michele was blossoming, so I decided to put my graduate studies on hold, and devote all my energy to my new job at Focus and my relationship with Michele. I had enough on my plate. I was the happiest guy in town.

After nearly nine months of treatment, I was cleared to resume driving. The sense of independence was refreshing. I ran errands and took trips to local malls to "people watch," and get out among the masses.

I was eager to schedule a visit with my friends and coworkers at Focus on the Family and reestablish my ties with them. After how those special people had gone the extra mile to support Michele and me, I was eager to go back and thank everyone personally. I missed them so much and missed the fun we had at work each day.

During the twenty-minute drive from our apartment to the Focus campus, my mind went a mile a minute. I thought about how incredible those folks were, and how cool it was to have our vice-president visit several times when I was in the hospital. I looked forward to sharing with them how their generosity helped us pay down our insurance deductibles and kept our heads above water.

I thought about how different I looked. When I left on sick leave, I had a full head of hair, and a mustache. I was also thirty-five pounds heavier. Nine months later, I was bald with a moon face thanks to the steroids, walked like a wino, and wasn't at the top of my mental game by any measure.

I was sharp as a cork. But I was strong enough to visit my friends. That's all that mattered.

I arrived at the Focus campus in the late morning, so my visit dovetailed with the lunch hour. After being gone for so long, I felt like a first-time visitor driving onto the campus, and winding my way through the parking lot.

Focus employed several hundred folks at that time. I hadn't worked there long before I knew a lot of people, at least by their first names. Within the division where I worked, the vast percentage of those roughly one hundred folks I knew well and considered good friends.

As I made my way through the main entrance and up the stairs, I was greeted by a group of folks who took part in the blood drive, the bake sales, and other fundraisers held on my behalf. It was so great to connect with them, some of whom I had exchanged only a quick "good morning," and a wave or thumbs-up as we entered the building each morning.

As I stood talking with a few of those folks at the top of the stairs, Dr. James Dobson, the founder and president of the organization emerged from the administrative offices and approached our gathering.

Though I had worked there for a couple years prior to getting sick, I had never formally met him, but when I was on the unit at City of Hope, our vice-president brought me a copy of the biography he had written about Dr. Dobson, and his life and ministry.

On the inside cover, Dr. Dobson wrote me a very special note:

Hey Rob, your friends here at Focus are holding you up in prayer. I don't know why you have had to suffer, but I do know that God has not lost track or control of your circumstances. Keep the faith–and get well quickly! Your friend in Christ, Jim Dobson.

Someone mentioned I was visiting that day for a reunion with my fellow employees in the Communications Division. A warm smile came over Dr. Dobson's face. "This is Rob Henslin? You are the most prayed for guy I've ever seen!"

He patted me on my back, and told me it was great to see me doing well. He told me to get back to Focus soon; that they needed me. It was a tremendous shot in the arm.

Pumped up by that brief meeting, I headed down the main hallway on the second floor and opened the door to the Communications Division. Unbeknownst to me, my crazy friends had a well-coordinated plan in place to welcome me back in a manner they knew I would find familiar and comforting.

Besides an almost constant stream of practical jokes, and plenty of laughs as we went about our work, we had a special tradition within the division. Late in the afternoon, if it was a birthday, anniversary, or other significant day in your life, you and your entire cubicle were bombed with wadded up paper balls, usually accompanied by other scraps of paper as well. At 4:30 p.m., everyone stormed your office and dumped their trashcans over the walls of your cubicle. It was always a wonderful mess.

I was a recipient of just such a bombing on the occasion of my last day as a single man in early February 1989. I have a great photo of the aftermath.

On the day of my visit, just seconds after I greeted one of the two gals who worked in the front reception area, wads of paper balls came out of nowhere. I was bombed from every direction. Employees were hidden strategically throughout the area, behind walls and plastic foliage, with paper wads at the ready.

I never saw them. They got me good—real good. I just stood there in the middle of that mess, cracking up as they cheered and clapped.

Welcome back bro!

A short time later, we gathered in the department's conference room for lunch. The room was filled with conversation, laughter, smiles, and lots of wisecracking, just like it always had been. The group asked me to share some thoughts. Some called out "speech."

I wanted to let them know how much Michele and I appreciated all their love and support. But when I stood up and looked around the room at that gathering of friends, I was suddenly overcome with emotion and couldn't get a word out.

The tears flowed—a huge release of all the "stuff" I had pushed down deep in order to stay focused on treatment and getting well. I realized at that moment just how much I missed and loved those folks, and how deep was the sense of loss I felt.

I struggled to speak. "I'm sorry you guys. I can't get a word out."

The room that just a few moments earlier had been filled with joking and laughter had grown very quiet, and lots of folks were crying. The sudden realization of the heaviness of the situation hit us all right between the eyes. Yet, the room overflowed with joy over God's blessings. Someone called out to me.

"We love you Rob. Keep fighting!"

The visit to Focus that day provided some needed perspective and reconnection, and helped me understand I had made progress. With each day's passing, I was one step closer to returning to work and perhaps some semblance of normalcy. It was so good to be with those folks and feel a sense of solidarity with them.

They continued to be a prayer force, and a source of encouragement to Michele and me as my treatment continued. When I had bad days, I leaned heavily on the knowledge those folks were in my corner. I didn't want to give up. I didn't want to disappoint them.

35

Clueless

After just over a year of chemotherapy and steroids, my treatment concluded. My job was done, at least the daily grind, and the invasive, painful, mind-altering treatments. Michele and I felt a huge sense of relief when we reached that milestone.

As I continued to feel better, I faced new challenges. Because of the brain radiation, I had short and long-term memory loss that drove Michele crazy. She got so frustrated when I couldn't recall what she had said only moments prior. Plans we made and marked on our calendar weeks in advance came as a total surprise to me. I had no clue we had any plans.

I had no clue.

The treatment wreaked havoc on my body, and on our relationship. It took many months for the chemo and it's side effects to work themselves out of my system to where I felt really good—dare I say normal? Michele would argue even now those effects never really worked themselves out. I suspect there is a fair amount of truth to that.

In the years following my cancer treatment, I had to rely on family members and friends to help me recall much of my childhood. In many cases, I was able to find the memories I thought had been washed away.

But to this day, I struggle to simply recall the events that prior to brain radiation and chemotherapy were vivid and fond memories. The good news is that there is apparently plenty of room for all the new memories I make each day, as I have no problem accessing that data in what remains of my brain. That is an awesome blessing.

36

Upside, Downside

My treatment schedule was scaled back to bi-weekly visits to the City of Hope for checkups, coupled with a daily pill regimen that would last nearly three years. At one point, I was taking sixty pills per day.

Bottles of prescription meds lined our kitchen counter, like soldiers waiting to march into battle. They served as a daily reminder of the milestone we had reached, and also that our fight was not over.

As Michele and I embraced a life more free of the oppressive cloud of treatment and sickness, we rode a wave of several new dynamics in our life.

On the upside, we had an opportunity in August of 1991 to travel to London for a few days, where we attended the wedding of one of Michele's friends. After a couple days there, we met up with Michele's family in Paris and enjoyed nine days of fun, prior to my returning to work.

My cancer, and its watershed consumed our lives for nearly two years. Our travels abroad were a wonderful reward, a chance to clear our heads and refocus.

Like our trip to Vancouver and Victoria, we were blessed with beautiful weather during that vacation. I never saw a sky so blue as the one that enveloped London's Big Ben clock tower as it came into view upon our exit from the underground subway.

Paris was beautiful as well. We toured the Eiffel Tower, the Palace of Versailles, numerous museums, and enjoyed nightlife in the Latin

Quarter, a part of the city near Notre Dame cathedral that buzzed with jugglers, street musicians, chalk artists, and incredible restaurants. We ate crepes, falafels, and fresh bread and cheese. A week after we returned home, I returned to my job at Focus on the Family. Michele left oncology for a new position in home healthcare.

On the downside, the role changes we had experienced during my illness created tension, arguments, miscommunication, and issues left unresolved. I transitioned from being the sick patient to something more resembling a husband. At least I thought as much at the time.

Michele gave up much of her role as advice nurse and caregiver and was quite ready to migrate back to wife mode and devote her energies to anything other than my (our) medical problems.

We struggled to figure out exactly who we were, who we had become as a married couple. There was a level of detachment from one another that, at the time, I thought I understood and was comfortable with. I thought I knew full well the difficult road Michele had walked during the very trying times of my illness.

She had worked in an oncology unit in a hospital, and then came home each night to her cancer-ravaged husband. She lost some of her spark and was far less affectionate. I figured after what she had been through with me, part of her was just not ready or able to make much of an emotional investment in our relationship.

My leukemia was in remission, and I was on the road to recovery, but I struggled to maintain a focus on the positives rather than on the "what ifs." I tried not to think a whole lot about the cancer monkey asleep on my back.

I hoped with time and God's grace we could shake off much of the residue of my illness and the upheaval it brought our marriage.

I thought we could reclaim lost ground in our relationship, but it was a struggle. We never really had a chance to just enjoy being a young married couple. That hacks me off to this day.

But looking back, I see how God worked to keep us moving forward together. He did it in a very special way.

37

It's a Girl!

Lauren Clae Henslin was born June 26th, 1992. She was a perfect, healthy little girl. She was a genuine miracle. Michele and I became parents. We became a family.

When I was first admitted to the City of Hope, one of the tough pills we had to swallow was learning that because of the nature of chemotherapy, we would most likely not be able to have children. *Ouch.* It wasn't what either one of us, in our mid-twenties, wanted to hear.

When my doctor broke that news to us, I slumped back in my chair. It was one more, bad thing in a long line of bad things we had to chew on. But in October 1991, a home pregnancy test confirmed Michele was pregnant.

We both flipped out in a good way. It was as if we had found a gift, wrapped up with ribbons and bows, hiding under the (artificial!) Christmas Tree after the other gifts had long been opened. It was so much fun sharing the news with our family and friends, something positive and completely unexpected to be excited about, and look forward to after our long struggle.

God blessed us with the precious gift of Lauren, and it drew Michele and me very close. Fast. We had a new focus, a new way to work together. It strengthened our bond. We were a family, and we felt blessed—incredibly blessed.

My Dad was 86 years old when Lauren was born. I don't think he thought he would live to see the day he would welcome a granddaughter into the world. It was an amazing time.

Did I mention our daughter was perfect?

Even as I wrote this memoir, I was overwhelmed with emotion *(what a sap)*. At the time of this writing, Lauren was a high school senior, making plans and contemplating her future as adulthood approached.

She's a smart, beautiful young lady with a love for children, has strong opinions and an independent spirit. She has a knack for making friends, and bringing people together. She is a daily reminder for Michele and me of God's blessings in our lives. I love her so much.

Miracles really do happen.

38

Don't Waste My Time!

When I left Focus on the medical leave of absence, several freelancers covered my position. I was told my job would be waiting for me whenever I was ready to return. Incredible. Following our trip to London and Paris, I returned to the organization as the department transitioned from "old school" art production and design to an electronic, Mac-based computer platform. I was as happy as a clam at high tide to be back, contributing to a cause I believed in.

On one occasion our Art Director, Brian, called a planning meeting to discuss a new project request that came directly from the organization's Board of Directors—high-level stuff.

For reasons unclear to me at the time, I had a very negative initial reaction when Brian described the piece. It was not going to be anything Focus offered as a resource to help strengthen families, but rather (in my humble and oft ignorant opinion) was something someone thought would be nice, but the piece lacked much value beyond that.

It was an "oh brother" moment.

The meeting adjourned, and we had our marching orders to get the job off the ground. Over the next week, the editors wrote copy, and the art department staff developed the design and built the page layouts. With each passing day, I developed more and more of a chip on my shoulder.

After being patient, and I think cutting me some major slack in light of my time away battling the illness, Brian called me into his office and confronted me. "Dude, what is your problem? I'm sick and tired of your bad attitude!"

I had a moment of clarity.

I was never angry with God over getting sick. I never spent any time asking "Why me?" But I realized the booklet project felt like a big waste of my time.

"You know Brian, I honestly didn't know why I've been acting the way I have until just now," I said. "The booklet project for the Board members seems stupid and pointless. I guess I really don't want the time I have left on the planet to be wasted."

He sat silently for several minutes. Tears welled up in my eyes, and I got really quiet. He looked at me and nodded his head as if to say, "Okay, I can understand where your head is." It was quite a moment.

I apologized to him for my attitude, and told him I would square things away. I have no specific memories of the balance of our conversation that day, but I do recall my portion of work on the Board project was handed off to someone else, and I turned my attention to other projects.

I appreciated the way Brian handled the situation. Looking back on that time in history, I realized I had allowed an attitude of "don't waste my time" to became a part of who I was, and in part, the person I am today. I'm not sure if that's a good thing or not.

My cancer odyssey taught me life was precious and stirred in me a deep desire to do something meaningful with my life. That was the upside. But unfortunately, my desire to not waste my time manifested itself as impatience and callousness towards others—towards my colleagues at work. That was wrong.

Thankfully, God allowed me to have that moment of clarity when Brian called me to account, and I was able to recognize my bad attitude for what it was. I'm thankful for that gift.

39

Heading North

In the second quarter of 1991, Focus on the Family relocated from California to Colorado Springs, Colorado. Employees were invited to stay with the company and relocate. Many chose to do so. For me, it wasn't the move to make.

When I was sick, I decided before I turned thirty, I wanted to work for myself if possible and provide graphic design services to my own clients. When Focus relocated, I saw it as the opportunity to pursue that goal.

By mid-August of 1991, my work at Focus concluded. I purchased a slightly used computer system, worked hard to build a client base, and established my business.

Michele and I talked often about our mutual desire to move to the Bay Area when the timing was right. She was eager to return home to family and friends, and I had long thought living in that part of the country would be a welcome change from the congestion, heat, and smog of the San Gabriel valley.

By June of 1992, Michele left her job on maternity leave. It was a special time. We spent lots of time together, playing with baby Lauren. We also made sure her grandparents had as much quality time with her as possible.

With me working freelance and Michele home from work, a window of opportunity opened for us to get serious about a move. We packed up as much of our stuff as possible even though we did not have a specific moving date scheduled or a place to move to. We opted to be proactive and set the wheels in motion by packing ahead of time. Slowly our garage space, and then our living room filled with boxes.

We took several trips to the Bay Area to search for a suitable rental, and eventually worked out all the details to secure northern California digs. In September of 1992, we packed up our rental truck (to the brim), tucked baby Lauren into our car, sedated our cat, and hit the road.

Leaving southern California was exciting, and at the same time a bit unsettling in light of my strong connection to and dependence on the City of Hope. My buddy Gordon joined me for the trip. We talked a lot about our times together, and all that had transpired in our lives since we'd first become friends in high school.

Gordon was a tremendous bulwark of support when I was going through treatment. There were times when he called me at the house, and right off the bat told me if I needed to go throw up he was cool with that. He didn't mind waiting on the line while I took care of business. Too cool.

I will always cherish his friendship, and the support he provided when I was going through that hell. We had some good conversations and lots of "laugh 'til you cry moments" on the trip north. We remain good friends to this day.

For Michele, the trip north with Lauren was far less amusing. Though our cat had curled up into a ball and was sleeping soundly, Lauren decided it would be more fun to simply cry; not every now and then, but for the entire 400-mile trip.

Gordon and I passed Michele several times, driving our Isuzu Trooper as we made our way up the Interstate in the truck. Each time, the look on her face seemed more haggard and strained. At one point she came along side us and rolled down her window. "Want to trade," she asked.

My response was quick, and Gordon had my back. Almost in unison, we yelled "No thanks" and hit the gas.

After the long trip north, the cat woke up (nursing a hangover),

Lauren stopped crying and fell asleep, and we spent our first night in the Bay Area at the home of Michele's parents. We spent the next couple of days moving our stuff into the rental house with help from Gordon, Michele's family, and our friends in the area.

Our rental house was pretty cool. There was a park just a few blocks away, our neighbors had two young kids who were very friendly, and the house had lots of garden space for Michele, and room for Lauren to play.

I had my office up and running within a week, reestablished contact with my clients, most of them in southern California and some out of state. I developed plans for marketing my services to the wide range of companies in the Silicon Valley.

In 1993 Michele accepted a position as Weekend and Relief Nursing Supervisor for a homecare and hospice agency in Mountain View, about fifteen minutes north of our place in Sunnyvale. She spent the balance of her time being Lauren's Mom.

Michele was an awesome Mom. She was a natural, and one heck of a gardener as well. She spent lots of time working the raised planting beds in our backyard. She planted a dwarf orange tree. I still wonder from time to time if the landlord kept it and allowed it to grow.

We settled in well to our new locale and moved forward with life as a family. We were thankful for the blessings of restored health, a marriage tested by fire but hanging in there, our beautiful daughter with her easy smile and twinkle in her eyes, a good job for Michele, a growing business, and simply being a family.

Every day I thanked God for the gift of another day. I prayed I would not waste it. At least once each day, my thoughts turned to the cancer monkey asleep on my back. *How long would he hibernate? What would we do if he woke up?* Sometimes those thoughts were overwhelming.

There were days when I thought, *What's the point? What is the point of acting like my life is okay, when it most likely won't stay that way? The monkey will wake up, and I'll be toast.* Other days, I was able to accept my situation for what it was, and focus on the present rather than the "what ifs" that may or may not be in my future.

40

A Second Unexpected Miracle

Two years after Lauren was born, we were blessed once again with another unexpected miracle. Kristen Marie Henslin was born June 1, 1994. She was as cute as a bug. She was perfect. Lauren was so excited to have a baby sister. I was blown away by the thought I was the father of two beautiful daughters. We brought Kristen home from the hospital and began life as a family of four.

Did I mention baby Kris was perfect?

During the weeks that followed, I wondered what the girls would be like when they grew up. *What kind of personalities would we see develop in them as they began their journey as sisters?* I pondered also what God was teaching us through that incredible second miracle. *How should we respond? What about the sleeping cancer monkey?*

Whenever I thought about Lauren and Kristen, I saw them as a sign from God that everything was going to be fine—everything—for all time; wishful thinking on my part. I believe it was fueled by a desperate desire to once and for all wrap a big red ribbon around the ordeal that Michele and I had been through.

Can we just move on? Write the book already. Print it, bind it, and park it on a shelf somewhere. Done.

In my mind, Kristen's arrival into our young family, and watching our daughters grow so close was icing on the cake. How could I explain the blessing of two children we were told by the medical community we would never have? I could not without considering the realm of the miraculous.

It had to be a sign we were out of the woods.

Sure Rob. You bet.

The better, more theologically sound approach for me to take was to see my girls as a daily reminder that miracles happen. I really had no idea how things would play out in my life. Who did?

I had to exercise my faith on a daily basis, chill out, and take things as they came. Ultimately, I had to try to be less of a piece of work, and choose to recognize and enjoy God's blessings, regardless of circumstances. That was my path to peace.

41

Leap of Faith

Michele and I got about the business of being a family. But we lived tentatively. We were hesitant, perhaps subconsciously, to make too many bold moves. We rented rather then entertained any ideas of home ownership.

But by early 1998, mortgage interest rates were at an historic low. An opportunity arose for us to consider the possibility of buying a home. Without much hesitation, we got the wheels rolling and figured if it was meant to work out it would. If not, we had given it our best shot.

We were pre-approved for a home loan, and Michele began looking at houses with Gail, our realtor. I joined in on the hunt as my project deadlines allowed. After looking at close to one hundred homes *(yes, 100)*, Michele found a place in a great neighborhood in San Jose.

The house needed some big love, but it was easy to see the potential. We knew we could make it a home, where we could raise our girls, put down some roots, and plug into the community.

When the day arrived to meet with the mortgage broker and sign the nearly three-inch high stack of loan documents, Michele and I were struck with the heaviness of the moment.

It was not just the financial obligation we were taking on, but the realization that we were making a huge leap of faith, shaking off that tentative, safe existence we were then living.

Michele was fired up, eager to dive into our new place, and make it the home we both knew it could become. The day Gail handed us the keys was like the turning of a page.

It was the beginning of a new chapter in our lives. I spent the first two weeks working on the place in the evenings, then on July 4th weekend, 1998, we moved in. Four-year old Kristen insisted on being the first one to walk through the front door.

42

Making Memories, One Day at a Time

What seemed like a never-ending list of home improvement projects, some more critical than others, occupied much of our time in the years that followed. With the help of family and friends, we turned our little fixer-upper into a warm and welcoming home.

In the midst of that flurry of activity we raised our girls, with everything that implies: belly button piercings, birthday parties, bunnies, Christmas, dance team, Halloween, hamsters, homework, kittens, make up, puppies, school events, sleepovers (*I'm so glad we installed solid core bedroom doors*), soccer, summer camping trips—and boys. It was mayhem and magic.

Our neighbors, raising their own kids, became good friends. We gathered for backyard barbeques, birthday parties, late night flyover viewings of the Space Shuttle and International Space Station, yard sales, and an annual New Year's Day Rose Parade Breakfast Extravaganza.

At the strong urging of my wife, we had an office built in our backyard where I could operate my graphic design business. This also made it possible for our girls to have their own bedrooms and provided some physical separation from my work and home life. It allowed our home to be just that, without my business pressing in.

Life felt really good. Each day I thanked God for another opportunity to be there for my wife and my kids, be the provider I yearned to be, enjoy time with family and friends, help my clients be successful, and enjoy life in the Bay Area.

What Michele and I had been through so many years prior had a profound influence on how we lived our lives. But in all honesty, there were times where I didn't give the sleeping cancer monkey much conscious thought. With so much time past without any health problems and life feeling so normal, I thought perhaps he would never wake up. I thought we were out of the woods.

But I was dead wrong.

For a second time, after nearly twenty years, my leukemia returned, and our lives were changed in an instant.

Against the backdrop of that nightmare, with our world turned upside down, other issues bubbled up and in some cases exploded on the surface. Hurts and pains suppressed and held onto tightly for decades and never dealt with, were revealed.

The cancer monkey indeed woke up, but very quickly became only one component of a much larger mess. There wasn't just one monkey but a whole bunch of them. They had been having a sleepover.

This time around the challenges, heartache, pain, revelations, and blessings in the midst of it all, would far surpass anything we could have possibly imagined.

"Courage doesn't always roar. Sometimes courage is the little voice at the end of the day that says I'll try again tomorrow."
—Mary Anne Radmacher

43

Relapse

It is never a good thing when your doctor calls you at home, especially when you just met with her a couple hours earlier. Doctors do not call just to chat. At 1:50 p.m. on October 20th, 2008, my office phone rang. It was my primary care physician, Dr. Shan.

"How do you feel, Rob?"

"Oh, I feel pretty good, doc. No complaints, why?"

She began to discuss the lab values, how this number looked really good, and this one and that one as well, but then mentioned my white blood cell (WBC) count. There was a brief pause on her end of the phone line.

I got a lump in my throat as big as my shoe.

"Your white cell count is very elevated at sixty-five thousand."

"My what! My white cells are what?"

"I think your leukemia has come back, and that you have had a relapse. Do you understand what has happened?"

"A relapse? What?" I quickly spun into a fog. Michele came out to my office. The doctor had first called our house phone, and Michele told her I could be reached at work—my office in our backyard.

Michele stood in the doorway, her eyes as big as saucers as she listened to my half of the conversation with Dr. Shan.

Once doc said the white cell count was elevated, I checked out. I really only remember a few phrases from the balance of our conversation.

Doc mentioned something about connecting me with a really good Hematologist within the Kaiser system, the need for me to come in (the next day) to meet him, and something about a bone marrow biopsy to confirm the diagnosis—all just a blur.

The room spun.

It was a typical, beautiful fall day in the Bay Area. Though Silicon Valley felt the pinch of another economic downturn and a growing national recession, my business, in spite of absorbing its share of hits over the course of the year was doing well.

I worked with a great group of clients on a wide variety of projects. My production schedule for the final quarter of the year was booked solid.

Michele worked at the Vaden Student Health Center on the Stanford University campus. Our daughters were a month and a half into their freshman and junior years in high school, were plugged into the high school group at our church, and life had been humming along nicely.

All of that vanished in a heartbeat, washed away by the utterance of a single word: relapse.

That morning I'd had an appointment with Dr. Shan at the Kaiser medical offices just a few miles from our place in San Jose. It had been a routine visit. Since it had been some time since I had any blood work done, Dr. Shan asked me to stop by the lab, and have a full panel drawn before I left the clinic so we had a fresh baseline on file.

Simple enough, or at least it seemed that way at the time. I was in and out of the lab in just a few minutes, and headed home to resume work on several big jobs that were on my plate. But they would have to wait.

As soon as the doctor received the lab results that same afternoon, she called me. She rattled off lab values, doing her best to be sure I was on the same page with her, and that I understood what had happened. My head was spinning as I listened to her speak.

With a trembling hand, I hung up the phone a few moments later, and with a huge lump in my throat broke the news to Michele.

"Doc said my white count has gone through the roof. She thinks my leukemia has relapsed."

I could hardly get the words out of my mouth.

We just stared at each other in stunned disbelief, and then we lost it. We cried and hugged each other and just freaked out, both of us in shock. Within a few minutes our girls came home from school with friends in tow. We hastily pulled ourselves together and waited for the right time to break the news to them.

What a mess.

In an instant, the positive energy of that beautiful day was shattered. We felt consumed by a dark fog. The cancer monkey woke up from his long slumber.

I didn't think he would.

I thought I was in the clear. Our minds raced. We tried to get a grasp on what we needed to do, what wheels to put in motion, and what could wait. Instant priority shift, just add bad news, and stir to a cloudy consistency.

Looking back on that day, I have pondered what was worse: the original diagnosis twenty years prior or receiving word of the relapse. I decided the latter was worse.

Life (from my perspective) was going well, and there had been so many years without a hint of medical problems, let alone anything leukemia-related. There was no two-month-long "ramp up" to slowly digest the fact I was being eaten alive by a disease. The relapse came right out of left field.

This time it wasn't just Michele and me in our little rental apartment in Azusa. This time there was a mortgage, a car payment, and a business to run. We were parents to two wonderful girls. We were a family. There were bunnies, a cat, and dogs. One moment we were bread, the next moment toast.

We never saw the toaster coming.

After a few minutes to get a grip, Michele left my office, and headed back inside the house. She greeted the girls and their friends just as she always had when they exploded through the front door. I sat stunned for a few minutes in my office and tried to digest the horrible news we just received. Then I got out of there to go think for a while.

I was right in the middle of a huge web site design project for one client, and a batch of product marketing collateral for another. Both were hot projects near completion, but right then my head was nowhere close to being in the game.

I don't recall much of the balance of that day. I suppose I went back to the office after that break, but I doubt much was accomplished.

That evening, Michele broke the news to Lauren when they were out running errands. Lauren took it hard.

I had an opportunity to sit down with Kristen later that night. When I knocked on her bedroom door, my mind was racing. I had no idea what I would say to her.

The minute I made eye contact with her, I lost it. The news crushed her like a tin can. It hurt so much to see her so upset, and to know Lauren was also carrying the weight of my bad news. My girls did not deserve that.

It was the worst day of my life.

44

A Painful Email

L ate that night I was wide-awake in bed. I stared at the ceiling as I thought about the business with all the open projects and loose ends that had to be tied up. I could not believe my leukemia had relapsed. I was sad and mad at the same time.

Sleep was a myth. I went out to my office around 3:30 a.m. and drafted a painful email to my clients and vendors to alert them of the bad news, and the implications relative to their projects in my production pipeline:

To my wonderful clients, vendors and business associates,

I write this note to let you know that I received some bad news today that has huge implications. I had routine blood labs done today and rather than hearing from my doctor that my cholesterol was a bit high or that my blood sugars were out of whack, I was told that it looks like the Leukemia that I have been in remission from for almost twenty years is back. My wife and I received the call around 2 p.m. today and have been in shock and emotional basket cases ever since.

I'll know more specifics tomorrow, once my doctor has had an opportunity to consult with the oncologist (Kaiser), and based on that information, will be able to make a call as to how best to handle the completion of currently open projects with many of you, or to arrange for the collection of files for handoff to you or your other vendors for completion. I've tried to work through today and complete as much work as possible, but there will be loose ends to tie up and in some cases, the need for me to completely bow out of projects discussed but not yet executed.

The potential long-term implications relative to if and when I can return to my work and when I do, for how many hours per week are huge and at this point unknown. Based on what I had to go through twenty years ago, a point came a couple months down the line where I wasn't worth much and was too sick from the treatment to be of any use to anyone. So, needless to say this is a horrible, awkward and sad time, but I wanted to let you know right at the outset what was going on and assure you that I will do my very best to see that our open projects are either completed or handed off cleanly so that you can keep your respective programs moving forward.

My faith is strong and my wife and two daughters very supportive, and I plan to get my game face on again as I did twenty years ago and fight hard. I will certainly keep you all posted in the days ahead, especially as the remainder of this week unfolds.

I will probably be in and out of the office a lot over the next several days but will check messages and emails as often as I can. Thank you for your understanding during this rough time. I appreciate you all very much!

Best, Rob

I had no idea just how few or how many days I would have to wrap things up. In light of history, I figured that boat would sail sooner than later. It took me a half hour to write that message. After I sent it, I sat in my office for a while and thought about the sudden turn my life had taken.

The night was very still, eerily so. I glanced at my stack of project files, pictures of my girls pinned to the bulletin board next to my computer, and my model rockets displayed on wooden stands. Each of those items represented a part of my life that brought me great joy. But on that night, I had a crushing realization my life was no longer about those things.

I was in for the fight of my life.

I made a solo trip to Kaiser Hospital the next day. It was a sprawling, state-of-the-art facility. I walked into the clinic building adjacent to the main hospital lost in my thoughts.

Physically I felt fine; there was nothing wrong with me. I hadn't time enough to really grasp all that had transpired over the previous twenty-four hours, let alone consider what delightful events loomed on the horizon.

I just knew things were different—again—and that it only affected every aspect of my life. Though I felt fine, I knew that within a few days I wouldn't. And I knew I wasn't getting out of that place until someone had plunged a needle into my backside.

45

Clincs, Fourth Floor, Department 400 Hematology and Oncology

I found my way to Department 400, checked in with the gal working the front desk and took a seat in the waiting area. I sat there, flipping out on the inside, and trying not to let my emotions get the best of me.

I was as big as a Redwood and sat there with tears welling up in my eyes like a five year old lost in a department store. I couldn't believe my cancer had returned. Images of Michele and my two daughters and scenes from our life flooded my mind.

I leafed through a few *Modern Yachtsman* magazines until my name was called. A medical assistant led me to an exam room to ponder life for a few more moments. I felt totally alone. During that time, I thought about how quickly things had changed; how they would never be the same. I needed to get my game face on and fast. I prayed the doc who came through the door would be someone in whom I could place my full faith and trust.

My prayer was answered. Dr. Robert entered the room, and got right to it. "So, is your head spinning or what? You received some bad news yesterday."

His directness, and at the same time his compassion was the perfect combination. He looked me right in the eye. His words cut right through the fog in my head.

"Yeah, it really is spinning, doc. Right now I really don't know what to think, what to feel. I'm kind of numb."

It only took a few minutes of conversation for me to realize the guy was top drawer, a perfect fit. He had years of experience dealing with my type of cancer, was beloved by the department staff, had an awesome bedside manner, and was a wisecracker.

A full head of wavy, graying hair capped his slender face. He was very animated when he described how far treatment for leukemia and lymphoma had advanced in the twenty years since I was first diagnosed.

"Back then it was a different story. You're going to need a BMT— a bone marrow transplant—since you've relapsed. Today, it's quite possible for it to be curative of your leukemia. We couldn't say that twenty years ago."

That was big news. Huge. I recall acknowledging what doc shared. But almost at the same time, while my head nodded in approval, my brain tapped me on my shoulder and whispered, *He just said you are going to need a bone marrow transplant since you relapsed.*

I had heard the term before. When I was a patient at City of Hope, my brother was tested to see if he was a match. Had he been, his bone marrow would have been harvested and transplanted into me, effectively giving me a brand new immune system. That would have been the best possible treatment.

But my brother wasn't a match, so my doctors treated me with chemo and steroids and hoped for the best. They'd had extremely high hopes.

With the realization I was facing a BMT burning into my consciousness, doc slid his stool over to the computer terminal to input my medical history.

Throughout our exchange, he explained in great detail what the plan would be moving forward to get me back into remission. One minute I tracked his every word; the next, my brain was thinking ahead six months.

I asked him to tell me about the bone marrow transplant. Looking back on that meeting, I realize I probably asked for too much information. It was way too overwhelming to process at one time. I think Dr. Robert knew as much, but he was very cool about it, and did his best to provide answers to my questions that wouldn't completely spin me out.

He spent considerable time walking me through the plan. During our chat he told me he and Dr. Steve at City of Hope were colleagues and would be talking about my case just as soon as my medical records arrived from City of Hope.

It was very comforting to think two of the sharpest doctors on the West coast would be collaborating on my case.

One knew me well. The other was a quick study. I was in good hands.

Dr. Robert quickly became my new favorite person on the planet, effectively holding the keys to the kingdom relative to how my life would play out in the months to come.

Following the initial consultation, we moved to a treatment room down the hall where doc performed a very smooth, and relatively pain-free bone marrow aspiration and biopsy. Unlike Dr. Frankenstein so many years earlier, he leaned over me at every step in the procedure, told me what was coming next and asked if I was okay.

"Yep. I'm fine, doc."

"Man, you're a tough guy."

I assured him it was much more about him having the touch. "I'm not a tough guy doc. I'm doing all I can to simply maintain my sanity."

Though the procedure itself was fairly uneventful, the experience was a reality check; a shot across my bow of sorts. I used it to mentally prepare for what I knew would be at least months of poking and prodding with sharp instruments, into places typically resistant to such invasions.

I will always appreciate the investment of time Dr. Robert made that day to be sure I was cool with everything—as cool as I could be. He knew my head was spinning, and that I was doing my best to hang on until the ride came to a full and complete stop.

As I got to know him over the months that followed, Dr. Robert was always the same great guy, always taking time as if I were his only patient, and always filled with great stories, and some kind of wisecrack. He helped me make it through the day with some laughs and a smile.

46

Closing My Business

I had just three days to get my affairs in order before I was admitted to the hospital to begin the Induction phase of chemotherapy. Beyond the very personal, emotional issues Michele and I dealt with during that frenetic time, I had to find a way to shut down my business without leaving my clients up a creek. I handed off digital files for active projects as well as archives of older work.

Over those three days I prepared packages for overnight delivery, uploaded massive data files to my clients, or the vendors they had lined up. In some cases, clients received backups of projects that dated back ten years.

I pushed through and got it done, but by Saturday evening I was mush. In the quiet of that night, I was hit with a deep sense of isolation, and a realization that the relapse had severed me from my work, my clients and vendors, and the joy I felt running my own show.

It was the first real sense of loss I experienced as a result of the relapse. Like that first bone marrow aspiration after nearly two decades, it was another reminder of the grim reality Michele and I faced.

47

And So, it Begins… Again

My email Inbox was flooded with replies to the alert I sent. The responses overflowed with shock and disbelief, but they also included encouraging words about hanging in there, being strong, and fighting hard. Digital encouragement.

A groundswell of support rose up seemingly out of thin air. Emails, cards, and letters of encouragement poured in. People wrote checks, gave us gift cards for stores and restaurants, and sent handwritten collections of Bible verses for me to keep close as I began treatment.

Our friends organized a dinner delivery network online through Yahoo Groups. A homemade dinner was delivered to our place every Monday, Wednesday, and Friday. Michele didn't have to worry about cooking.

I don't think the folks that provided those meals will ever know what a tremendous help they were. Their selfless acts and willingness to meet a need was a real sanity saver.

On Sunday, October 26, 2008, I exchanged nervous banter with my wife in a small office in the Kaiser Hospital admissions office. The admission specialist input my patient and billing information into her computer and rang up the first of what we knew would be several hefty admission charges on our credit card.

A few minutes later, she led us to the elevator, and we made our way to the third floor, Medical/Oncology unit.

What a horrible feeling. My mind darted from thought to thought as we made our way down the long corridor to the unit entrance. I dreaded the notion of multiple rounds of chemotherapy and other procedures I knew would be part of the mix. I thought about my girls starting a new week of school with their heads full of concerns about what the future held.

Was their Dad going to die or what?

Michele spent a lot of time with me that Sunday afternoon. She was a real comfort. After nearly twenty years free of any kind of leukemia-related issues, reorienting our brains took some time.

Beyond the medical realities I faced, Michele had her own long row to hoe to keep all the plates spinning on the home front and at her job. We talked that afternoon about what, beyond the total upheaval of what we had known to be our life for the past twenty years, our life might look like in the months to come.

In the days that followed, we texted or talked frequently. I updated Michele about my treatments, she told me about her day at work and our girls' activities. I focused on getting through each day relatively unscathed.

Have I mentioned Michele was the greatest wife and mother to our girls a guy could ever ask for?

48

Packing Sanity in a Duffel Bag

When I packed my bag for the first admission to Kaiser, I took some deliberate steps to ensure I would be able to muster the focus needed to push through the chemo cycles.

First, I packed sweat pants and tee shirts as I firmly believed hospital gowns were nothing more than the cruel invention of a twisted mind. I hated them twenty years prior, and knew I would hate them again. They made me feel like I was sick and in the hospital.

I also packed a small notebook to journal my thoughts and keep track of lab values or other important information. Tucked inside was an envelope with pictures of my girls and our family. I spent a lot of time looking at those photos. It pumped me up for battle.

My family was the reason I needed to stay strong. They were the reason I had to fight.

Along with the photos, I included a hand-written collection of Scripture verses one of our friends had sent me in a card just a few days prior. They centered my soul. Taped to the inside front cover of the notebook was a yellow sticky note with two phrases:

Eye of the Tiger. One Day at a Time.

I learned the first phrase watching the movie *Rocky* in 1976. It was the mantra boxer Rocky Balboa's cornerman used to focus Rocky's mind between rounds. He needed Rocky to get hungry, like a steel-eyed tiger stalking it's prey. He needed him to dig deep to find the strength to overcome his adversary. Those words—Eye of the Tiger—fired Rocky up to do battle. They fired me up as well.

When I learned of my relapse, that phrase popped into my head almost immediately. I knew it would become part of my mantra as I began my treatment, that, and taking things one day at a time.

Each morning when I woke up, and many times in the quiet moments when my head filled with worry, I repeated those phrases out loud and looked at the pictures of my beautiful family to get focused. Focus did not always come easily, but having those items helped me ride that emotional roller coaster.

49

The Caring Bridge

M ichele and I looked for a good way to keep folks updated on my status. I recalled several years prior the stepdaughter of a friend of mine went through a heartbreaking illness. His family used a web site to keep family and friends abreast of their daughter's condition.

It provided a conduit for a flood of support his family needed at that critical time. When we were hit with the relapse, our first thought was to get something similar in place.

We decided to use CaringBridge (www.caringbridge.org). It was a donor-supported service, so it cost us nothing to set up our personalized pages. Michele made contact with one of our good friends, Suzanne, whom she worked with at the student health center at Stanford. Suzanne offered to help set up our personalized CaringBridge web site at: http://www.caringbridge.org/visit/roberthenslin.

One day during my first week at Kaiser, on one of her days off, Suzanne made the trip down the peninsula, and helped me write the "background story," and the first of many journal entries we would post over the next year.

Suzanne took my handwritten notes home, and keyed them into our web page. It was a tremendous labor of love I will always appreciate.

Once the site was up, our family and friends were able to read our Journal entries and post their own messages of love and support.

Reading those messages helped me keep my head in the game. I didn't want to give up my fight and let those folks down. The site proved to be an invaluable way to bring folks together in the midst of our cancer chaos.

50

Into the Deeper Woods

I stayed in touch with my daughters in the midst of all the treatments via text messaging over our mobile phones. I told them I loved them, wished them a good day at school, and bugged them about getting their homework and chores done so their Mom didn't go crazy.

My "Dad" vibe was alive and well even though I didn't feel all that great. It was a real shot in the arm to be able to maintain contact with them. My apologies to any teachers or other school officials who got bent out of shape because my girls used their phones during school hours. You'll get over it.

After just two doses of "the juice" that first week, my white blood cell count dropped from nearly 65,000 to 24,600. I was encouraged by my body's initial response. I prayed it wouldn't put up a fight.

With the chemo coursing through my body, Zofran became my new favorite pill. Of the handful I forced down the pipe each morning, it was the only one I looked forward to taking, as it did an amazing job controlling the nausea.

I walked several times each day; twenty-one laps around the unit was a mile under my belt. It was one thing I could do, one point of control over my situation. For a change of scenery, sometimes I walked right out of the unit and down the main corridor of the hospital, pushing my IV pole with me.

When I returned from one of those adventures, my nurses were not happy with me at all. Apparently I had an appointment with a sharp object, and no one could find me. They were just about to call hospital security when I rolled back onto the unit.

Hi guys. Why all the furrowed brows?

It's not good to be tardy when someone is eager to stick you with something sharp. It just gets them agitated.

The chemo infusions concluded within a week. In my head, I thought I would be discharged over the weekend to spend a couple weeks at home.

But several of my "clotting factors" were way out of line, which caused excessive bleeding. I spent a second week at Kaiser as the doctors tried to get a handle on that complication.

Things got pretty dicey for several days. There was a very real concern I might bleed out. I received countless blood and platelet transfusions. When the nurses came into my room, their concern was painfully obvious. I never mentioned to Michele just how intense things got. Perhaps she knew anyway.

Learning I would not be going home when I thought I would, coupled with the somber realization I was in real trouble with complications made the second week a tough push—a real soul-sucker.

Hanging out in my room, staring at seven channels of nothing on TV, reading magazines, and watching the bio-hazard waste can in my room fill to the brim with blood-soaked gauze bandages just about drove me crazy.

It was as if there was a dark cloud hovering over my room. I felt very alone and out of control. Each day I endured a downpour of crushing bad news. I recall one day during that second week, asking Dr. Robert if my situation was unique or out of the norm in any way.

His response was direct and to the point. "No one gets through their Induction chemo without complications. As we attack the leukemic cells, they scatter throughout your body and just wreak havoc. In your case, the blood clotting problem is your big complication, but we'll get a handle on it."

His words provided some needed perspective. A little bit of sunshine broke through the thick layer of clouded uncertainty.

Eye of the tiger. One day at a time.

A few days later, Dr. Robert came into my room on his morning rounds. He leaned up against the wall, his arms crossed in front of him holding my chart close to his chest.

"So, how are you doing today, Rob?"

"I'm pretty angry and doing a lot of looking over my shoulder, doc, you know?"

"Yep. I know. That's understandable."

"This is not how my life was supposed to play out."

"But it did."

"Yeah, it did, and I'm really pissed off."

It was at that point doc heaved a bit of a sigh, paused for a moment, and then shared a story with me. He told me about growing up in New York, playing basketball with his buddies.

"When we put a good lickin' on the other team, the guys would whine and complain. We would tell them, 'You got beat. It is what it is'. You need to get to the point where you can say the same thing about your life and this relapse. It is what it is."

Five simple words.

It was perhaps the most honest and helpful thing anyone has ever said to me. He continued. "Sometimes in life, stuff just happens, like your relapse, and it will really help if you can get to a point where you just acknowledge that it is what it is, then focus on fighting hard. Don't fight against it. Fight it."

I took those words to heart. Since doc shared them with me, there have been numerous occasions where that was precisely the best perspective to take, the best way to cope, and still move forward.

Thank you for that, doc.

51

Mike and Alma

On one of my walks, I passed a man talking quietly on his mobile phone just outside the room next to mine. I nodded as I passed him, and he was quick to respond with a smile and nod of his own. The door was closed. It was usually open.

On those occasions, I saw a relatively young woman in her bed with an array of multi-colored fluids suspended from her IV pole, a cloud of pillows enveloping her. She didn't look like she was doing well at all.

Each time I passed her room I prayed a quick prayer that God would grant her peace, and give her comfort in what was clearly an awful time.

About four laps into my push for the day's mile, I once again approached the man standing outside that room. As I drew closer to him, he concluded his call, slipped his phone back into the holder clipped to his belt, buried his head in his hands and began to weep.

I stopped and asked him if he was okay or needed some help. He looked up at me with tired eyes. "My wife is not doing well. The doctors told me there is nothing more they can do for her."

A confused look came over his face, and he continued.

"She has this… acute lymph… lymphoblastic leukemia. She has leukemia. She is only 46 years old, and I am 50. We are of the Greek Orthodox tradition, and I am praying to God for her healing, but she is so sick."

I was frozen for a moment, like a deer in the headlights, not sure how to help or even knowing if I could.

"I'm sorry, my name is Mike and my wife is Alma" he added, and apologized for not properly introducing himself.

"I'm Rob and I have A.L.L. as well. Don't even worry about not introducing yourself to me. You have other things on your mind."

Mike had a Kleenex in his hand and wiped the tears from his eyes. A faint smile came over his face.

"You're right, Rob, I do have these other things on my mind, like they are pressing in on me, and I feel like I can't do anything to help Alma."

Mike was the most genuine, soft-spoken, and humble man I have ever met. He was a man broken by grief. He just wanted to help his wife. We talked in the hallway for several minutes. He wanted to know about my case. We decided to walk just outside the entrance to the unit where several benches lined the wall of the corridor.

We sat for a while, and I told him of my original diagnosis in 1989. I shared how just a week prior I learned that my leukemia had returned, that it came out of nowhere, and that it was my first stay in the hospital. Mike seemed to take great comfort in knowing I was dealing with the same disease as his wife.

I freaked out on the inside, because Alma was about my age. He asked me all kinds of questions: What did the doctors tell me about my chances? What was I most concerned about? Was I scared about what the future held?

I tried to be honest with him about my own fears and struggles. I guess my role that day was to simply be there for him, and let him know he and his wife were not alone. I told him I was a Christian, that God gave me peace in the midst of the struggle, but there was still the struggle to endure.

I told Mike I had plenty of fears, and a mind that raced at times with all the "what ifs" and "if onlys" that are part of the baggage that comes with such a traumatic experience.

Mike told me they were advised by the social worker to make

149

arrangements for Alma to receive hospice care, which meant she didn't have long to live, perhaps just a few weeks. Mike and I talked for a few more minutes then he was called back in to his wife's room. He smiled and shook my hand.

"Perhaps we will have another opportunity to talk, Rob."

I told him I looked forward to it. We had a few more conversations as my stay on the unit was extended for that second week.

In mid-November, when I returned to Kaiser for the second round of chemo, Alma was still in the same room. It was always full of family and friends and even some smiles and laughter. Mike and I had more occasions to talk. He told me Alma's condition had improved.

She was responding to the treatments he had pleaded with the doctors to continue. He fought for his wife's life. When I discharged a week later, Alma was still there, but when I returned for a third round of chemo in December someone else was in that room. I never found out what happened to Alma.

From time to time—surprisingly often I find—my mind reviews the events of those brief encounters with Mike and Alma, and it moves me to tears each time. I hope I was able to help them. I wish I knew how things turned out.

Frustrating.

The experience had a profound impact on me. I guess not knowing will remain one more item in the long list of holes and tattered edges, where the holes don't get filled in, and the tattered edges are never cleaned up.

Was that just a chance encounter with another cancer patient? My brain can't dismiss it as simply that. Was it a divine appointment—a "God Thing" as some folks like to call such events?

I think so, with all that is in me.

Perhaps I was meant to endure that second week of blood-clotting problems so Mike and I could have more time to talk. I hope and believe that was the case, and whatever help I was able to provide Mike brought him and his wife some degree of comfort.

52

An Outpouring of Love

In the midst of all the medical madness of that first two-week hospital stay when my head was spinning and my spirit riding waves of ups and downs, family and friends rallied together to support my family. Two pastors from my church dropped by one day for a visit. We talked for quite a long time, me wearing my mask to avoid potential infection risk.

The three of us talked about adjusting to life in a hospital, family, faith and the importance of trusting God for each day, one day at a time. They asked me what I was most concerned about, and how they could best pray for me.

I told them I worried about Michele and my girls, how they would hold up under this pressure. I told them I didn't have a good feeling about my treatment going so well this time around. Their taking time to stop by and connect with me early on in my hospitalization helped ground me for the fight ahead.

When Michele stopped by for visits, she brought in stacks of cards that had come in the mail, all filled with notes of encouragement and support. One day she brought in a large cardboard box. It was from my niece and nephew in New Hampshire. Inside was a collection of toys that made me laugh out load.

There was a little jet plane, a plastic tiger, one of those wooden paddles with the little red ball attached to it, and Silly Putty; just a bunch of goofy fun stuff to put a smile on my face. It sure did. Ryan and Erin, I love you two so much.

Late one morning, one of my nurses came into my room with a large, green tote bag and approached the side of my bed.

"Someone dropped this off for you at the nurse's station."

Inside the bag was a book of crossword puzzles, a National Geographic magazine, a Reader's Digest, a package of mints, and a huge chocolate bar. It was too cool! Also in that bag was a note from my friend Elizabeth. She lived several hours south of the Bay Area, but was in the area with her son, and took time to put that goodie bag together and drop it off for me. What a friend.

I talked with my buddy Tom about how things were going on the unit, and mentioned the hospital rooms had flat screen TVs, but only seven channels, and the program pickings were slim. Tom, learning there was a VHS/DVD player attached to my TV, brought me a grocery bag full of videos to help me pass the time. It was awesome.

I was bleeding out from every orifice in my body, and the days were filled with lots of uncertainty, furrowed brows, and faces of concern. But because of the thoughtfulness of special friends, I was able to enjoy some great movies and make it through a very difficult time.

I wasn't the only one on the receiving end of that huge outpouring of support. Michele's coworkers at the student health center essentially passed the hat and presented what had been collected for her in a gift bag. It was full of cards and notes, cash, gift cards for restaurants, groceries, and gasoline, and other items to help us through what everyone knew would be tough times for the foreseeable future.

We were blown away.

As the months played out, Michele put those gifts to good use. That gesture of love and very practical support from her colleagues and our friends went a long way in helping her keep the roof over our heads, gas in the car, and the lights on.

53

The Cheap Date

One morning late in the second week of treatment, Dr. Robert came into my room on his morning rounds, and looked at me with a big smile.

"Hey, you're a cheap date," he said.

I was puzzled.

"What do you mean, doc?"

"I mean I only had to wine and dine you for two weeks and your system responded!"

I cracked up and he laughed as well. He was very excited. The latest lab values indicated the chemo was effective and doing battle against the leukemia. It was great news, and along with it, doc told me my clotting factors were stabilizing.

He also brought up for the first time in any real detail, the issue of the bone marrow transplant. Though we didn't have a deep-dish, Chicago-style discussion about the matter, doc wanted me to know the search for a donor had begun, but finding a match could take several months—or longer. The "or longer" was the heavy portion of what he shared that morning.

I learned there were cases where folks had waited a very long time—many months or even years—for a donor match. During that period of waiting, those folks had to continue their cycles of hospitalizations and chemotherapy to stay in remission.

That was a tough nut to ponder. I did my best to acknowledge it as a real possibility, but hoped to high Heaven my donor would be found before too long. I couldn't think too much about multiple hospitalizations and chemo cycles and all the baggage that came with it.

He told me in light of the improvement in my clotting factors, I was "much closer" to going home. Doc didn't want me to spend a lot of time thinking about the bone marrow transplant. He urged me to focus on taking care of myself one day at a time, and getting out of there.

54

Trick or Treatment – A Tradition Put on Hold

Our family had a long-standing tradition of making home-made, slow-cooked chili and cornbread for dinner on Halloween night. It's something we started when the girls were very young, as Halloween nights in the Bay Area could be cool and sometimes rainy.

A bowl of something hot and hearty like homemade chili was the perfect solution. The girls always enjoyed it, even if in more recent years, they only wolfed down a quick bowl seconds before they bolted out the door to meet up with their friends for the night.

But in 2008, the chili chef was absent from the kitchen and present in the hospital. The only Halloween fun I enjoyed was with the nurses on the unit, who played their own twisted version of "trick or treat," knocking on patient's room doors, and asking for "treats" in the form of the hard candies, mints, and gum they knew we had stashed at our bedsides.

It was actually a ton of fun to have them come in, carrying little plastic pumpkin "loot buckets" and acting like goofs. But the thought our chili tradition was on hold at least for a year bugged the heck out of me.

Twenty years prior, I was in the hospital at City of Hope during Halloween. I have memories of hearing *The Monster Mash* playing at the nurse's station on Wing Six.

Twenty years later, it happened again, and this time around there was far more to miss; not just a steaming bowl of chili. I missed being with my family, watching the girls interact with their friends, and all the drama that came with getting their costumes just right, the laughter, and just being home to hand out yummies to the kids that came trick-or-treating.

The girls brought me photos from Halloween night on one of their visits a few days later. It was good to have at least some connection with them and the events of that night.

55

Home to Recover

After two weeks in the hospital I was discharged late Friday night, around 10 p.m. on November 7th. The first blast of cool night air on my face when the hospital lobby doors opened was pure heaven.

It was the first fresh air I had breathed in two weeks.

When I did my daily walks on the unit, I often stopped at the windows, and stared out at the lush, green foothills that surrounded the area.

I watched raindrops land on the large panes of glass and trickle their way down to the window sill, knowing soon enough I would be discharged, and able to breathe in that fresh, fall air.

It couldn't come soon enough after two weeks on the unit.

It's funny how the simple things, like breathing something other than artificially conditioned air became causes for major celebration. I guess it is the simple things in life that really matter: the sweet smell of cut grass, rain on your face, a beautiful sunset; all freebies and all too often missed.

Maybe I was wrong. Maybe there are some good things in life that do not come with strings attached.

I don't want to take them for granted ever again.

I was in a Neutropenic state with a white cell count of 400. The normal range for a healthy individual was 10-12 thousand. We implemented the vending machine diet from two decades prior. Foods like applesauce, cereal, crackers, fruit cups, juice, mayo, milk, mustard, pudding, tuna, and peanut butter and jelly were purchased in bulk packs of pre-packaged containers. Like I did twenty years before, I enjoyed fresh-cooked meals, but I avoided leftovers due to the bacteria exposure risk.

I spent most of my time in one of the bedrooms in the front of our house. It was converted into a "day room" of sorts, with a recliner chair, sofa, and TV. I had to be mindful of avoiding potential infection risks.

I washed my hands frequently, had folks wash their hands with antiseptic hand wash before they came into our house, asked friends to stay away until they were over colds or the flu, and asked everyone to leave their shoes outside when they came over for a visit.

56

A Formal Introduction to the Long Road Ahead

I had an appointment at Stanford on Wednesday, November 12th to meet Caroline, the social worker assigned to my case, and (a new) Dr. Robert, the head of the Blood and Marrow Transplant department. I felt a little better than the day I came home, but wasn't at the top of my game. Michele joined me that day. It was an eye-opening and emotionally draining day for both of us.

Caroline addressed several issues. She asked about my emotional and mental state as I pondered the transplant that loomed on the horizon. We discussed our support systems, home life, and the impact such traumatic experiences had on family and friends.

Spiritual issues were also covered. We let Caroline know we both had a strong faith and were plugged into a local church.

Before she concluded her time with us, Caroline provided a glimpse of what life on the unit would be like for me, once I was admitted. Her description of the typical daily routine was overwhelming to put it mildly; it was too much reality in one sitting.

I sat with my mouth wide open, catching flies the whole time she was talking. At the same time, what she shared was necessary, and helped us process things a bit and prepare.

With each topic Caroline addressed, my anxiety level grew, but I was also filled with confidence and hope. I was sad and happy at the same time. I suppose that was a natural response but what a roller coaster ride.

Following our hour-long meeting with Caroline, Dr. Robert entered the exam room and stuck out his hand. He was a very distinguished-looking fellow, with graying hair and a gray beard to match.

He made eye contact right away, and his eyes looked right through mine. I like him instantly. His first comment to me was rather startling.

With only a hint of a grin, he said, "I want you to know in the history of my medical practice I've never seen a case like yours; never seen anything like it. No one goes 19+ years on a first remission. How did you do that?"

"Never seen anything like it" was a phrase I would have rather heard expressed by someone who discovered a three-headed cat or dinosaurs living in a mobile home park in Montana.

"I have no idea how I did it, doc, short of clean living and God's blessings," I replied with a smile.

Doc smiled back. I asked him the million-dollar question, "Is it a good thing or bad my case is nothing you've ever seen before?"

"I guess we'll find out soon enough," doc responded. "Right now, we kind of don't know what to do with you."

Great. He'd never seen anything like my case, and did not know what to do with me. It was a "one-two" punch that for just a moment sent my brain to the mat. He was supposed to have the answers, not the questions.

Then doc mentioned something he and the entire team of transplant doctors, all professors in the Stanford Medical School, were extremely curious about.

"The really interesting aspect of your case is the presence of what's known as the Philadelphia Chromosome. You are Philadelphia Chromosome positive."

"I'm what?"

He explained it was a mutation of the DNA, first discovered in 1960 by two doctors in Philadelphia. The mutation made folks susceptible to Chronic Myelogenous Leukemia (C.M.L.), but in some instances, Acute Lymphoblastic Leukemia (A.L.L.). Why the mutation occurred was not known, but it was present in 25 to 30% of adult patients with A.L.L. I was a member of the elite 25 to 30% club.

What an honor. Do I get a membership card or premium tee times, or something?

Dr. Robert and his team were curious about when the mutation occurred in me and what triggered it. Stress (or should I say "potential stressors" and how I chose to respond to them) was a huge factor and could have been the trigger in my case.

Since they did not test for it back in 1989 when I was at the City of Hope, there was no way to know for sure when the mutation happened—but it happened—and that ultimately opened the door for the relapse.

Doc was very interested in gaining insight into the mutation, and other aspects of my case that might have contributed to my long remission. My case was perplexing, since I had not had a bone marrow transplant back in 1989. Had that been the case, Dr. Robert told me it would have been much easier to explain. He was quite stunned.

"Several months prior to your case being referred to Stanford, we treated a young gal name Sylvia who went eleven years on her first remission. We thought that was incredible. When we read your case history, we couldn't believe it," he said.

Doc concluded our time together with some encouraging words for me about hanging tough through the next rounds of chemotherapy. "Take things a day at a time, as much as you can, and we will see you soon enough, Robert," he said, and shook my hand with a confident grip.

I left that appointment somewhat puzzled and confused. At the same time, I felt like I was in the best hands, that all my doctors were top drawer, so I tried not to allow the seemingly confused nature of my situation to get the best of me.

57

Round Two

Knowing what was ahead, I dreaded heading back to Kaiser's Medical/Oncology unit. Beyond the chemotherapy, there would be a second lumbar puncture, and of course, the possibility of more complications. I was frustrated that an entire team of doctors at Stanford had no idea what to do with me. The open-endedness of it all was quite unsettling.

Dr. Robert at Kaiser told me I needed a bone marrow transplant. Dr. Robert at Stanford was scratching his head. I was caught between the two of them, but had to focus on working my "fry and release" program, perhaps for many months.

On Sunday, November 16th, Michele and I made the familiar trip to Kaiser, and I was admitted for the second round of chemotherapy, known as Consolidation.

Same song. Second verse.

On Monday morning, Dr. Robert entered my room.

"Welcome back" he said, with a mischievous smile.

"Thanks doc. I can't tell you how happy I am to be here."

Doc got my attention fast. "I wanted to let you know that eight hundred folks have been identified in the preliminary search for your bone marrow donor."

"Eight hundred people? What does that mean?"

"It means the ball is rolling. That number will be refined further and further, until a final determination is made regarding the best match for you."

He was really amped up. That was tremendously positive news, but I tried to keep in mind what doc told me previously—how the search for a compatible donor could take months or even years. "Or longer" was still a very real possibility.

"How much energy should I spend thinking about this, doc?"

"Not much. But I wanted to let you know the search was underway. I thought it might pump you up."

It was good news. I tried to simply embrace it as such and leave it at that, but my mind was locked on it for most of the day.

On Wednesday of that week, I received a phone call from Michele around 5:00 p.m. She was at the Chevy's restaurant in our neighborhood.

A fundraising event had been planned where folks were sent flyers about my situation. With that flyer in hand on the night of the event, 25% of the proceeds from their dinner purchases were donated to the National Marrow Donor Registry in my name. How cool is that?

Michele and I talked for a couple minutes, and then several of my clients, vendors, former co-workers, and friends jumped on the line to wish me well. There was plenty of laughter and joking on the other end of the line. I wished I could be there to party with them.

They raised a nice chunk of change that night; money that would help cover the cost of finding matches for all those in need of a marrow transplant.

I didn't have a mobile phone with me when I was a patient at the City of Hope. I had a phone in my room, but using it was awkward at times. Twenty years later, my mobile phone was like an extra appendage.

Having the freedom to leave my room, leave the unit for that matter, and have a conversation with family and friends away from the reminders of my reality was a pure blessing.

I must say, there were times when as much as I wanted to have folks visit, a phone call was a better option when the face-to-face dynamic was too much.

58

When a Lumbar Puncture Goes Bad

My second stay at Kaiser was supposed to be just a four-day gig, then I would be discharged to recover for a couple of weeks. At least, that was the plan. The first spinal tap during my initial hospitalization went very smoothly. But during the second one, I experienced the "dark side" and my stay turned into a big headache.

I was on my stomach, with several pillows placed under my hips and knees. I couldn't see much of what was happening around me, but heard the sound of the surgical technicians tearing open plastic packages of sterile drapes and the "clank" of various instruments being placed on a metal tray near my feet.

The doctor entered the room. He walked around the procedure table and tapped me on my leg. "How are you doing, Robert?"

"I'm good doc, just chillin' out. Is everything cool?"

"Oh yes. We're waiting until we get a couple more vials to collect the spinal fluid. We'll get underway in just a few minutes."

After a short time had passed, doc began the procedure, and without much effort, located a spot where he wanted to insert his needle. Unlike the set up at the City of Hope, the arrangement of the room at Kaiser did not allow me to watch doc do his thing. I felt the "pop" as the needle punctured the spinal sack.

No sweat I thought to myself. *You've done this seven times before.* As that thought was still resonating in my mind, I felt one of those electrical "shooters" thunder down my left leg. I winced a bit but didn't dare move.

"Yikes, doc. You just lit up my leg."

"I'm sorry, Robert. I'm pretty close to a nerve, but I'm getting a good fluid return."

"You're close all right, but if you're getting a good tap, that works for me. I've planned a busy afternoon of laying around and contemplating my future, doc, so as soon as you can get me out of here…"

He laughed.

"I appreciate your sense of humor. You seem to be pretty upbeat about all this."

"Hey doc, as long as you have that needle in my back, you'll get my best material. I'll be here all week. Try the veal."

In my head, I thought I would be out of there in just a few minutes; a little more spinal fluid out, some Methotrexate in, a few more laughs and I'd be on my way.

Thanks guys, it's been a blast hanging out with you.

I was wrong. I heard doc say something to one of the surgical assistants about the fluid return stopping, and wanting the procedure table raised at the head end to enlist the help of gravity.

After another minute had passed, he apologized to me *(uh oh)*, and told me he needed to find a second location. The tap had gone dry.

I felt a second "pop" as the needle punctured the spinal sack in a new spot. By then, one of the nurses was sitting at the end of the table. She asked me questions about my family, my pets, what I did for a living; anything to distract me from what was becoming an unpleasant, nerve-racking event.

Doc's needle hit my nerve again—a couple times—and more electricity shot down my legs. I muttered under my breath. "I'm removing you from my "A" list for Christmas cards, doc." He laughed, and apologized again for the hassle.

Just when I thought we were coming out of the woods, I heard doc say, "Shoot." That is never a good thing to hear, especially coming from your doctor, and even more so if that doctor has a needle stuck in your spine. But he did in fact say, "shoot," so I braced for impact, glanced over at the nurse who was squeezing the life out of my hand and asked the doc what "shoot" meant?

"Well Rob, you're really not going to like me now. The second tap has also gone dry and we still need a couple more CCs of spinal fluid from you, so I'm going to have to try a third tap." Prior to hearing that news, I was ready to sell the doc my children, and confess everything.

The table was tilted up even more, to the point where I could no longer hold myself in position by grabbing the end of the table. All the blood drained from my skull and pooled in my toes.

It was kind of comical, on one level. Given the steep angle of the table, I must have looked like an anti-aircraft missile ready for launch. On another level, it wasn't funny at all. I was done with it, and my coping skills waned.

The minutes seem to crawl by. More bolts of electricity shot down my leg, and more adjustments were made to the angle of the table. *How 'bout I just stand up and lean against the wall?* The nurse who had been merely sitting by me, holding my hand, continued asking annoying questions to distract me.

Eventually I told her I didn't want to talk anymore about my dogs or my job or my kids. I just wanted to wrap things up and get back to my room and take a massive dose of drugs. She understood and tried to be consoling. "I know this is a rough one for you Rob, but you're toughing it out," she said.

"I'm trying to keep my game face on and stay focused, but I'm losing it. If I slip you twenty bucks, can you make the doctor stop?"

She laughed, and Doc went in for the kill. I thank the Lord in Heaven above he was able, almost instantly, to get a good return of fluid into his syringe. But in the process, he landed dead on top of a nerve. The pain was like nothing I had ever experienced before. It felt like an "ice cream" headache that ran the entire length of my leg.

I spent thirty long seconds swearing under my breath and cursing the medical establishment. Doc tried to keep my head in the game, but I could feel my tongue splitting into a fork at the end and a rattle growing out of my gluteous-I've-had-enough-of-this. Then suddenly he was done.

Doc leaned over and put his hand on my back. "Okay. That's it. I got a very good return on the last tap, so you're out of here."

"Okay doc. You seem like a good guy, so perhaps I'll add you back to the 'A' list and send you a Christmas card after all."

After roughly a half hour of "rest" back in the pre-surgery area to return blood flow to my brain, followed by fond farewells to the team in the Radiology department *(yeah, right)*, I was sent back to my room.

Good to be home after a busy day at work.

59

Rosemary's Chicken

Rather than transferring from the gurney, I asked if I could just be rolled into my room next to my bed and rest there for a couple hours. I was wiped out from my dance with the Devil in Radiology and drifted off to dreamland.

I woke up as my dinner tray was delivered with no idea what I had ordered. I wondered if it would sit well with me. I wondered if I still had a spine.

Whatever was hiding under the plastic dome smelled pretty good, so I got help transferring to my bed. I settled in, cranked it up into something resembling a sitting position and got busy with my dinner.

Just as I finished removing the plastic utensils and the salt and pepper packets from the little plastic bag, the front and back of my head began to throb.

Can I just saw my head off? I think I would feel much better.

I stopped what I was doing, hit the button on my bedside controller unit, and got horizontal. When I did, the pain went away almost instantly. *Uh oh. Now what?*

I chilled out flat on my back for a few minutes and pondered my next move. I was really hungry and wanted to partake of the splendor under the dome. But it was difficult to eat as I was frozen in my tracks with fear.

After some strategizing, I decided to eat dinner that night (it was

Rosemary Chicken) riding "side saddle" in my bed, almost horizontal to avoid onset of the migraine. For the rest of the evening, I hunkered down and relaxed, hoping that more horizontal time would resolve the headache issue.

Later in the evening, I sat up very slowly and waited for a moment to see if my head would explode or visions of my ninth grade world history teacher would flash across my mind. Nothing happened. It must have been something about the way Rosemary prepared her chicken.

But whenever I tried to stand up, the headache hit again like a lightning bolt through my skull. I can report that everything I had been told about how bad those migraines could be was 100 percent accurate, perhaps even understated a bit. The front and back of my head ached like it was being crushed in a vice... by my world history teacher.

I wanted to unscrew my head from my body and leave it in the bathroom until it could come back out and play well with others.

I could not get out of my (very small) room for walks and wasn't the least bit interested in watching the seven channels of nothing available on TV. Over the next few days, I developed a bad case of cabin fever with an attitude chaser.

Make mine a double.

With Thanksgiving looming on the horizon and no cash on hand to buy my way out, I essentially pleaded with the docs to discharge me. They were hesitant to release me, but I nagged them every chance I could until finally Dr. Robert came by for a visit to see what all the fuss was about.

"What happened Rob," he asked with a perplexed look on his face.

"I was nailed with a post-tap migraine a couple days ago doc. Rosemary's chicken helped some, but now I'm just going crazy and need to get home. That's all."

"I don't know if that's a good idea. Maybe we should keep you here to be sure the migraine resolves."

I was insistent. "I can recover from the headache at home, even if it takes several more days. If it doesn't, I can always come back for a visit. I need to be home for Thanksgiving or I'm going to go crackers."

Dr. Robert did me a real solid. He discharged me on Wednesday evening before the holiday. I felt like a bus—a very large bus, driven by an angry circus clown and carrying a load of anvils—had knocked me flat. But I was home. That was all that mattered.

Headache, shmeadache.

We had Thanksgiving dinner at our place. My in-laws joined us for a very quiet, enjoyable get together. What a welcome change from that tiny hospital room.

Much to the relief of our turkey, I was unable to eat more of him than a forkful and similar portions of stuffing and sweet potatoes. I really didn't care about the food. Being with family was more satisfying than any meal could ever be.

60

Making Lemonade

On a beautiful Sunday afternoon, December 7th, 2008, a bone marrow donor drive was held at Hope Christian Church in Los Gatos. It was a great way to make lemonade from the lemons we had been dealt.

While I underwent chemo treatments at Kaiser, my family and friends worked behind the scenes to make the event happen in an effort to find me a donor. It was amazing to learn about all the folks involved in the project and what they had been up to in order to make it happen.

My good friend Tracy worked her PR/Marketing magic to build "buzz" about the event and worked with our local community paper to post an article about my need for a donor. Other friends secured their church facility as the location for the event. The church provided coffee, and folks brought cookies and other snacks.

Though the intent of the drive was to find a marrow donor for me, it really wasn't about me. The real story was about the thousands of folks in need of donor marrow.

The people who came that day and registered to become potential donors could get a call at some point in the future and possibly have the amazing opportunity to save someone's life.

Fifty-one people registered that day, and cash donations to cover the administrative costs of processing their applications were raised as well. In addition, friends and relatives living outside the Bay Area or out of state who heard about the event, located events in their part of the country and signed up as well. Once again, family and friends rallied behind us, and the many others on the planet with the same need. Incredible love.

61

The Best (Early) Christmas Gift Ever

Amid-afternoon appointment on Friday, December 12th had me back up to Stanford to meet with Dr. Robert. Something was up. When I met with him, the picture became clearer.

Though Christmas Day was still a couple weeks away, what I learned that day was pretty much the best (early) Christmas gift ever.

Michele had to work on the day of the appointment, but Suzanne, our good friend and Michele's coworker at the student health center accompanied me to be my eyes and ears.

She had helped us early on, setting up the CaringBridge web site and was such an encouragement. I felt the effects of the second round of chemo and was not at my cognitive best by any measure, so it was great to have Suzanne with me to be my brain for the day.

It seemed like any time I met with my doctors, whether at City of Hope, Kaiser Hospital or at Stanford, my head was always left spinning when the appointment was over, fogged by information overload. Half the time, I only caught part of what those well-meaning folks told me.

Given my condition, I knew I needed someone with me who could pay full attention to what Dr. Robert had to say, and ask the questions I might not think to ask. The stakes were far too high to let even the smallest bit of information slip through the cracks.

When Dr. Robert entered the exam room, he looked at me with a straight face.

"Well Rob, do you know why you're here today?"

"No, doc. All I know is that you guys needed me to complete a block of tests and exams, but I have no clue what it means."

Doc took a seat and leaned back against the wall. The expression on his face changed. He became very serious.

"We don't have a donor for you," he said, and just stared at me for a second.

I glanced over at Suzanne. Then doc got a big grin on his face.

"We don't have a match for you. We actually have four, and what is really amazing is that all of them are perfect matches with the ten genetic markers we use to evaluate potential donor compatibility, so this is very good news."

I had four perfect donor matches!

It was the best possible news four times over. I looked at Suzanne, and we both grinned from ear to ear. Tears welled up in my eyes. Doc had to mess with me a bit. He got me good.

We covered a lot of ground that day. There was a ton of information to absorb. Suzanne kept very detailed notes that Michele and I reviewed later that evening and in the days that followed.

Had I tried to keep record of all that was presented, the end result would have been something more resembling chicken scratches—or Hebrew—rather than English.

After sharing the good news about the matches that had been found, doc's comments took a more serious tone.

"So, the ball is pretty much in your court now, Rob."

"What do you mean?"

"Our transplant evaluation team reviewed your case. A couple of the doctors were reluctant to recommend a bone marrow transplant for you, but they ultimately agreed with the rest of the team it would probably be the best treatment option, and give you the best chance at long-term survival. So you have been approved for the bone marrow transplant, should you decide you want to go that route with your treatment."

My happiness over multiple donors was quickly tempered by the realization that my discussion with Dr. Robert about a transplant had transitioned from the abstract to the concrete. *Holy cow!* We weren't just talking about a transplant, out there on the horizon, at some future point in time.

We were talking about MY transplant.

"What made those two doctors hesitant to recommend the transplant," I asked.

Dr. Robert leaned forward in his chair.

"We were all amazed how long your first remission lasted," he said, and continued. "Those doctors believed it possible for you to live many years having gotten back into remission a second time. Given your long first remission, they were reluctant to put you through the ordeal of the bone marrow transplant."

"That's funny, doc because I'm reluctant about it as well."

Doc tapped me on my leg. "You have a lot to consider, Rob. You and your wife should take some time and think it through." He was very encouraging and upbeat.

So the ball was in my court. I had to make a decision—perhaps the biggest decision I've ever had to make in my life. Talk about a sudden change in focus. My future became my present, in the blink of an eye. It was staring me in the face.

Even then, my mind was pretty set on moving forward with the transplant. When doc discussed the five-year survival rates for those in remission who chose not to have a bone marrow transplant (2%) versus those that did (60%), the choice was crystal clear, at least from a statistical standpoint.

But beyond the numbers, there were the matters of the heart. I had to consider the impact the transplant would have on my family. *Would it change who I was as a husband to Michele, as a father to my girls? What would our life look like if I survived? What if I didn't make it through?*

The bottom line: I had to just suck it up, shoot for the best odds possible and hope for the best. Dr. Robert gave me some advice that day that I still cling to.

"If you decide to go forward with the transplant, Rob, it is very important as you and I begin working together that you make decisions and do not look back. Do not spend any time looking back over your shoulder."

His words really struck me. He continued. "You'll drive yourself crazy if you spend a lot of energy second-guessing your decisions."

He explained transplant patients sometimes compare themselves to other transplant patients—patients who pursued a different course of treatment, who might be doing better or healing faster or who have returned to work.

Such comparisons only led to frustration and caused patients to lose focus. I had to focus on my situation, make my decisions, put my head down, and move forward. It was pretty meaty stuff. Many times over the months that followed I drew upon doc's counsel to make it through rough times.

62

Reality in a Three-Ring Binder

The last person we met with that day was Suzanne, the Nursing Care Coordinator for transplant patients. She was a new Suzanne in my life, a sharp gal, very knowledgeable, and compassionate with an easy sense of humor.

It was her job to go "deep" with me about the nature of the transplant, beyond what the social worker had shared. I braced for impact. She spent considerable time answering our questions and provided detailed information about the transplant process.

The real "meat" of our session with Suzanne was my formal introduction to The Binder. It was three inches thick and weighed as much as a pair of my shoes. It was chock full of everything I never wanted (but needed) to know about having a bone marrow transplant.

When Suzanne handed me The Binder, she did so with a gentle urging that I try not to be overwhelmed by it, but it was hard not to be.

It was like telling someone their house was scheduled to be burned to the ground, and all of their possessions lost, but hopefully a new and better house would be built in its' place—hopefully.

"Give it a 'once over' and then put it down, come back to it another day, and digest a bit more of it," she said.

I flipped through the sections and scanned the contents.

"This is brutal Suzanne."

"I know. It can be very overwhelming. But it's important that you read the entire document before being admitted for transplant. Michele and anyone else who will be involved in your day-to-day care post-transplant should read it as well."

The Binder was divided into twelve sections, covering every conceivable topic: how to prepare, and the emotional, mental, physical, psychological and social challenges patients and their families face.

There was information about every drug that may or may not be part of my treatment, and every treatment that may or may not be part of my protocol.

Check, please!

Thorough descriptions of the known, expected side effects, and short and long term implications of the transplant were also included.

Additionally, there was information for caregivers, in my case Michele, my in-laws, and several of our friends.

There were flyers about special classes for caregivers, for the transplant recipient, and information about coping with life after the transplant.

There were frank and vivid descriptions of the wide range of complications that could occur, and contact information for a host of counseling, medical, physical fitness, and other resources within the Stanford system and local community.

The only thing that binder lacked was coloring sheets for the kids.

Color the picture of the evil Leukemia monster being killed by Captain Marrow and His White Cell Troopers!

It was absolutely overwhelming.

Walking out of that meeting with The Binder stuffed into my back-pack, I thought again how quickly the transplant had become a reality.

Fasten your seatbelts and please observe the "NO FREAKING" sign.

Over the next week, Michele and I digested the contents of that package of information.

I completed the battery of tests Dr. Robert had requested: a blood draw, pulmonary function test (PFT), resting cardiac echo (ECHO), chest X-ray, twelve-lead electrocardiogram (EKG) and a bone marrow biopsy (OUCH). Those tests were part of the pre-transplant evaluation process.

With the reality of the transplant looming on the horizon, I used the time at home to set up our Living Trust documents. It was something Michele and I had talked about for years.

There was simply too much at stake to put it off any further: our home and other assets, my business, our girls, and who would care for them should anything happen to Michele and me. My goal was to have the work completed before admitting to Stanford for the transplant. LegalZoom.com to the rescue.

The process was as smooth as silk, but as Michele and I signed the various documents, I felt like I was signing my life away. I was already scheduled for a very bad day. The paperwork seemed like a formality before the plan could be implemented. Very strange.

It was as if a banker, a lawyer, and the Grim Reaper were all waiting in the wings; each one was eager for the chance to get a piece of me. It was only the Trust documents separating Michele and me from a world of hurt.

When I was a patient at the City of Hope, I remember completing an Advanced Directives document. That simple document spelled out in specific terms what my wishes were in the event I had a heart attack, stroked out, or otherwise became incapacitated.

Nothing will thrust you faster into adulthood than that document.

I was a young man back then. My conversations with Michele were about what movie we wanted to go see or where we wanted to go for dinner. When I got sick, those discussions turned to more weighty matters.

Michele worked through the form with me. "Do you want to be kept on life support in the event you end up in a vegetative state? Do you want to be put on a ventilator that will breathe for you if you are unable to do so on your own?"

"Gee, hon, I don't know. Right now I'm still trying to understand what's happened to me."

Instant grownup. Just complete the form, and you're a member of the club.

That document was placed in my chart so my doctors and nurses were aware of my wishes. At the time, the Advanced Directives document covered all our bases. Michele and I had no "estate" in the classic sense of that word. Twenty years later, it was a different story. We had to get all of our affairs in order.

It was difficult to think about death and dying, and how I wanted things to play out in my final days. But the thought of my wife and family forced to make such emotionally charged decisions on my behalf, was motivation enough for me to suck it up and complete the paperwork.

I put myself in their shoes, and tried to imagine how I would feel should something happen to Michele and she was not able to speak for herself. Doing so allowed me to get past the emotion and embrace the Advanced Directives form as a positive, proactive way I could have some level of control over my situation—my life.

63

Round Three

On Sunday, December 14th we made our third trip to the admissions office at the Kaiser Hospital for a round of Maintenance chemotherapy. Barring complications, my stay at "Club K" was to last just five or six days. I would be home for Christmas.

The second round of chemo had been a tough ride. I wondered how the third round would play out. We signed the admitting form, dinged the credit card with yet another whopper charge, and made our way, once again up to the Medical Oncology unit.

Same song, third verse.

Michele came by for a visit on Monday evening, after my first full day back on the unit. We had to discuss the bone marrow transplant and make our final decision. Once I called Suzanne at Stanford and gave her the thumbs-up, the ball would start rolling toward my transplant date.

Huge decision.

My emotions were running thin. I was 100 percent committed to moving forward with the transplant, and at the same time consumed with an overwhelming sense I was never going to get well. Sometimes the lump in my throat was so big it blocked the view of the hope that lay on the horizon.

I was a person, not a statistic. Michele was also a person. We both had feelings and hopes and dreams. Part of me wondered about the physical toll the transplant would have on me. *Would I ever get my strength back? Was Michele prepared for me to come home in a zip-top bag, after a month on the unit, like a spoiled batch of mashed potatoes? What about all the complications and side effects?* The Binder was rather explicit about those. The transplant would take me to the edge of death.

What if I fell over the edge?

So on one hand, Michele and I considered the numbers—the stats. They painted a very clear picture: Have the transplant, and most likely live longer than those that chose not to. From that standpoint, Michele felt it was the best move I could make.

We didn't talk much about the impact the transplant would have on our relationship and our family, but both of us knew it would bring a unique set of challenges.

In retrospect, we should have talked more openly with each other about just that dynamic. Like any traumatic event, the bone marrow transplant would change us.

We had no idea how much it would effect the course of our lives.

That other stuff—the emotional wanderings of a mind on the edge—had me wide awake long after Michele headed home. I called Stanford and talked with Suzanne the next morning to let her know I was onboard.

I pushed through the balance of the week, completing the chemotherapy infusions and the third lumbar puncture. None of the nasty side effects or visions of my ninth grade world history teacher became an issue.

There is a God.

I was discharged on Sunday, December 20th, in time to be home for Christmas *(thank you, Lord)*. I was given several weeks off to regain my strength. My legs had turned to mush after the three hospital stays and all the chemo and meds.

I spent much of the time at home walking up and down our street, trying to regain some muscle strength. It was slow going. I found myself looking down at times to see if my legs were actually coming along for the walk, or had decided to wait it out in my front yard.

Since October of 2008 I'd shed close to sixty pounds—the hard way. My appetite was on-again, off-again, but eventually it came around enough to where I could put down a pretty good load of calories each day. I had to get as strong as possible. According to The Binder, the forthcoming "Preparative Regimen" would pretty much gut me like a trout.

64

Teaching for Transplant

Michele and I experienced a rude awakening in early January of 2009 when we attended the *Teaching for Transplant* class. It was one of the classes highlighted in The Binder as essential for the soon-to-be-transplant recipient and the primary caregiver(s) as well.

A nurse addressed our gathering. "If you do have a day where you throw up a lot of blood, it just means your body needs platelets to help your blood clot. We can make that happen for you." I felt like curling into a ball under the table after hearing those words.

The nurse who led the class worked on the E1 unit. She spoke truth, in volumes.

I recalled my experience with blood clotting issues at Kaiser, and the bags and bags of blood products I received. It was not a pleasant memory, so I leaned heavily on her reassuring words. She was the calm before the storm.

The nurse continued to assure us we would be in great hands and not to worry too much. It was reassuring to hear her describe, in a very straightforward manner, all the weird stuff that could happen, and yet have such a calming way about her.

I glanced over at Michele on several occasions during the class and also looked around the room. I wanted to see how the others present dealt with the information the nurse was sharing. As I sat there and took it all in, I was struck several times with a wave of dread. I thought, *Oh man, what have you gotten yourself into?*

When the nurse concluded her formal presentation, a bunch of us stuck around, introduced ourselves, and compared notes about what type of leukemia, lymphoma, or other illness had brought us to that place. We shared stories about how long we had dealt with our diseases, who our doctors were, and more.

Several of the folks attending the class were Dr. Robert's patients from Kaiser. We learned he would be retiring within several months, so we dubbed ourselves his "Final Referrals." I met a young gal named Megan. She was in her mid-twenties and was hit with leukemia just a couple years prior.

After a relatively short remission, she relapsed and needed a transplant. She was a newlywed. Michele and I empathized with her and her husband, having ourselves been in our mid-twenties and a newly married couple of just several months when I was hit with my illness.

Megan was a real trooper. She always had a smile on her face, and she did her best to maintain a positive attitude. Her Mom was a terrific lady, also full of life, grace and smiles. With her husband and family rallying behind her, Megan had a great support system in place.

I drew a lot of inspiration from her.

Michele was able to answer several questions and alleviate some concerns among the group following the class. She provided them with a great deal of comfort and peace that evening. I'm not sure if she noticed as she was talking with them, but I did.

I always marveled at how sharp Michele was when it came to her nursing abilities. She knew her stuff. Whenever family members and friends of ours had medical questions, or a sick child or some other strange medical situation, they often called her for advice and her expertise.

She was really good at what she did. It was pretty amazing to consider how many folks she had helped over the years, beyond those she cared for on the job. She's impacted a lot of lives on the planet, both professionally and personally.

After nearly an hour or so of our group talking and exchanging email addresses and other contact information, we gathered our things and said our goodbyes. One of the men present that night was a fellow named Sergio.

He spoke very little English. A Spanish language interpreter translated the nurse's presentation for him so he could follow along.

When Sergio got up from the table and stood in the doorway with his family, he waved goodbye to us. "Good night my friends. All the best to you," he said. "God will see us through this."

It was quite a moment. The room drew quiet then we all smiled, waved back at him, and thanked him for his kind words. That pretty much made my night. I had been preoccupied over the course of the evening with the thought that I really didn't want to be one of the folks who vomited up a pint of blood.

Sergio's positive attitude and quiet confidence shifted my focus to a more positive realization: God was well aware of my situation. He had me in his grip, and would see me through this trial.

Thank you, Sergio, for conveying such a powerful message and for being an example of how to live joyfully in spite of circumstances.

65

Lemonade With a Radiation Chaser

On Sunday, January 25th a second marrow donor drive was held, hosted by my Chiropractor, Dr. John, and his partner, Dr. Mark. Just like the first event, many of our friends showed up to support the effort. In addition, many folks from the local community came by to register as potential donors. I attended the event, but was preoccupied with thoughts about the upcoming Preparative Regimen at Stanford.

Ten people registered that day, and additional cash donations were collected as well. We raised $1300, and registered sixty-eight new potential bone marrow donors between the two drive events.

I hoped one of the folks that signed up would get the call one day and learn they had been matched with a recipient. It would be one of the greatest days of my life.

A week after that drive event, I began the Preparative Regimen. It was the big step in the pre-transplant process, about which the orientation binder contained a wealth of descriptive (read: frightening) information.

The regimen consisted of four days of total body irradiation, where I would receive a monster dose of radiation three times each day, for four consecutive days.

The treatment would effectively destroy my immune system and kill off most of my blood and bone marrow. *Swell.* Following those four, fun-filled days, I would be admitted to the E1 Transplant unit. At that point things could get rather dicey.

About the same time I would begin my radiation treatment, committing myself to a fragile existence at death's door, my donor would undergo the marrow harvesting procedure somewhere on the planet.

Death would take me within a few days, if the donor decided at the last minute he did not want to go through with the marrow harvest after all, or some other situation arose preventing the transplant.

I have to believe the doctors and others involved in coordinating the harvest and donation logistics had confirmation my donor's marrow was harvested before they began my radiation treatments. I hope that was the case, but in all honesty, I really have little knowledge of how all of that went down.

Life on the edge.

As I pondered all the pieces of the puzzle that had to come together, the miracle of the transplant became more astonishing.

On the morning of Tuesday, February 3rd Michele and I made the trip to Stanford's Cancer Treatment Center. It had become familiar ground to both of us.

For the previous week I had been connected 24/7 to a portable infusion pump that provided constant hydration to flush my system. There were no medications or vitamins or anything like that, just IV fluids. It was like fattening up a pig for slaughter.

Our road trip that morning was quite similar to the one we made twenty years prior, when we drove from Huntington Hospital to the City of Hope. Michele drove, and I rode "shotgun," this time with the pump suitcase nestled between my legs.

Our conversation was minimal and light with occasional moments of purpose-driven living bubbling to the surface. Either Michele or I said something about taking things "one day at a time" or "keeping our heads down and moving forward."

Conversation reduced to bumper stickers.

Once we arrived, we were led to a treatment room to await my first appointment with The Beast downstairs in Radiology. It would fry my system in three ten-minute doses, scheduled several hours apart.

A few days prior to that Tuesday morning appointment, I had been to the Radiology department in the basement *(how poetic, right?)* of the Cancer Treatment Center for what was called "Radiation Simulation." It was similar to the simulation I went through at City of Hope.

In this case, however, it was not just my brain that was going to be fried. It was certainly going to get its share of action, but the rest of my body was invited to the party as well. *Bring the whole family. There will be pony rides for the kids. RSVP regrets only.*

I tried to focus on the fact that in spite of what I had already been through, I was still very much alive. I didn't feel very alive, but the most recent lab results made a strong case for that being my current state.

A medical assistant led me to a tiny waiting area just outside a very large, thick, metal door. There was a yellow and black label stuck to the face of the door that read, "Radiation Hazard."

Like a welcome mat for would-be burglars that read "This Home Insured by Smith & Wesson" the sign on that door was yet another reality check and provided an unwanted moment of clarity.

I had begun the end of what I knew to be myself, the older model with leukemia, the dent in the fender, and the bald tires. As hard as it would be to go through it and the transplant that followed, I knew down deep it would be worth it.

The possibility of life, measured directly against its rather stark alternative, regardless of statistics and percentage points was a far better option in my mind than giving up and giving in. When I got into the thick soup of the transplant that is something I had to remind myself of almost daily.

In the radiation treatment room, there was a phone booth of sorts; a three foot square, wooden structure about seven feet tall, with two "saloon-style" doors on the front made of thick acrylic.

Inside the booth, a canvas sling hung from two hooks that were screwed into the ceiling. The sling had holes for my arms to pass through, and two pockets to hold lead shields to protect my lungs.

The sling held me vertical and still, staring eye to eye with The Beast. We needed no formal introduction. I recognized him from twenty years prior. He hadn't aged much.

I wondered if he still had that odor control problem that had me running for the restroom after each of my brain radiation treatments at City of Hope.

The Beast would fire his invisible death ray from nearly twenty feet across the room. The tech spent several minutes explaining what the procedure would be each time I had a treatment. I would face forward, then face to the rear of the booth, then forward again. We would repeat that for four consecutive days.

Of all the information I received that day, the most memorable was the tech's suggestion that I feel free to bring in some CDs of my favorite music to listen to while I was receiving treatment.

Radiation Serenade in D.

The tech informed me. "You'll be hanging here for ten minutes each time, and the machine can be kind of loud once it spins up. We've found patients like being able to concentrate on the music rather than the sound of the machine, which is really like a loud buzzing noise."

I nodded my head in approval. It sounded like a good plan to me. *Why not?* I would be hanging in a canvas sling, suspended by two iron hooks, wearing only my underpants and my lead shields inside a wooden and acrylic phone booth. All I needed was a really good soundtrack playing in the background.

I went home from the simulation with a head full of information, unsure how I would describe my day to Michele. I couldn't have made up a more bizarre story if I tried. A plywood phone booth, a canvas sling, and me in my underwear—that was great material!

So there we sat a couple weeks later on that Tuesday morning, waiting for my first "at bat" against The Beast. I had my CDs in hand, and my trusty hydration pump by my side.

Locked and loaded. Bring it on.

They did. I was called downstairs and within no time had stripped down to my underpants and socks, like Clark Kent, not quite able to make a complete transformation to his Superman alter ego.

I was hung in the sling with my shiny new lead shields in place, just like the techs had promised. I realized at that moment the total body irradiation procedure was a great equalizer of sorts.

Everyone was the same when we faced the Beast, whether a banker, lawyer, corporate vice-president, ditch digger, or balding graphic designer. No amount of money, not the most savvy negotiating, not even corporate stock value skyrocketing through the roof could shield a man from that necessary evil.

We were all the same when we were hanging in the canvas sling.

I handed the tech my musical selection for that first day—some vintage James Taylor.

After several minutes adjusting my position in the booth and focusing the business end of The Beast using crosshairs projected onto my chest, the techs loaded James into the CD player, cranked up the volume, and hit the "play" button.

As the gals walked past the booth, they told me I needed to remain very still and if I felt funny for any reason (*funny beyond being nearly naked, hanging in a canvas sling from two metal hooks*), I should simply call out to them and let them know. The booth was equipped with a microphone so we could chat during the procedure if need be.

So ladies, do you come here often? It's my first time in this place, and I feel like I'm on fire!

The techs closed and sealed the heavy metal door at the end of the corridor like they were securing the building for the Apocalypse. An oscillating red light was mounted to the wall above. I felt like I was at NORAD and we were about to launch a nuclear strike.

The Beast switched on and flashed its ominous warning beacon throughout the room as if to say, "Don't mess with The Beast. He's awake now, and he's hungry."

After thirty seconds a voice came over the intercom. "Okay

Robert, here we go. This will be a ten-minute exposure. Be very still. The time should go by quickly, just concentrate on your music."

With that, The Beast woke up, and got busy on me. "Exposure" was really a nice way of saying "sear" which is what I did to hamburgers on my grill at home. *Perhaps they will baste me with garlic butter before "exposing" my backside on my second visit to the dungeon.*

A loud buzz filled the room, like a swarm of bumble bees nursing a hangover. Like many times in my childhood, when I "sang along with Mitch (Miller)" at my grandma's house in Morro Bay, I sang along with James for the balance of the exposure.

When the techs shut down The Beast and reentered the room, they smiled. "How do you feel Mr. Henslin?"

"I feel fine. No place I'd rather be than right here, partying with you gals, in my underwear, suspended by these hooks!"

"We heard you singing. You have a nice voice!"

"Well thanks. I think it's the booth. Great acoustics. Do you think by the time you gals are done with me, I'll still have a voice?"

Both gals laughed—and also dodged the question. I was left wondering if there was a part of their sinister plan they had not revealed.

That was how it went two more times that day. We returned the next three days in a row and went through the same drill. There was no basting but plenty of searing.

I crashed hard Friday night. The decompression from the stress of the week got the best of me. But in the middle of the night, I found myself wide-awake with my mind racing. I glanced over at Michele, out cold and sawing logs, perhaps even building a cabin. She was gone.

I realized after that night, we wouldn't be together in our home for something on the order of a month. A month! Beyond that, I would only have limited contact with my daughters.

I didn't know if they would even want to come see me on the E1 unit. It might be too much for them. It might be too much for me. They might not even be allowed to visit, given their ages. I didn't know.

With each step in our journey towards the transplant, Michele and

I kept them informed. They maintained a level of detachment from much of it, not wanting to know the details, but they were concerned and unsettled.

They leaned heavily on their friends for support to maintain as much "normal" in their lives as possible. I hurt for them every day and wished I could tell them something positive and definitive, such as things looked really good and everything was going to be all right. But I couldn't do that.

So darn frustrating!

Those late night realizations were crushing. Even as I wrote this, a year and a half post-transplant, the tears flowed. I couldn't even see the keyboard to type. Do they make windshield wipers for prescription glasses?

66

Day -3: Admission Day to Stanford's E1 Unit

Saturday, February 7th, 2008. Admission Day. *Welcome Rob, to the last days of your former life.* Getting out of bed that day was a chore, both mentally and physically. I felt like I had been pulled through a pasta maker and left out on the kitchen counter over night.

Approaching the double door entrance to the E1 Transplant Unit, not for an orientation meeting as we had done several weeks prior, but because it was game time, was something that will forever be emblazoned into my memory.

I kept thinking, *Dead man walking.* I wondered if I would emerge from those doors after that "typical" twenty-five to thirty-day stay I read about in The Binder, and what shape I would be in.

With the radiation treatments completed, I knew I had played all my cards. I could only hope everything was going well with the harvest and delivery of my donor's marrow. There was no turning back. It was what it was.

I felt like I was walking into a funeral home to make final arrangements following a loved one's passing, but stood a pretty good chance of needing my own pine box and bouquet of flowers.

Oops. I guess we'll need two coffins, Lyle. This poor fellow just collapsed in a heap.

We entered the unit, walked down the corridor to the nurse's station, and introduced ourselves. "Henslin, party of two. We have a reservation."

Michele and I were met with smiles and warm greetings. The way those folks conducted themselves was impressive and an amazing comfort. They helped us settle in, answered the many questions we had, and helped us get our heads on straight.

As she had done before when I was admitted to Kaiser, Michele stayed with me for quite a while before heading home. Saying goodnight to her really tore me up.

It was hard enough during the Kaiser hospitalizations, but at Stanford, on the transplant unit, knowing within just a couple hours high dose Cytoxan chemotherapy would begin, was almost too much.

It was surreal in a way, like some kind of dream, but I couldn't just snap my fingers and make the pain go away. It was the real deal, the last lines being written in the book about the life Michele and I had known for two decades.

Saying goodnight to the woman I loved was more than I could take. After Michele left, I thought about my first night as a patient at City of Hope when she called me from our apartment. I felt that same feeling of helplessness. There wasn't a stinkin' thing I could do about it, other than pray... and wait.

It's bad enough in life when we hurt someone by our words or actions; usually we can make amends and move forward. But pondering things from my bed on the E1 unit, I felt my illness had inflicted hurt and pain on Michele, my girls, and my family and friends.

I felt incredibly guilty for what I was putting them through. I felt like I would never be able to make amends.

It wasn't clear thinking. I know that's not what they thought about me or about the situation, but it was very difficult—and sometimes still is—to shake those feelings of guilt.

Cytoxan chemo began that night around 10 p.m. to kill off the remnants of my immune system. Chemo was also administered on Sunday (Day -2). No treatment of any kind was scheduled for Monday (Day -1) so my body could rest for a day (*yeah, right*) before the transplant on Tuesday (Day 0).

The total body irradiation coupled with the high dose chemo would take me to the edge of death, where I would sit precariously for a couple days. I remember the stark realization of that fact impacting me during a conversation with one of my nurses.

"Once the chemotherapy is completed, the bone marrow factory in your bones will be out of business," said the nurse.

"How do I stay alive if everything is dead?"

"The only living blood cells remaining will be those already present in your bloodstream and internal organs. They will die off soon as well."

"How soon?"

"Well, the timing of the transplant is critical. We have everything timed so you receive the transplant within a certain window. There is some overlap built in to the schedule."

There was a "window," and the need for essentially perfect timing. Kind of a scary thought to say the least. But it was not a theoretical discussion I had that day with my nurse. I was in that window and in need of that perfect timing.

Having read through The Binder and attended the class with Michele we were both well aware of the huge risks. It was unsettling to dwell on the "what ifs" and often difficult to dismiss the thought I was riding the razor's edge.

But there was also a calm, matter of fact way in which those days right before the transplant played out that didn't allow me much idle time to dwell on the subject. I think the professionalism and incredible caring of the staff on the E1 unit made it so.

They kept me focused on what I needed to do: eat as much as I could, hydrate, hydrate, hydrate (along with lots of diuretic medication to flush the Cytoxan from my kidneys), get out of the room frequently for walks, and so on. My body was at death's door but I had a "to do" list. Tally ho!

It didn't take long at all—perhaps just a day or so post-radiation—for all sense of taste to vanish. I had zero appetite. Over the course of my life, that had never really been a problem. Meal trays were brought in three times a day. Nothing on them ever looked enticing.

Overall the food served at Stanford was pretty doggone yummy, but under those circumstances, they could have served steak, pizza and burritos (selections from all three major food groups) and I would have waved it off.

Not even the Jell-O cups, applesauce, crackers, or the small bottles of juice had any appeal. My system was fried big time, and it would be some time before things returned to any semblance of normal.

During the first couple days on the unit, beyond the chemo, hydrating and walking, there were large blocks of time devoted to teaching. There was a wide range of "stuff" I had to get a handle on prior to undergoing the transplant.

I was visited by what seemed like a never-ending stream of folks: dieticians, nurses, physical therapists, social workers, and if memory serves me correctly, a tiny car filled with circus clowns.

I learned the importance of performing oral care five or six times each day to prevent mouth sores, a process affectionately referred to as "swish and spit" using small cupfuls of sterile water.

Toothbrush? Not anymore, not for quite a while. Flossing? Don't even go there.

I would need to shower and change all my clothes every day regardless of how I felt. It was all about staying as clean and germ-free as possible.

The housekeeping crew would be in a couple times each day to mop the floors and clean all the fixtures and surfaces. There would be long periods of time where I would probably not be able to eat anything. That obstacle would be overcome with infused total body nutrition hung on my IV pole along with all the other bottles and bags.

A physical therapist taught me exercises I could do in my room to maintain some level of strength. Once I was transferred to an isolation room there was no coming out for a walk around the unit until my white blood cell count reached a certain level. That typically didn't happen for several weeks.

Those first days on the unit, from Saturday evening through the end of the day on Monday were really something. All of the teaching and to-dos, coupled with the emotional and psychological adjustments I had to make, left me feeling like an old candle—burnt to the end of the wick with the wax in a softened, viscous mass. And I hadn't even received the transplant!

The chemotherapy coursed through my body and killed off my immune system. The IV pole positioned next to my bed had a tangled jumble of bottles and bags hanging from it—various fluids—medicines to prevent infection, provide hydration, total body nutrition, potassium, magnesium, some clear, some colored, you name it.

There was tubing all over the place. All of it ultimately ended up attached to me through the central catheter line inserted in my chest shortly after I arrived on the unit.

Several pumps were attached to the IV pole to infuse all that juice into my system. Various indicator lights on the pumps flashed incessantly. At night, the display screens cast a creepy blue light throughout my room.

Periodically, alarms sounded because of air bubbles in a line or the completion of an infusion. Sometimes they went off for no particular reason. It was just the mood they were in.

I called the IV pole my "mobile command center" because it looked like the kind of thing an astronaut might strap on his back to explore the surface of some distant planet.

By Monday night, I was pooped from my day of rest. Though I was tired and wanted to sleep, I watched TV long into the night, and thought about my donor. *How did the harvest and transport of the marrow play out?* I wondered how he fared through the procedure. *Was he in any pain? Did he have any regrets?*

I thought how amazing it was that a bone marrow transplant was even possible—that folks actually survived. I knew the marrow had probably already arrived at Stanford. It was in the hands of the laboratory folks, who worked their voodoo to wash, filter, supplement, fortify and otherwise prepare it for the infusion.

My nurses described the transplant as a blood transfusion, and said it would take several hours to complete. In my head, I pictured essentially a bag of blood hanging from my IV pole, on a slow, half-day drip. When I actually got into it, I learned it was just a bit more complicated than that.

67

Day 0: Transplant Day

Tuesday, February 10, 2009 was my second birthday. I woke up to find my nurse for the day, the lovely and talented Farrah, at my bedside taking my vitals. She was an amazing gal, an RN with a Master's degree from UCLA. She was lovely. She had a great personality and a rye sense of humor. She was a joker—we hit it off right away.

She stood at the foot of my bed, and input my vitals into her computer on wheels or "COW." I did my best to wake up fast. A fellow from Food Services brought in my breakfast tray. Farrah told me to get as much of it down as I could. She wanted me strong for the transfusion. It was 7:30 a.m. The transplant would begin around 9:00 a.m. We would be best friends for the whole day.

It was "go" time.

I slammed down my breakfast as best I could, although much of it went down the pie hole without even registering on my taste-o-meter. I remember some eggs and a strip of bacon, and some home-style potatoes.

Farrah brought me two cold cans of Ensure, a liquid nutritional supplement that provided a huge load of both calories and vitamins. She asked me what flavor I preferred, chocolate or vanilla? I told her probably chocolate. She handed me the can and a cup full of ice cubes.

"Cool. Drink this as you eat your breakfast. You might have to get used to the taste, but most patients seem not to mind it too much if it's cold. My favorite flavor is the milk chocolate but they have a dark chocolate as well."

"What's the point of drinking the Ensure when I already have a couple cans of juice and a milk to throw down?" I asked.

Farrah glanced at me with a knowing look. "Ensure will probably become your new best friend in the weeks ahead, Robert." She continued. "It's loaded with all kinds of vitamins and minerals, and most of all, calories."

She smiled, and told me within just a few days, it was likely I would not be able to eat anything from the meal trays. The doctors and nurses would urge me to drink as many Ensures during the day as I could handle. "Have one now, while you are still able to taste it, and get used to the whole notion," she said.

I finished my breakfast—the stuff I couldn't taste at all, and the can of Ensure as well—which had a pretty good chocolate flavor, but also a strange chemical after taste.

It was as if the folks who manufactured the stuff knew they had to come up with something that closely resembled chocolate milk, but also knew they had to screw it up with modern chemistry just enough that it complied with long-established guidelines for the taste and texture of hospital food.

After "brushing" my teeth, I donned my HEPA filter mask, and took a walk around the unit. Barring a fire drill, natural disaster, or impromptu clown show, it would be the last time I came out of my room for some time, perhaps many hours. I wanted to get some legwork in before Farrah came in to start the transplant.

Shortly after I returned to my room, Farrah came in with a huge bag of what looked like whole blood. I had received many blood transfusions over the past several months, but had never seen such a bag as the one she hung on my IV pole that morning. It was literally the size of a small watermelon.

She hung that sucker on my command center IV pole, ran the tubing through the infusion pump, and keyed-in the volume and dose rate.

Then she turned toward me, grabbed my hand in hers and squeezed it tightly. "All right Robert, are you ready to get started?"

It was a heavy moment. Up to that point the morning had been fairly tame, but when I saw that enormous bag of dark, red blood, and realized it was the harvested marrow from my donor, things took a rather somber turn.

Farrah was all set to hit the "start" button on the infusion pump. But it wasn't just the pump she was poised to start. It was my whole life. My future.

I got really choked up as the gravity of the situation hit me. I had difficulty getting any words out. Farrah noticed I was losing it. "Oh, I'm sorry buddy. I know this is hard. But I want you to work with me today and have a positive attitude, okay?"

"I will Farrah. I'm fired up. I'm just feeling the heaviness of the moment."

It had already been quite a journey to get to that point. She took my vitals again, and told me she would be in every fifteen minutes to check them, to be sure I didn't have a reaction to the infusion.

Reactions are bad things. Been there, done that.

"This bag is the first of what I think will ultimately be three or four bags that will be infused. I think it will take the better part of the day to complete the transplant."

The whole day?

That sounded crazy, but was in fact how things played out. We started the transplant at 9:10 a.m. and didn't finish the last of the three bags until after midnight. After that, Farrah hung two additional bags of whole blood just to top off my tank. It was a long day, but the deal was done.

I was still alive. So far, so good.

68

The Long, Strange Trip

One day following the transplant, I was moved to an isolation room. It had a double door entry. Whenever my nurses or family and friends came to visit, they had to enter through the first door, wait for it to close completely, gear up with gowns and facemasks, and then open the inner door.

It wasn't quite a sealed airlock, but was darn close to it. The room measured fifteen feet square. There was room for my bed, a recliner chair, and an additional chair for visitors. Along one wall, a waist-high bank of storage cabinets ran under a wall of windows.

The view from my room was of a beautiful triangular-shaped garden space surrounded on three sides by hospital buildings. Circular rows of brilliantly colored flowers bloomed at the base of tall evergreens that filled with shafts of filtered sunlight each afternoon.

There were a couple Cherry trees in the garden as well. Their branches were covered with bright pink blossoms.

Outside Stanford's Emergency Department was a heliport where helicopters brought victims of traumatic injuries. I could hear the choppers arriving and departing several times each week. When they did, the Cherry trees in the garden outside my window blew violently in the wash of the helicopter's rotor blades.

For a few moments, the entire garden filled with a swirl of pink "snowflakes," as the blossoms blew off their branches. That scene continued until the helicopter gained altitude and cleared the heliport. It was fun to watch, like shaking a giant snow globe.

There was a small counter on the wall opposite the wall of windows with a sink and more storage cabinets. Off the main room was a bathroom with a shower stall equipped for wheelchair access.

That was it—my home for a month. And there was no coming out to play until my white cell count said I could.

One thing I realized early on in my stay in that happy little space was how having to drag the mobile command center everywhere I went made the simplest things big events that required pre-planning, thought, and FDA approval.

What had been the simple act of taking a shower became an hour-long argument with water, IV tubing, and washcloths. I spent forty-five minutes tap dancing with the numerous infusion lines attached to my IV pole.

Water sprayed all over the bathroom, dousing my pumps and IV bags, and sometimes the fresh change of clothes I placed on a shelf along with my towels.

On several occasions I stood in the shower, tangled up in my tubing with soap running into my eyes, laughing, and thinking, *Oh man, this is pathetic.* Other days, it really got to me, and I had zero tolerance for it and just got mad.

Several days post-transplant I experienced the onset of some weird psychological changes. I was almost consumed with a feeling that there was a person living inside me. It's difficult to describe, but I recall occasions where I made my menu selections for the next day's meals, and thought, *I like Jell-O, but does the new guy like it?* I called him "Gus."

Those types of thoughts crossed my mind all the time. I asked my nurses if it was something they had seen before with other transplant patients, or had I pretty much blown the last bolt on my manifold cover? They assured me it was quite common for such psychological changes to occur, all part of the adaptation-acceptance process patients go through as they come to terms with the transplant. Eventually those weird feelings and thoughts went away, but for a couple weeks I felt out of my head and way too deep into someone else's.

There were often days when I was struck almost out of nowhere with a sense of hopelessness. I'd be watching the Food Network on TV and would think, *What's the point of writing down this recipe? I'll probably die before I have a chance to bake this stupid dish.*

Lots of patience and encouragement from my nurses kept me grounded. It was absolutely essential to ride the train all the way to the last stop. I know those gals worked overtime to keep me motivated. I'm so thankful they did, because I did not have a good handle on things.

One minute, I was happy and fired up. The next, I was completely despondent and didn't care if I lived or died. There were radical emotional swings, from one end of the spectrum to the other.

I prayed each day for a level head.

There were good days on the unit. Saturday, February 21st (Day +11) was just such a day. Michele visited me and brought with her a brand new Macintosh laptop computer that had been purchased by a couple of extremely generous friends.

Now I could connect with the outside world and post journal entries to the CaringBridge web site. It was such an awesome gift.

Being in that isolation room, unable to go out for walks until my white count recovered, and feeling like the walls were closing in on me was quite constricting. Having that computer and being able to connect with friends and family was a breath of fresh air—a blessing at just the right time.

Side effects did manifest themselves, including medication-induced high blood pressure and diabetes. An endless flow of medications maxed out the capacity of my over-burdened IV pole command center.

If the world had come to an end at that point, and the only means of survival was a hefty supply of plastic infusion bags, I would have had a corner on the market.

I received countless blood and platelet transfusions, along with a course of Intravenous Immunoglobulin (IVIG), a plasma-like product that helped manufacture antibodies and ward off infection. Those efforts paid off. The transfusions gave me more energy for a few days, and I remained free of infections.

Near the end of my third week, I was really down for the count, physically and mentally. The complications had pounded me like a railroad spike. I had no appetite, threw up all the time—in spite of the constant flow of anti-nausea meds—and my mental outlook was in the tank.

I spent a lot of time out of my bed, which my nurses encouraged. I got in what walking I could manage in that small space. It amounted to little more than a half circle around the foot of my bed, retraced over and over in fifteen-minute pops.

I felt like Steve McQueen in the movie *Pappion,* pacing back and forth in his cramped prison cell, unable to take more than eight steps before turning around. Beyond that, I watched TV from my recliner and pondered life.

One day my favorite angel, nurse Anne, who always wore pearls along with a smile on her face, came into my room. She had reviewed the latest entries in my chart and learned of my sorry state. She told me she was not going to let my situation get the best of me. She was going to work with me, and we were going to work together to get on top of things.

"Robert, it's really NOT all right that you continue to have nausea. It's really NOT okay that you can't sleep at night," she said.

I was pretty spaced out. Anne continued. "We are going to get a plan together and get you back on track. I want you to tell me everything. If you can't keep something down, I want to hear about it. Don't just throw it up and sit back in your chair. Don't assume that is the way it has to be. And please do not feel like you are taking up all my time if you need to talk with me about a problem, okay? That's why I'm here."

Her words hit home. I suppose they shook me out of the funk I had descended into. *How 'bout I just throw this can of Ensure through that window, Anne? Would that be okay?* There was so much bad and very little good happening. I will always love Anne for helping me through that difficult period.

We developed new strategies for dealing with the nausea, the sleepless nights, the lack of appetite. Within a few days things took a more positive turn. I was refocused on fighting the fight. And it was a fight—every single day.

After just a couple weeks, the central line in my chest became infected and was removed. A day later a new line was placed in my left arm. The course of broad-spectrum antibiotics—anti-bacterial, anti-viral, anti-fungal, anti-gravity, antidisestablishmentarianism, you name it—continued for several weeks.

69

March Madness

There were many nights on the unit where my mind raced with thoughts about what the future held, images of my wife and daughters and better times, and feelings of loneliness and despair. On those nights, I usually sat in the recliner next to my bed and watched TV for a few hours, trying not to freak out and hoping I would drift off to dreamland.

I discovered the simple pleasure of popsicles, as they were often the only food item that had any appeal. On those nights when I was going stir crazy, my nurses brought me popsicles. Frozen comfort food. It was always a nice treat.

College Basketball's "March Madness" dominated the TV programming, but the madness was not limited to the tournament hardwood. There was plenty of it on E1. Popsicles and other refreshing frozen treats went a long way in providing relief from the often crushing weight of the transplant experience.

You just can't help but feel better when one of your cool nurses enters your room at 3:00 a.m. with a popsicle in hand, a big smile on her face, plops down in a chair, and hangs out with you for a while to talk about life.

Thank you, Ashley. I will always love you for your care and compassion.

By March 11th my white cells reached the required 1000 count benchmark. I was allowed to get out of my room for as many walks each day as I could tolerate.

Liberation Day!

After thirty-eight days in isolation, it felt great to get out among the living. I would even have been happy to see the carload of clowns.

Late in my stay on the unit, I developed abdominal pain. The doctors ordered a variety of narcotics for pain management, and an abdominal CT scan was attempted, but I was in too much pain.

The narcotics didn't do much for me by way of pain management, but apparently they did a real number on my brain. Within a day or so of those meds being administered in a continuous IV drip, there was concern over what was referred to by my doctors and nurses as my "impaired cognitive status, and labored breathing."

From everything I've read, it's never a good idea to have impaired cognitive status, especially when you also can't breathe. I was given oxygen through a nasal cannula, and connected to an O_2 saturation monitor so my nurses could gauge how much oxygen was getting to my brain. It seemed like a noble pursuit.

As the NCAA basketball tournament advanced to the "Sweet Sixteen," "Elite Eight" and "Final Four," the March madness continued on the unit. I wandered out of my room in the middle of the night on two occasions, completely spaced out (read: cognitively impaired) without wearing my protective mask.

I have no memory of that whatsoever.

By March 13th, my white cell count had reached 1600 (1.6). There was new concern that I had a viral infection affecting my brain and lungs. *Just great. Does this train ever come to a stop, or does it just keep getting robbed?* A brain MRI was performed, but the results were unremarkable.

By March 21st the abdominal pain dissipated so my doctors once again pressed me to have the CT scan. It wasn't a painful procedure, that is, if you could lie down for it. But it was interesting.

I was positioned on a cold, metal table wearing nothing but my birthday suit and a towel. The heated, padded leather table and the salmon appetizer were apparently unavailable.

The table passed through the center of a machine that contained a giant electron magnet. Visions of my sixth grade science project flashed across my mind. As my facial extremities passed within millimeters of the inside of the long tube the magnet spun at high RPMs in a circle around me, and captured my soul.

The CT, like the MRI, was unremarkable. It's quite remarkable how unremarkable all those tests proved to be as there was clearly something going on. My doctors were determined to get to the bottom of it.

Up to that point, they had not been able to nail it down. And they were still very concerned about my lungs, so they scheduled a Bronchoscopy for March 23rd. The fun just kept on coming.

For that procedure, a nurse spent fifteen minutes spraying numbing medication into the back of my throat (and I mean loads of it). She had me recline back on the treatment table, not quite fully horizontal.

She asked me if I could feel anything in the back of my mouth. I told her I couldn't feel my legs.

The doctor who would perform the procedure dropped the head of my bed into a horizontal position and shoved a very large pipe-like instrument into my mouth, and down the back of my throat. I thought it was a telephone pole.

Turns out it was a fiber optic camera connected to a video display that probed the deepest, darkest recesses of my lungs. I'm almost certain it chronicled my family's genealogy as well.

I didn't feel any pain, but it was awkward to say the least, and ran completely counter to what common sense told me should be happening at that time. If you put something that big into someone's mouth, they're going to choke, regardless of how much numbing medication was sprayed.

Halfway through that procedure, my brain tapped me on the shoulder. *What they're doing is just wrong and needs to stop. You need to get out of this closet of horrors and run away from these people as fast as you can.*

It took everything in me to keep from gagging on the throat cam, but luckily when I got to the point where I knew a serious change in our relationship was about to occur, doc said, "Okay Robert, we're all done." I wanted to express my thanks, but I was too busy gagging on my lungs. I thought they were supposed to be attached down there.

Just as quickly as he had stuffed that camera into my mouth, he pulled it out, and propped the head of the table back into an upright position.

Several small nodules were found, along with irrefutable evidence that the alien spaceship crash in Roswell, New Mexico decades prior, really happened. I was kept on the big dose of anti-fungal meds for several more days.

I slowly became less of a space cadet, but just to keep things interesting, still exhibited a significant level of mental confusion from time to time. My nurses asked me several times each day if I knew where I was, what year it was, the name of the current U.S. President, and other simple questions a kid should know the answers to. I batted around .350 with my answers.

They gave me partial credit for coming up with "Osama" for the President's name.

70

Discharge!

After forty-eight days on the unit (nearly double the time estimated in The Binder), I was stable and clear-headed enough to be discharged. After many heartfelt and difficult goodbyes, and lots of tears, I checked out of the hospital on Thursday, March 26th, just three days before my 47th birthday, a goal I had set in my mind a couple weeks prior.

Leaving the E1 unit was both scary and exhilarating at the same time. That place and those people kept me alive. They kept me from losing my mind.

Part of me feared life outside the unit. At the same time, it was an incredible feeling to exit through the same double doors that a month prior ominously welcomed me to an uncertain future.

With Michele walking next to my wheelchair, I made my way slowly down the main corridor of the hospital and into the welcoming freshness of spring outside the hospital's main entrance.

Like that first blast of air after my initial stay at Kaiser several months earlier, the cool breeze blowing across my face as I waited for Michele to bring the truck around was a special moment—a feeling I will always cherish.

Michele entered the circular driveway and stopped in front of the hospital. I climbed in for the trip home. As we drove away, I broke down in a huge release. I was so happy to be alive, to have made it through the transplant, and finally be heading home to be reunited with my family.

On the way down the freeway, I thought a lot about Anne, Ashley, Farrah, and the other nurses, and George and the medical assistants, and the many other folks on E1. What amazing people they were. I wanted to remember all of their names and faces and burn them into my memory. But that was impossible.

Much of my time on the unit is a blur. I suppose that is a good thing. I'm thankful for the memories I do have—the good and the bad—because in spite of all the challenges and heartaches, there was plenty of compassion, friendship, love, smiles, and other blessings.

I certainly hope the days I spent on E1 pushing through the transplant cured my leukemia and gave me a solid second shot at a long life. Only time will tell.

But beyond survival, I wanted it to have made me a better person, more compassionate with empathy for those in similar circumstances. However I was able, I wanted to do something with the time I had left on the planet to help those folks on a very practical level.

I had no idea what that looked like, so I tried to keep an open mind, and let that wish rattle around in my fried brain. But as I began my new life post-transplant, I quickly realized there were several monkeys, wide awake following their long slumber, waiting in the wings. Each one had a load of issues to unleash and each one challenged me to further embrace those five, simple words: It is what it is.

Rather than entertaining thoughts of how I would spend my time when I returned to work, dealing with those issues would consume my thoughts, time, and energy.

The notion of a short road to recovery on the medical front or smooth sailing at home was wishful thinking on my part, but not a shred of it was grounded in reality.

"Today is not yesterday: we ourselves change; how can our works and thoughts, if they are always to be the fittest, continue always the same? Change, indeed is painful; yet ever needful; and if memory have its force and worth, so also has hope."
—Thomas Carlyle

Home Again for the First Time

Though I was no longer the "boy in the bubble," I maintained a level of isolation at home to avoid potential infection risks. My immune system was almost non-existent, so I spent much of my time in the day room.

We installed a child safety gate in our hallway to effectively cut off that area from the rest of the house. When the gate was closed, it sent the message folks shouldn't venture any farther.

Our daughters' friends hung out at our place, which kept the energy level high. After spending so much time in isolation, the sound of my girls having a ball with their friends was like music to my soul. When folks dropped by for a visit, the laughter and conversation was welcomed therapy.

I wore my mask or everyone else did whenever folks came over.

Most of the time it was easier for me to pop my mask on than ask a room full of folks to don masks and converse in muffled tones.

But when it was everyone else with masks on their face, it was like a scene from a summer camp competition where campers stuffed their mouths with soda crackers then tried to whistle.

"So how are things going for you now that you're home?"

"How's that?"

"Now that you are home, how are you doing?"

"Oh, doing well. And yes, it's now a dome. Hair won't grow up there for sometime."

"Not dome, home."

"Yes, it's great to be home."

"It must have been tough to be in isolation for that long."

"I couldn't make out what you said."

"You were in isolation for so long."

"Oh, so long. I'm sorry you can't stay longer."

I didn't want those times to end. It was vibrant and cheerful, like a home should sound and how life should be. Life wasn't supposed to be me in a recliner, sequestered in the recesses of our house, feeling like a used dishrag, and unable to make much of a contribution to the cause.

The fatigue was unrelenting. I had been warned about how bad it could be post-transplant. There were posters on the walls of the E1 unit warning of the need to get considerable rest following discharge and to be prepared for a level of exhaustion unlike anything I had ever experienced.

They weren't lying.

What made it so bad was compounding the stress of the hospital stay—draining enough on its own—with the fact my immune system was literally rebuilding itself from the ground up. Every resource was being channeled into growing new blood cells and fortifying my organs and muscle tissue.

There was no budget surplus for after school programs!

I felt like I had fallen from the top of a Plum-tuckered tree, and hit every branch on the way down. If I tried to walk the hallway in our home for more than just a couple minutes, my body would pull me aside and we would have a little chat.

"Um, okay. We understand you want to take a walk."

"Yes, I do. I don't want to be any trouble. I just thought I could make it to the end of the hall, and then…"

"And then? And then what? Hello! You'll collapse."

"Really?"

"Really!"

"Well, I suppose that's possible."

"Possible? You don't get it. If you want to do anything, you need to talk to your body first. We don't like surprises—and we're not even your adrenal glands. You were warned about this."

"I'm sorry."

"That's better. We are working just as hard and fast as we can in here to rebuild you. The job is much closer to a reconstruction than a remodel. We're not just adding a room to your existing floor plan, pal!"

"Again, I'm sorry. This is all new to me."

"Well, okay. That's fine. But no more monkey business, okay?"

Beyond the fatigue, I was unable to eat, much less taste anything, but like survivalists preparing for the end of the world, we filled our pantry with cans of Ensure and items from the infamous vending machine diet plan, as Neutropenia was always a possibility.

During the first week at home, I had positive realizations I had survived the bone marrow transplant, but I also grappled with thoughts about how long and bumpy the road to recovery would be.

Michele and I knew full well it could take six months, a year or even longer to recover to the point where I could return to work.

Relief from the crushing fatigue could not come soon enough.

Like twenty years prior, there was a considerable pile of pills to take each morning and evening. Sleep did not come easily due to severe low back pain because of too many days in a hospital bed.

I had no legs under me at all. It took everything to stand up from a sitting position. The notion of taking a walk outside was a joke. It wasn't in the cards. Not then, not for a while.

At night, when the rest of my family was in bed, I was often wide-awake in the day room, yearning for sleep to come. In those late hours the house was still and lonely.

The day room was bathed in a flickering blue haze, cast by the TV that sat atop a simple "Euro-style" storage cabinet. It was the throne upon which sat Lord God Video, dispenser of mind-numbing white noise. The droning of folks hawking their kitchen storage containers and miracle hair restoration products each night from that box nearly drowned out my two snoring dogs. Nearly. That was my life at home. I clung to any shred of normal I could find.

72

The Outpatient Regimen

There were daily appointments in the ITA for blood draws, IV hydration, blood, and platelet transfusions; whatever was necessary to keep me going and my immune system growing stronger.

I couldn't drive due to the massive amounts of medication coursing through my system, and relied on a network of folks, including Michele when she was able, my in-laws, and friends and neighbors who signed up to provide rides as needed.

They were needed almost every day.

I leaned heavily on those folks. Each day we made the trek back up the freeway to Stanford. Often the days were long and draining. When I arrived back home I was wiped out. I so appreciated the sacrifice (and investment) of time my family members and our friends made to help me.

For the longest time, part of me felt guilty about "burdening" my family and friends with my needs. But in time, I realized those folks wanted to help, and didn't view their helping me as a burden at all, but rather a way they could contribute and help out at a time of real need.

It was quite humbling.

73

Complications

Houston, we have a problem. I had incredible pain "down there," and was not able to empty my bladder, but I bled, and I bled a lot. It was horrible. There was blood everywhere. The pain was sharp, like being cut repeatedly with a piece of jagged glass. It was all I could do to contain myself.

It was late at night on Friday, April 10th. Michele was asleep on the sofa in our living room, as it was impossible for her to sleep with me up every few minutes and constantly tossing and turning in bed. She was exhausted. I did not want to wake her up.

In hindsight, I should have called her for help. I should have let her know I was in real trouble. We should have headed back to Stanford to be readmitted to the unit then and there, *(duh!)*.

Instead I chose to tough it out in hopes that whatever was happening to me might pass as quickly as it came on. *Good thinking Rob.*

I guess I just really did not want to acknowledge the possibility I would need to be hospitalized again so soon after discharge. I would get past it. Two weeks of outpatient visits were under my belt. This complication came on without warning.

I spent that night popping out of bed every five minutes to use the bathroom. After each trip, I had to wash blood off my legs, hands, and feet, and mop up blood from the bathroom floor. It was like a scene from a horror film.

I somehow made it through the night. The next morning, I told Michele about what happened. She was very concerned. I was exhausted. We made our way to the ITA for a scheduled hydration appointment.

I told my nurse about the overnight blood bath. She wasn't happy about that news at all and quickly alerted the Physician's Assistant on duty. My nurse was frustrated with me as well, and righteously so, for taking the risk I did in thinking I could handle the problem on my own.

"Jeez Robert, why didn't you call us? That's why we're here."

The lesson here: Don't be a hero. If you begin to bleed (*from there or anywhere else*) and you experience excruciating pain, seek help immediately. It's really not cool to hack off your nurses with feeble attempts at self-diagnosis and treatment.

Additional lab panels were ordered to check the status of my kidneys and bladder. The news was not good. I was readmitted to the E1 unit that day with a raging case of Post-Transplant Hemorrhagic Cystitis, essentially, bleeding from the bladder wall.

It was a fairly common complication of the high dose Cytoxan chemo administered during the Preparative Regimen. Remnants of the chemo hung out in the tissues of my bladder wall, like a bunch of gangsters itching for someone to beat down. The blood clots shut down my urinary function.

Let the beating begin.

There was no standard treatment to deal with the problem. My doctors said it was more about a game of "skilled trial and error" to find the right fix and that took time.

74

Intimate Encounters With the
Sisters of Suction

When I was admitted, a catheter was inserted... all the way
(*down there*), and a series of collection bags attached to it.
Those bags and the plastic tubing were secured to my IV
pole. I spent two and a half weeks on the unit dealing with bouts of
incredible pain that struck like lightning—where I least wanted it.

I thought I would go out of what was left of my mind on several occasions. When the pain came on, I hit my call button. When the nurses
came, there were usually three of them with bottles of saline and giant
syringes in hand, the kind I'd seen veterinarians use to nurse farm animals
back to health.

Painkillers please. Make mine a double, with ice.

The nurses encouraged me to take long, slow, deep breaths, and
do what I could to reinsert my eyeballs back into their sockets. I
encouraged them to hit me over the head with a hammer.

A nurse flushed saline into the line, and then drew back on the
syringe in hopes of extracting the massive blood clots that had taken
up residence in my bladder.

I had visions of my internal organs locking arms and holding on
for dear life against the suction. Given the level of pain, I wouldn't have
been surprised if a chipmunk had dropped into the collection bag.

Flush and suck. Repeat.

It was insane. I was flat on my back with my hospital gown

gathered up around my neck, a hopeful eye fixated on the collection bags. Though every effort was made to keep the curtain that encircled my bed and our intimate gathering in place, it never happened.

With three nurses huddled over me, sometimes requesting additional backup, and the door to my room wide open, all sense of modesty and personal privacy was lost in nothing flat.

On more than one occasion, my roommate's family members and friends were treated to an eyeful of the most sensitive of medical procedures. I'm sure my nurses enjoyed a silent giggle during those encounters.

"Hi folks. Good to see you tonight."

"Oh my God that hurt."

"Oh, I'm fine and thank you for asking. Sorry about all this."

"Well, you're very understanding. I wish I wasn't flapping in the wind for you."

"Wow. That one hurt. I am taking slow, deep breaths, Anne!"

"Yes. I'm enjoying getting to know him as well. He's a great roommate."

"Holy Moses! Is that saline or battery acid in that syringe?"

"All right. You folks have a nice visit. Youch!"

One episode was especially memorable. Several nurses wielded syringes like members of an elite squad of hydro-warriors ready for battle. Blood and Saline dripped all over my bed linens.

My hospital gown became a bath towel. That curtain? Forget about it. In the midst of the flurry of activity, I stared up at nurse Anne with a smile.

"Anne, you and I have history, but I never envisioned our relationship deepening to this level. It's rather compelling."

"Robert, you crack me up. Don't worry about it. We do this all the time."

"I've tried to keep it modest and not scare you gals to death, but it just isn't working."

I thought I had experienced the utmost in awkward vulnerability when I was in isolation for forty-eight days, cognitively impaired and all. Was I wrong. My sessions with Nurse Anne and the Sisters of Suction set a new standard.

After a few days of trial and error, we had a procedure worked out to get the best results from the declotting efforts. We moved clots through the line like teenage girls work through a mall. It was one heck of a ride.

No chipmunks were ever found.

Unlike my time on the unit for the transplant, I fled the confines of my room and walked several times each day, pushing my IV pole with the four collection bags attached to it, and the large plastic tubing from my catheter hanging out for all to see.

I looked like a balloon animal maker and plastics recycler all rolled into one. On those occasions, I cursed the design of hospital gowns.

There really wasn't a foolproof way to keep all those hoses and bags and tubes, and my best side from causing a spectacle as I made my way around the unit.

Full moon over E1. I think I can see where the astronauts landed!

After pillaging the supply cabinet in my room, I found a way to keep it all contained; nylon straps with plastic clips on each end. They were used to restrain combative patients who cursed the design of hospital gowns.

The straps worked really well as a belt. I asked for a second gown so I could "double up" and have front to back coverage. Total eclipse of the moon.

75

GoLytely Into That Dark Night

With the Cystitis and other post-transplant dynamics in play, my doctors ordered *(say it with me)* more tests. They wanted to check me out from what remained of my stem, to stern. A Colonoscopy was slated—my personal favorite of all the oscopies. The preparation for it was actually far worse than the procedure itself. *Go figure.*

The night before the procedure, nurse Ashley came into my room around 9:00 p.m. with an enormous container in hand. It looked like she was participating in a disaster preparedness drill and was responsible for stockpiling the drinking water.

She set it down with a thud on the tray table next to my bed, and asked me if I was feeling a little thirsty. I looked at her with a grin.

"No, I'm not feeling all that thirsty right now. What's up, Ash?"

Ashley smiled her amazing smile, and informed me before the colonoscopy could be performed I had to consume all the fluid in the canister—half of it before midnight, and the balance before 9:00 a.m. It wasn't water. I'm not even sure it came from this planet.

It was called "Golytely," and was designed to clear the GI track like a school gym was cleaned before a Homecoming dance.

Golytely *(Who names this stuff?)* was unlike any other liquid medication I had taken. With the other meds, it was apparent at least an effort had been made to flavor the concoction with some type of fruity blend or other palatable mix. GoLytely tasted like a pair of old gym shoes, flavored with fermented licorice apple juice.

Three gallons worth.

Ashley told me the stuff was "nasty." Apparently that was medical terminology. There was no way of getting around it. I had to get it down the pie hole.

Ashley tried to walk me through the process. "What we usually do is pour it over ice cubes in a cup, and have patients take small drinks and just keep doing that until they're done. It seems to go down more easily when it's cold."

Go down more easily when it's cold—victims of shipwrecks did the same thing in the open ocean. The whole time Ashley was talking, her nose was wrinkled up and she had a bit of a furrowed brow. Just talking about it made her queasy—and she was the nurse!

Ashley poured my first tall, frosty Golytely over ice. I toasted her and took a swig of the liquid gym shoes, and was promptly revisited, along with my gown and bed linens, by that swig. Seemed smaller on the way down.

Uh oh. Now what?

Ashley was very encouraging. "Well, try it again and maybe this time just take a little sip."

I thought I had done just that.

"If I make my sips any smaller, the suction will tear my lips right off my face."

A man can only pucker (at that end) so much.

"Well Robert, there is another option we could try, but I'd like to see if you can get it done the easy way."

Ashley was a doll. She had an amazing ability to gently "pre-warn" with her words, almost in a melodic, southern drawl. She said it would be best if I could get the stuff in me the "easy" way, which meant something far less appealing loomed on the horizon. I didn't even want to think about that.

When Ashley returned twenty minutes later, she asked me how I was doing. I told her I was engaged in a heated argument with my gag reflex, and so far, it was winning the debate.

"Well, it sounds like we will need to go to option B. We hate to do that," she said, with a frustrated look on her face.

She patted me on my shoulder as if to say, "It was really nice knowing you. You're a great guy. I'm so sorry things turned out this way."

"So, Ashley, what exactly is option B," I asked hesitantly.

She told me I wasn't going to like her much anymore. I told her that would never happen. She looked at me apologetically. I hate when nurses do that.

"Okay Rob, option B, and we hate to do it, is insertion of a Nasal Gastric (NG) tube in order to bypass the gag reflex. Many patients just can't tolerate the Golytely. The NG tube is really the only other way to get the stuff into your system."

Here's how that worked: a small diameter, flexible rubber tube, approximately twenty-four inches in length that only felt like it was the size of a radiator hose was shoved into my face through my nose by my nurse and former buddy, Ashley.

It stopped for a moment at the base of my brain just to say "hi" and have a short visit on the way in, and then descended against the back wall of my throat.

And all of that happened as Ashley and another nurse she called in to assist, apologized for the brain-splitting pain they knew I was experiencing.

They knew this because as they told me to "swallow, swallow, swallow" and fed the line into my face, I swallowed and also embedded my fingernails two joints deep into the mattress on my bed.

The few hairs that remained atop my head braided themselves into cornrows and every one of my toenails curled into tight little balls at the end of my feet. I could swear I saw the carload of circus clowns speed past my room. They were laughing.

That procedure only took a minute to complete. The cornrows took a week to recover. It felt far worse than the root canal I'd endured several years prior. There was no pre-med, no anesthesia. Only apologies. Next time, just clock me upside the head with a bed pan, and then insert the line.

With the tube in place, the nurses used one of those giant veterinary syringes to draw up small quantities of the liquid gym shoes, and then they connected it to the end of the NG tube that extended a few inches out of my nose.

I know. It's bizarre.

They pushed the juice through the tube, and right down the back of my throat. Each time they shot the stuff through the line, the base of my brain received a five-second "ice cream headache."

Since I didn't have to drink the stuff and argue with my gag reflex, we plowed through all three gallons long before dawn. Before the end of her shift, Ashley was nice enough to pull the NG tube back out of my face, which was almost as much fun as the insertion had been.

I'll leave it at that.

Mission accomplished. I spent the balance of the night making frequent trips to the bathroom, as all that Golytely had to "go-some-where" once the gym had been cleaned for the dance.

At 10:00 a.m. the next morning, I was sent to the Radiology department for the Colonoscopy, and I'm happy to report that it was smooth sailing.

I remember being greeted by a very nice nurse who checked my vital signs and gave me a couple pills to sedate me. She had me transition from my bed to the exam table, roll over on my side and think happy thoughts.

The next thing I knew I was being stirred back to consciousness by that same nurse, and shortly thereafter was rolled out of the treatment room back to E1. I was relieved that things had apparently gone smoothly, perhaps even "lytely."

Both ends of my GI track were scoped, but ultimately nothing was found either in the initial exam or indicated in the pathology report that followed several days later.

Another bullet dodged.

I was discharged from the unit on Thursday, April 30 with marching orders to drink like a fish. No syringes required. If I didn't keep my kidneys flushed, the gangsters could return with attitude. If they did, they would be looking for payback.

76

My Apologies...

As I wrote this memoir, and recounted the seemingly endless flow of medical appointments, examinations, and treatment regimens, I had to pause. A little voice whispered to me in the back of my head, *Hey, Rob, you're overwhelming your readers without providing any happy content to give them a break from all this madness.*

I wanted to write beautifully descriptive, upbeat paragraphs about times Michele and I got away from all of the oppressive medical mess for a while. I continued the conversation with myself.

"Isn't there something you can write about that's happy and positive?"

"Well, I'm trying to include the positives, because there were plenty of them. I wish I could write we traveled to Europe, or we even went two hours down the coast from our place to Carmel and enjoyed a few days together."

"Okay. That's good stuff. Write that."

"Well, if I did, it would be a lie."

The honest truth is once the leukemia returned in 2008, the entirety of our life became a non-stop roller coaster ride. It was quite literally one thing after another.

So I must apologize here mid-stream, if you find yourself shaking your head or putting a gun to it, asking if this was really how life was for us.

The challenges we faced were unrelenting, with precious moments of hope, laughter, and blessings sprinkled along the way. My hope is those gold nuggets will inspire you to keep reading, and drink in the positives. Marvel at the big picture of how God brought me through even the darkest times, and all of that in spite of my often-faltering faith.

77

100 Days

Thursday, May 21st—Day +100 post-transplant! It was a big deal. When I was on the unit, I didn't think I would make it to day twenty-five. I had an appointment at Stanford for a big time work up. There was no sign of leukemia in my marrow.

Good news (great news!) as that was the prime indicator the transplant was a "good graft" and was doing its job, following all the chemo and radiation.

I received even more good news several days following the appointment. A chromosome study was performed on the marrow to determine what percentage of my DNA remained in my immune system and how much of my donor's DNA had taken over.

The test indicated 100 percent of the marrow contained my donor's chromosome base with no detectable trace of mine to be found. In one sense, I no longer existed.

Wonderful and strange!

My platelets and white cell counts improved as well to the point where the possibility of slipping back into a Neutropenic state was very unlikely. My immune system was slowly building strength.

But my red cells struggled to build a respectable level. Dr. Robert called it a "hemolysis problem." I wondered how soon I would find myself surrounded by syringe-wielding nurses.

Since my blood type was B-Positive and my donor was A-Positive, new red cells failed to thrive because remnants of my own red cells generated anti-bodies and killed them off. When I learned of the four donor matches that were found, Dr. Robert told me while all of them were perfect genetic matches, none were blood type matches, and that could cause problems down the road.

Every medical decision weighed the risks against the benefits. In the search for a bone marrow donor, the benefit of having the genetic markers in alignment outweighed the risk of my donor not having the same blood type. Doc wasn't too concerned.

"If you run into problems because of blood type incompatibility, we can deal with that. We'll cross that bridge when we get there."

We had reached that bridge. It was Custer's last stand playing out inside me.

The Battle of Little Big Horn on the cellular level.

Doc described the problem as a "bump in the road" all things considered. He assured me the problem was quite common, and it usually resolved on its own over a period of several months. Ultimately my blood type would change from B-Positive to A-Positive. *Bizarre.*

The red cell hemolysis problem continued. It left me in an almost constant state of anemia, easily wiped out, beyond the "normal" post-transplant fatigue. I needed frequent blood transfusions. I was so extremely exhausted there were days when I wanted to hail a cab to take me from one end of the house to the other.

78

Changing of the Guard

I was sad when Dr. Robert retired. We had become good friends. I put my full faith and trust in him as he worked his craft, and got me back into remission in the latter part of 2008. I was his "cheap date." I wish I had met him earlier in my years, as he was full of great stories and observations about life.

He taught me the value of embracing those five, simple words:

"It is what it is."

I wish I could have heard those words expressed to me when I was initially diagnosed with leukemia back in 1989. If I could have gotten that concept into my head, it would have made my path a bit easier to travel. But I did not have that mindset back then.

I bucked the system, tried to hide from it in my room, and pushed back against it for a time, and that distracted me from getting my game face on and fighting my disease. I never had the *Eye of the Tiger* back then.

I received word via a friendly, personalized postcard from Kaiser alerting me of the appointment with Dr. Raji. She was taking Dr. Robert's place and would manage my post-transplant care and feeding. I really didn't know what to expect.

On Monday, July 2nd, I had my first meeting with her. We hit it off from the moment she entered the exam room. She was a wonderful lady, full of life and smiles. She was from India, and wore her long hair pulled back in a ponytail. She laughed easily at life and at herself.

What impressed me the most about her was very early on she told me though she had practiced oncology and hematology for twenty something years, there was still plenty she did not know.

She was perfectly willing to defer to the judgment of Dr. Robert at Stanford when it came to coordinating my post-transplant treatment plan.

"You always have to be willing to learn new things. None of us has all the answers," she said.

When she spoke those words, I was really blown away. Her candor and openness was refreshing. I think it took a lot of guts to say what she did, and she did so with a big smile on her face. Carefree and confident, not a bad combination.

79

Toughing it Out

I ate a lot of homemade soup, downed a lot of Jell-O, and drank a lot of Ensure. Eventually my appetite and ability to handle a more normal diet returned, but certain food restrictions remained in place: no raw vegetables or thin-skinned fruits like apples, grapes, or difficult to wash fruit like strawberries, and no fast food or take out.

Additionally, I had to avoid crowds, gardening, or digging in the dirt. I had to stay away from construction sites, sawdust, leaf blowers, pet droppings, and my neighbors when they mowed their lawns. I wore my mask during clinic visits.

As I began to feel better, I read a bit, wrote more of this memoir, called and emailed friends to reconnect, "got my chef on," and cooked some amazing meals with Michele.

It felt good to feel good.

I tried to savor those good times and remember them when bad days came.

My improved condition was due in part to the many blood transfusions I received following the transplant. It was normal to require blood, platelets, and other products at the beginning of the outpatient program. Because of the hemolysis problem, I received my share.

But too many transfusions could bring on a condition known as "Hemochromatosis," in laymen's terms "Iron Overload." That condition caused liver damage and affected other organs as well. In an effort to resolve the hemolysis problem, in October of 2009 I started what was to be a short course of Prednisone therapy.

I knew the steroid would do a number on me and hoped the daily dose wouldn't be nearly as much as the 125 milligrams I took each day back in 1990. At that high dose I was a train wreck—emotional, irritable, with a very low coping threshold.

I wasn't fun at parties.

Dr. Robert set my dose at 60 milligrams per day. Within two weeks I felt the effects kick in. I had trouble thinking clearly, sleeping, and got agitated very easily over the most insignificant things.

My bones ached, and my emotions ran thin. If I looked at a photo of my girls or thought about Michele and all she had endured, I lost it. But 60 milligrams per day was not 125.

I was only 48% as crazy as I was the first time around.

80

Pain and Gratitude

October 20th, 2009 was Day +252 post-transplant and also marked the one-year anniversary of the relapse. It was hard to believe I had ridden the roller coaster for twelve months. It felt like twelve years.

It was extremely painful to reflect on the events of that year: having to break the news of the relapse to our daughters, closing my business, and feeling a profound sense of loss and isolation, my wife bearing the full burden of keeping the bills paid and the lights on, dealing with multiple hospitalizations for chemotherapy, and enduring the tumult of the transplant, and complications following my discharge. Certainly 2010 would be a better year.

Along with the sadness I felt, I was filled with a deep sense of gratitude. I was alive, 252 days beyond the nasty, felt pretty good and had enough gray matter left to be able to consider all that had transpired. Every day was a blessing. I wanted to engrave that on my heart.

I often thought about my donor. I had to wait for a second year post-transplant to pass before I could make contact with him through Stanford Hospital and the National Marrow Donor Program.

All I knew about him was he lived somewhere on this big, blue marble, outside of the United States. He was one of those amazing, giving folks who stepped up as our friends had in hopes he could be the match for someone in need. He was.

I looked forward to making contact with him and perhaps meeting him face-to-face. I was not sure what I would say to him. Beyond "thank you," what would I say to the man who saved my life?

81

My "Out of Big and Tall" Experience

Thanks to what Michele and I referred to as "Dr. Robert's Miracle Diet Plan," I lost 125 pounds in eight months (down from a high mark of 330 pounds). I spent a month selling and giving away my 4X tall shirts, sport coats, pants, and shorts.

Now I looked like my Dad when he was seventy years old.

It took some time to get used to. Frightening. Along with being a "big-boned" fellow, I've also been, frankly, as big as a bus for most of my life. Weight control was always an issue.

I lost thirty-five pounds over the course of treatment in 1989, but I slipped into old habits as life returned to "normal." As the years went by, I had no problem putting that weight and more back on.

I squandered the opportunity to get a handle on it back then. I disrespected myself, and disrespected Michele as well. Not something I'm proud of.

These days I tip the scales at 225 pounds, which is about dead-on ideal. I work hard to manage my portions and make better choices when it comes to my diet.

I'm convinced most of what's gone, besides massive amounts of fat and muscle mass due to the chemo, radiation, the BMT, and nearly three months total time in hospital beds, is a big chunk of "stupid" I carried around for decades—stupid thinking, stupid rationalizations and stupid decisions relative to food and weight issues.

Stupid weighs a ton.

Because of the relapse and its fallout, a rare, second opportunity to get a clue and a handle on my weight presented itself. I wanted to make the most of it and once and for all put a fork in the pig and declare victory.

After wearing sweat pants and oversized, short-sleeved shirts for most of 2009, I didn't relish the idea of another Thanksgiving or Christmas wearing gym clothes. I headed out with Michele on a road trip in late October, and found some clothes that actually fit.

In my head, and when I looked in the mirror I still saw the big guy, with the big bones, and big gut, but Michele told me I wasn't that size any more. It was difficult to reconcile the two perspectives. My prayer was the Lord would keep me on the straight so I could remain narrow.

82

Family Dynamics

When my cancer relapsed, our family and our home life were turned upside down. In spite of us all trying to cope with our situation, there was tension. I worked hard to separate my medical life from home life but often that didn't work out so well. Surviving one day at a time was my life.

If I had a rough day at a clinic appointment and had a bad attitude as a result, I tried desperately to avoid bringing it home, and projecting my frustration on my girls or Michele. Sometimes that went well. Other times I failed miserably.

There were days when it was abundantly clear Michele was having a bad day, and wanted to get out from under the oppressive weight of the transplant, the complications, the challenges of recovery, and a life of constant stress. She longed for any semblance of normalcy.

The girls were affected as well. They were in the middle of their high school years, wondering where our runaway-train was headed. Lauren didn't deal well with medical issues to begin with, and was quite happy not hearing the gory details about hospitalizations, transfusions, biopsies or anything else. She was very encouraging during my recovery, always focusing on the positives.

Kristen was not quite as sensitive about the medical stuff as her sister, but she had her limits. Like Lauren, she tried to be understanding and encouraging, but I know it was difficult for both my girls to cope with all the upheaval and uncertainty. They spent a lot of time with their friends. They were gone more than they were home. Perhaps being away from all the strangeness was best.

I did the best I could to be a good Dad to my girls in the midst of that chaos. I hope I provided some semblance of an example for them to follow. Not knowing but hoping for the best is an uncomfortable place to dwell.

83

Restoring a Family Tradition

With the transplant behind me I was on a mission, bound and determined to restore the chili and cornbread tradition to our Halloween festivities. When the big night came, Lauren left with friends to work our neighborhood for loot.

How big IS that pillowcase you're carrying, hon?

Kristen and a friend tackled a couple bowls of a new chili recipe I whipped up, then headed out to seek their candy fortunes. They actually sat at the table. They used napkins. A short time later, Michele and I sat down with our friends and enjoyed dinner, with a hearty side helping of banter and laughs.

In our neighborhood, roving bands of teenagers stayed out all night, so it was essential to have some of the good stuff on hand late in the game. Pennies, dimes, little sour balls, and those pointless off-brand lollypops didn't cut it.

If we couldn't come up with a chocolate bar the size of a toaster, our house stood a good chance of receiving a dose of toilet paper, and our pumpkins would be blown up or kicked to the curb. It could get ugly.

So we manned the candy bowl, and answered the call of trick-or-treaters, and would-be pumpkin-kickers long into the night. It felt great to feel good, wear pants, defend our property against the onslaught of teenagers, and spend time with the folks I cared about the most. Mission accomplished. It was wonderful.

84

Much to Be Thankful For

The red blood cell problem continued through November. I was still on my high-speed ride on the Prednisone Express. At the time, Dr. Robert had no idea how long I would need to stay on that course of therapy.

The official plan was "indefinitely" as determined by the lab values at an appointment on November 11th and duly noted in my chart. Those labs also showed very elevated values for several of the panels related to liver function.

Hmm…

I was slightly jaundiced and the whites of my eyes were tinged pale yellow, but it was nothing like what I experienced back in 1989. It was a kinder, more-gentle jaundice. A new battery of tests was ordered, but I would have to wait until after the Thanksgiving holiday to learn my fate.

After the battle I waged over the previous year, I really looked forward to a fantastic Thanksgiving Day with the family. The year before, I was wiped out from the chemo treatments at Kaiser. I wanted to have a ball this time around.

It was a perfect day, filled with lots of laughs and good conversation with family and extended family, NFL football and wrestling with my young nephews.

Yes, Uncle Rob does need to breathe, so chokeholds are a no-no.

Turkey with all the trimmings, and a table full of awesome desserts brought us all to our knees. I had never been a fan of either pumpkin or pecan pie, but for whatever reason, I was suddenly a hardcore fan of both.

I wondered if that newfound appreciation for those treats was just the result of oxygen deprivation when I was nephew wrangling, or perhaps something my marrow donor passed on through the transplant. I joked with Michele that he was probably a fine southern gentleman.

We took a bunch of photos that day. I'll always cherish the memories of our gathering. It was such a treat after the challenges and setbacks endured over the previous twelve months.

85

Okay About Those Test Results...

I was nervous. The liver biopsy found the presence of Graft vs. Host Disease (GVHD). *What? A new disease?* I received that news on December 2nd at a clinic appointment with Dr. Robert. It was yet another "common post-transplant complication."

Of course it was. They all were, right?

GVHD manifested itself in both acute and chronic forms. The Binder addressed the subject in great detail. The donor marrow (the graft) attacked the organs or systems of the recipient (the host). In my case, I had a chronic form of GVHD that infiltrated my liver. It could be managed but not necessarily cured.

Dr. Robert's recommendation was I start a course of Rituxan therapy along with the Prednisone I was already taking in an attempt to manage the GVHD and possibly the hemolysis problem as well.

The good news: the GVHD was detected early. The bad news: the dosage of Prednisone would be increased from 60 milligrams per day to 80 milligrams per day. I knew it would do a number on me.

Rituxan was a fantastic drug used to treat Lymphoma, Rheumatoid Arthritis, Lupus, and other conditions as well. Its efficacy *(and safety, thank you)* for treating leukemias and certain post-marrow transplant complications was being explored through clinical research trials.

I was invited by Dr. Robert to be part of one of those "off-label" studies. The Rituxan worked in concert with the Prednisone, in a one-two punch of sorts. But there was one huge potential complication.

It could cause a fatal brain infection. *Thanks for that.*

I just happened to stumble upon that little nugget as I researched the drug online. I wanted to learn as much as I could about the short and long-term side effects.

Fatal brain infection—Surprise!

I talked with Dr. Robert to get his perspective on the matter. He tried to reassure me. "Statistically, it's a fairly small percentage of folks who develop the infection following treatment. What I can tell you is that no one we have treated with it has developed that problem."

Though still somewhat hesitant, I decided to sign on to be part of the research trial. I was frustrated over having to weigh the risks versus benefits and wrestle with the issue. *I survived the transplant. I did my job. Can you please just do yours, doc? Fix me!*

I didn't want to wade, chest-deep, through any more medical drama. Been there. Done that.

86

You've Got Mail... And it Will Shake You To Your Core

In preparation for the Rituxan therapy, the daily dose of 80 milligrams of Prednisone knocked me into the next area code. I was an emotional wreck. I felt like my brain had fried. It was difficult to process thoughts and carry on a simple conversation. It was like my circuits were overloaded.

We're sorry. Your brain is experiencing unusually heavy thought volume at this time. Your thoughts are very important to us. You may want to consider thinking at another time when we can better serve you. Thank you for using your brain.

I went online to check emails one morning, and ran across a new message from Michele. I opened it and was promptly blown out of the water. In it, she expressed disappointment and sadness about our relationship and my inability to fix what she felt were destructively negative attitudes and actions.

I read her words and went numb.

Where did that come from?

I didn't know what to think. She wrote she was at the end of her rope with me, and had planned an intervention in early 2008. She was ready to implement it, but then my Leukemia returned.

"Intervention." *Oh my God. What just happened to my life?*

What's wrong with Michele?

What's wrong with me?

As I have written previously in this memoir, Michele and I had our share of miscommunication and conflicts over the years. What couple doesn't?

But I didn't know what to do with her email. It came right out of left field. While I tried to digest what she had written, I struggled to see how things had gotten to the point in her heart and mind where she used those words and wrote what she wrote.

I stared at the computer screen and freaked out.

For the balance of the day, I puttered around my house like an angry hermit. Beyond shell-shocked, I was irate, frustrated by the timing of that message. Like there wasn't already enough on our plate to deal with.

Sure, let's add marital problems atop our already flaming pile of crap! Jeez.

Throughout the day I thought about Thanksgiving, and what a fantastic time it seemed to be with the family. *Did I miss something?* I had no idea.

I considered the events of the previous year: the hospitalizations, the bone marrow transplant, the complications, the numerous road trips Michele and I made to Kaiser and Stanford, and the weighty matters we met head-on and hard decisions we made.

I wondered how Michele felt on the inside. *Was she really just growing more and more frustrated and merely going through the motions with me as I faced the challenges of the relapse and treatment?*

A very hollow feeling came over me. I thought about my interactions with Michele and the girls. *What on Earth was she talking about?* It was a horrible day.

I had no idea at the time, but the days and months that followed would prove to be even more frustrating, with additional revelations that further spun me out.

Life was already insane. What comes after insane?

87

Lab Rat, Party of One

T he next day, I had an important (read: tedious and brain-draining) clinic appointment with Dr. Robert at Stanford to finalize plans and sign on the dotted line for the Rituxan/Prednisone clinical research trial. Time to commit.

I still had some reservations about that pesky "fatal brain infection" issue, and was frustrated that I couldn't get the straight dope in my online research attempts.

All I needed to know was how many forty-seven year-old, balding white guys, diagnosed with A.L.L., who were also Philadelphia Chromosome positive, who had received a bone marrow transplant and had GVHD and a red cell hemolysis problem as complications post-transplant, who had taken Rituxan with Prednisone at the prompting of their physician, were still alive one year following their treatment.

Breathe… Was that too much to ask?

Rituxan seemed to be the best treatment option. With an apparently low risk of acquiring the infection, better, I thought, to go for it and try to get the GVHD under control. *Risk versus benefit.* Those three words seemed to define my existence.

The word on the street regarding Rituxan was some folks experienced potentially serious side effects, including hypoxia, respiratory distress, and heart attack. *Swell.* Approximately 80% of fatal infusion reactions occurred during or within twenty-four hours of the first infusion.

Why couldn't the side effects be pimples, a sore throat, and a case of "the blues?" It seemed it always had to be the "biggies." Just once, I would love to have a doctor tell me following the eighteen-hour surgery to remove all of my major organs, I might experience a slight itch in my left elbow, but it would only last a day or so.

Rituxan was a wonder drug. There was plenty of wonder associated with it. I wondered if I would survive. But in light of what Michele wrote in her December 7th email, part of me didn't care if I survived or not.

My first Rituxan infusion took place on Thursday, December 17th at Kaiser. I walked out of the clinic still alive following the treatment. I took that as an encouraging sign. I was relieved that none of the known, expected, and potentially horrible side effects had reared their ugly head.

On Friday, I woke up, still alive *(an even better sign)* and felt okay until around noon. Then out of nowhere, which on a map is darn close to "out of the blue" exhaustion hit like a monster wave at the Bonsai Pipeline. Time to ride the big one, bro!

From that point on I took frequent naps during the day just to keep the batteries charged enough to function and maintain some level of rational thought.

When my buddy Lou was treated for lymphoma several years back, he and his wife Penny made the trip from their place in northern California to the Bay Area and stayed with us. He received his treatments at Stanford, in the same facility where I went for my outpatient appointments.

When he returned from his Rituxan infusions, he retired to our guest bedroom and slept off the buzz for six hours or so. Then he emerged later in the evening feeling pretty good.

I was thankful my response to the treatment was similar to Lou's, and nothing worse than massive fatigue was the big issue to deal with.

88

Not a Creature Was Stirring, Except Me

Following the first Rituxan infusion, my daily dose of Prednisone was tapered down from 80 milligrams to 60. I rode that dose for quite a long time. Insomnia and leg cramps were a major problem. I was fed up with all the meds and didn't want to take another pill just to sleep, so I kept long hours each day and took frequent naps.

Quite often I was up very late, right into the early morning hours. Other nights I went to bed fairly early, but the leg cramps popped me out of bed like a frozen waffle in a broken toaster.

During those quiet early morning hours it felt like it was just me and the stars in the pre-dawn sky.

I walked up and down our hallway and around the house to get the blood flowing. Sometimes I went back to bed and got in an hour more of sleep, but more often than not I had to stay up and stay active in order for the cramps to fully resolve.

I tried to do something productive with the time: cook some break-fast the girls could reheat when they got up, load the dishwasher, start a load of laundry, write a little more of this memoir—anything.

On December 22nd, killer leg cramps sprung me out of bed at 3:00 a.m., and almost immediately I started thinking about Christmas Day. As I stumbled down the hallway in our house, trying to stretch my muscles and not wake up the rest of the family, I wondered what kind of shape I would be in.

A year prior I was given the best Christmas gift ever, news four perfect bone marrow donor matches had been found. I would have a second chance at life. There's not a tree large enough to park that gift underneath!

I thought if I could survive the second dose of Rituxan and ride out the Christmas festivities, it would be the icing on the cake.

At the same time, I wished we could just skip Christmas altogether.

The previous two weeks had been such a drain, emotionally, psychologically, and physically. Michele's email had me thinking and re-thinking my history with her, wondering what else she would express to me in the days and months to come.

I kept asking myself, *Where have I been this whole time, that I missed this?* The words in her email kept rattling around in my brain. At times, I felt consumed by them. It was as if every aspect of my life was royally screwed up. There was no relief from it.

I wanted it all to be over, to return to some semblance of a healthy medical state, fix the marital problems, and get on with life.

I kept thinking about Thanksgiving and whether the smiles and laughter were real or not. I really didn't want to go through Christmas Day if it was going to be a big fakeout.

I was depressed, angry, and stunned over the content of Michele's email. The ache inside tore me up. I realized my take on our relationship and our life together was not even close to hers. We were worlds apart. Merry Christmas.

That realization cut to the bone.

89

What Nightmares May Come?

When I was able to sleep, I was hammered with the scariest nightmares—stuff that made Stephen King's writings look like Dr. Seuss. I knew the dreams were a side effect of the high dose Prednisone. The drug messed with my mind in a big way when I went through treatment at City of Hope, but not like this.

Rather than feeling wired all the time and "hyper-aware" of my surroundings as I did back then, the second time around I was an emotional basket case most of the time with nightmares so vivid, waking from them almost hurt physically.

It most certainly hurt mentally and emotionally.

Sometimes the dreams were in very living color, other times in black and white. I think those were worse. There were jarring images of splattered blood and sharp metal and faces of people I didn't know, up in my face screaming at the top of their lungs.

There were horrible places filled with shadows, completely void of light. Black on black.

There was no sense of direction, only terror. I had a feeling in those nightmares I should recognize the people screaming at me, but I didn't.

And there was usually a horrible, almost crushing sense of entrapment in that strange state, no doors, no way out. No one offered any help. No one said, "Come this way, and you will be okay."

Nothing but madness.

I think it's the closest a man can come to experiencing Hell. It shook me to my core every time. Most of the time I experienced the dreams "through my eyes," but sometimes I watched myself go through the experience from a perspective that felt almost out of body.

It was a hopeless, godless place. My only thought was for relief. It never came.

Eventually I woke up from those trips in our pitch-black bedroom. For a few moments, I couldn't figure out what had happened or if I was really awake. And when I realized I was awake and everything that happened was only a nightmare, the tears flowed.

I did my best to keep my uncontrollable sobbing as quiet as I could, so I didn't wake Michele. She was no fun if she was disturbed in the middle of the night.

One night I woke up from one of those nightmares and couldn't get a grip on myself for several minutes. I freaked out and prayed for a level head and for peace to come. It was a long time coming. I rolled over to try and find a comfortable position. When I did, I was face-to-face with my Pug, Riley.

Yes, we let our dogs sleep with us now and then.

In the middle of the night she usually snored so loud we had to bury our heads under our pillows to drown out her "buzz saw." That night, at least at that moment, she was wide-awake, and stared right at me as only a Pug can.

She was under the covers, only her head sticking out. The two of us shared a quiet, calming few moments together with me petting her head and trying to calm down. She licked my hand.

I think it was a God thing.

Within several minutes I calmed down and realized the nightmare was just that. Riley was real. I was in my bed, in my house. Sam, my German Shepherd, was laying across my legs at the foot of our bed.

Riley tipped the scales at a whopping eighteen pounds. She was as cute as, well, as a Pug can be. Often that was pretty irresistible. Sam on the other hand, was more on the order of eighty pounds. At night he let all of them hang out… all of them.

Dead weight.

But that night—that night especially—I couldn't have cared less my legs had nowhere to go, or even that I couldn't feel them under Sam's weight. After that nightmare, I was happy to still have legs.

The good news is the nightmares didn't hit during afternoon naps, only at night when I really wanted to rack some quality sleep. Life was no picnic. The ants always seemed to show up, and they brought their own utensils.

90

A Breakthrough?

Over the years following my initial diagnosis and treatment, Michele and I had many heated exchanges and times of frustration, but they certainly were not "deal-breakers" in my mind. We kept moving forward, raised two incredible daughters, bought a home and—I thought—were doing okay, all things considered.

All I knew for sure was I loved Michele, was committed to her and our relationship, and was her number one fan. Like many of our friends, I was amazed at her strength. She was my best friend and a real encourager as I went through cancer the first time around.

My relapse, three hospitalizations at Kaiser, the BMT at Stanford, and all of the fallout from it that permeated our life—the whole ball of wax—was more than a wife should ever have to deal with.

I felt so bad that her life, and our life together, had not been anything close to what either one of us envisioned.

After Michele sent her email in early December, we had a couple of occasions to talk briefly about our situation, and had one conversation in particular that in my mind was a breakthrough of sorts.

I felt like we were able to clear the air a bit. But through that conversation with Michele, I realized that fallout from a conversation twenty years in our past had become a seedbed for anger and frustration. It festered and finally bubbled to the surface, and at the worst possible time.

91

A Christmas to Remember

A former boss of mine once said, "Plans are made to be changed." You were so right, Dee. One of the many delightful side effects I experienced following the transplant was medication-induced diabetes. I had the Prednisone to thank for that gift. My doctor ordered the supplies I needed to monitor my blood sugar, and by Christmas Eve I had all supplies in hand.

Michele and the girls went to my brother-in-law's place for a Christmas Eve gathering. I opted to stay home and lay low to keep my batteries as fresh as possible for Christmas morning, and the big family dinner at our place later in the day. At least that was the plan.

Around 10:00 p.m., when the family arrived home, I conducted the first test of my blood sugar and registered a chart-busting 467. Somewhere around 100 would have been ideal. Anything over 300 and my marching orders were to call in to the hospital advice nurse for "instructions."

We capped off what otherwise had been a great night for the girls, and a low key night of chicken tacos and the Hawaii Bowl football game for me, with a run to the Kaiser Hospital ER. By the way, Southern Methodist University took the University of Nevada to the woodshed in that game, posting a final score of 45 to 10. What a game, but I digress.

We left for the ER at 10:50 p.m. and told the girls we had no idea when we would be home. We let them know the gifts we had intended to wrap for them and place under the tree, would most likely be handed to them unwrapped in their shipping boxes, somewhere around noon Christmas Day. They were cool with that, knowing the boxes contained fabulous prizes.

After several hours of testing, labs, IV fluids, and lots of paperwork, we returned home around 2:15 a.m. Christmas morning and promptly poured ourselves into bed. Did we have a nice Christmas Eve? Oh yes, and then some. But Santa did deliver a wonderful Christmas Day for our family.

The girls had a ball opening their gifts. I was really excited to see them spend considerable time flipping through a photo album I created for each of them. It was a collection of images that chronicled much of their childhood experiences through their junior high school graduations.

I began work on the project in October, scanning prints we had in shoeboxes and compiling them along with digital images I had on file. The result was two matching, one hundred-page, printed and bound albums.

The girls were fascinated by the collection of photos, some they hadn't seen in many years, if at all. The smiles on their faces, as they leafed through those books, is something I will always remember. It was like the closing of one chapter of their young lives and the opening of the next.

Later that day, my Mom, brother, and Michele's family met at our place, and we enjoyed a wonderful time together. As was the case at Thanksgiving, the photos taken that day showed a house filled with happy folks, great food and lots of smiles, and laughter, and more wrestle time with my nephews as well!

Memories of Thanksgiving ran through my mind as we celebrated Christmas, but I decided to take things at face value and not spend a lot of time second-guessing myself, Michele, or my family.

92

That's Not a Rash

I woke up in the middle of the night on December 26th and could hardly walk. The top of my left foot ached with a dull, annoying pain. I figured it was a flare up of Peripheral Neuropathy, a side effect of chemotherapy. The nerves in my hands and feet were frequently numb with a burning, tingling pain.

Some days it wasn't a big deal; other days I wanted to submerge myself in a tub full of ice until I was numb. Having experienced the pain of neuropathy, I didn't think too much of the pain in my foot. I didn't take off my sock until morning. It was 4:00 a.m., and I wanted to get back to sleep.

When morning came, I removed my left sock and discovered a raging, purple rash across the top of my foot and two silver dollar-sized spots on my left shin. Thinking what I had on my leg was an intense GVHD rash, I applied a steroid-based ointment twice over the course of the day.

By late afternoon, as I sat watching NFL football, the "rash" advanced up my left leg almost to my knee. My leg looked like a giant raspberry Popsicle.

I clearly was dealing with something far more serious than a neuropathy flare up. I was back into Stanford on a direct admission to the Medical-Surgical unit. *So much for having a nice Christmas and New Years holiday.*

It was difficult to pray at that time, to ask God for healing, for protection and safety, for peace—for anything really. I was mad.

On the drive up the freeway, Michele and I talked some, but I was preoccupied with the potential of another long hospital stay, the uncertainty of what lay ahead, and Michele's email of December 7th.

There was a growing sadness and frustration inside me over the realization she was fed up with me on so many levels. But God love her, she was still right there by my side as we faced that latest twist in the road. I struggled to see how things had gotten so bad.

Did Michele really feel some kind of intervention was necessary?

Weren't interventions a last resort to help people with drug and alcohol addictions or eating disorders?

I had so many thoughts, so much frustration and sadness. At the same time, I had to focus on dealing with the leg problem.

Upon arrival on the unit, I was greeted by Dr. Aaron. He took one look at my leg and promptly told me my condition was something he had never seen before.

Great. I had heard that before.

Nothing about my case had ever been run of the mill. I recalled Dr. Robert, my BMT doctor, telling me at our very first meeting he had never seen a case like mine in the history of his medical practice—the history of his practice!

Dr. Aaron was no different. He was really taken aback by what he saw, and almost immediately ran for his camera so he could send photos of my leg to his colleague in the Dermatology department.

It didn't take more than a half hour before that doctor arrived in my room, eager for the chance to check out the giant raspberry popsicle that only two hours earlier had been my lower left leg.

I was the latest freak show out of Stanford's Bone Marrow Transplant department. My case was like none they had ever seen. And now the freak was back in the hospital with yet another strange development for everyone to trip over.

At the time of my initial referral to Stanford, I was intrigued by all the hoopla over my case, and at the same time, concerned. Over time, that dance got old. When Dr. Aaron flipped out like he did over my leg, which was interestingly enough attached to me, a human being, I was frustrated on the inside, but I never showed it outwardly.

I just looked at Michele and shrugged my shoulders.

"Well, nothing has ever been run of the mill with my case," I said.

She looked back with an acknowledging nod and a bit of a twist to her lips. Dr. Aaron told us he didn't think the problem was GVHD at all, but rather it was some type of infection that had localized in my leg and then took off from there.

Dr. Aaron was a great guy and a competent physician. He was very compassionate and also very forthright about what potentially lay on the horizon.

I've always dealt better with bad situations if given some straight answers early on. Dr. Steve did that for me when I was at City of Hope.

In this case, within the timeframe of about an hour and a half, Dr. Aaron and the other doctors on the team laid a heavy load of reality on me that pretty much slammed me up against the wall.

There would be a number of tests and examinations, two delightful "punch biopsies" of my leg's muscle tissue performed at my bedside, and surgery most likely first thing in the morning to determine the extent and depth of the infection.

The docs also fully disclosed the best and worst case outcome scenarios. The best was I would be discharged from the hospital with both my legs still attached. The worst case was exactly what you're thinking. Not a fun word to throw around at parties. I tried not to dwell on the outcomes.

Michele left for the night after our first meeting with Dr. Aaron, once it appeared things were under control and the diagnostic ball was moving forward. I rested as a steady stream of doctors came into my room, examined the leg, and asked a lot of questions.

I'm not sure I gave any of them really accurate information, because I was trying my best to remain calm (*let alone joyful in spite of circumstances).* I tried to process the notion I might leave the hospital in X number of days without the lower half of my left leg.

They could have lit me on fire at that point and called it a medically necessary procedure, and I wouldn't have flinched. As much as I tried not to dwell on it, my brain thought a lot about the possibility of amputation. I thought I had a rash.

Eye of the tiger? One day at a time? Not right now, but thanks.

When I was first admitted, Dr. Aaron drew a perimeter around the area of discoloration with a black marking pen. I went to an X-ray and ultrasound procedure and returned an hour or so later. Within that timeframe, the infection spread 3/8th of an inch beyond those markings.

Doc looked at me with a stunned look on his face.

"Robert, this thing is amazing. We can almost stand here and watch it spread."

I don't recall how I responded, but I wondered if the team would be able to stop the infection from taking out my leg. It was really moving fast.

Various doctors from a wide variety of disciplines rattled off their theories over the course of the night, from Dermatology to Infectious Diseases.

I learned way more than I ever wanted about the problem in my leg, ultimately diagnosed as Cellulitis, a bacterial infection that had taken up residence in the deeper tissues of the skin.

The bacteria could have invaded the tissues through a spider bite, a cut, a scratch from one of our pets, or a myriad of other causes. With all the poking and prodding the docs did that night, I thought it quite possible for them to return to my room at some point and tell me I had been raised by wolves.

Dr. Aaron did tell me because of the speed at which the infection was advancing the team felt it was best to get me into surgery that night. I had an hour to collect my thoughts.

Yikes!

I called Michele right away to let her know my situation had intensified. It was 11:30 p.m. and she had just arrived home, but she drove back to the hospital. She also called Suzanne, the same Suzanne who had come to see me at Kaiser Hospital in October of 2008 to help me write the first content for our CaringBridge web site.

Suzanne and her husband lived within a stone's throw of the hospital. Without any hesitation or concern over the late hour, she came over just to be with me while Michele was en route back.

What a gal! It was a selfless gesture I will always appreciate.

We only had a few minutes to talk and enjoyed a few laughs and a hug before they rolled me out. Suzanne walked alongside my gurney for as long as she could until I entered the pre-surgery prep area.

With a big smile and a wave, Suzanne sent me on my way and returned to my room to meet Michele upon her return.

The surgeons were sharp as tacks; very professional and all business. They didn't mince words when they described what they might find when they opened up my leg. Cellulitis with only shallow tissue involvement would be the best news.

A deep tissue infection, called "Necrotizing Fasciitis," where the muscle tissue was dead, and required debriding, would be a very bad thing. The implications had the potential to be what the lead surgeon characterized as "significantly life-changing," another medical term.

I was a little stunned, but also totally confident in the team of doctors. After fifteen minutes or so, an oxygen mask was placed over my face, and I was instructed to take a few deep breaths. I don't remember a thing after that.

I woke up in the Recovery area and learned several incisions were made in my leg to determine the depth of the infection. At least I still had my leg.

My entire lower leg was wrapped in gauze dressing. It looked like a giant, mummified salami was laying next to me in bed. I had no idea what the incisions looked like, how big they were, or where they had been made.

After an hour in Recovery, my speech was no longer slurred, and I could complete a full sentence, so I was returned to my room, salami in tow.

A short while later, Michele and I were given the best possible news. The infection had not gone deep into the muscle tissue and was caught just in time.

If my body responded to the antibiotics, I would most likely be able to keep my leg. That was good news, as over the years I had grown very close to that leg, both of them really.

I spent the remainder of the week in the hospital. After forty-eight days in E1, that week felt like an eternity. I just wanted to ride out my time on the unit, pack up the salami, and get home.

93

Mr. Trin

I shared my room that week with Mr. Trin. He was Vietnamese and perhaps in his late sixties. He had a slight build, was frail, and moved slowly across the room. He was clearly a man who had been down a long road of illness and treatment.

We had many conversations over the week and gave each other a "thumbs-up" and exchanged words of encouragement whenever we could. One morning, when he faced yet another procedure and waited for a wheelchair to be brought to our room, Mr. Trin sat on the side of his bed.

"How do you make a decision about whether or not to go ahead with chemo," he asked.

It broke my heart.

I did my best to convey how I had processed that same question. I shared my frustration over having to weigh the risks against the benefits when a new procedure or treatment was suggested. Mr. Trin nodded his head.

I thought about Mike and his wife Alma at Kaiser and our conversations about similar weighty issues. Mr. Trin told me he was very confused and concerned about whether it would be worth it given his age and condition.

We had only a few minutes to talk before the man from Transportation Services arrived at our room, and Mr. Trin had to leave. He expressed his thanks for what I had shared and told me it was a big help to him. He sat down in the wheelchair and within a few moments was down the hallway and off the unit.

I was discharged midday on December 30, in time to ring in the New Year and enjoy the day with family and friends. I never saw Mr. Trin again after that last brief conversation with him.

He was the nicest man. My hope is that all turned out well for him. That was another of life's holes that will never be filled.

As was the case months earlier, when I was on the unit at Kaiser and had my conversations with Mike about his wife's struggles with leukemia, I suppose at least one of the reasons I developed the leg infection was to have my conversations with Mr. Trin.

I really can't say for sure, but it gives me some comfort to think that even in the midst of that madness (*you might not be walking out of here, Rob)*, I was able to be of some use, some good to someone in need. Certainly not the ideal circumstances for good conversation, but that seems to be how the meat of my life is chewed.

94

A Blessing and A Curse

The bone marrow transplant was both a miraculous blessing and a tremendous curse. On one hand, it offered the invaluable gift of a second chance at life. On the other, it opened me up to a variety of complications and problems that simply came out of nowhere. The Cellulitis was one such complication.

After my discharge, I struggled to keep a positive outlook. As 2009 drew to a close, I found myself at times feeling a bit paranoid, waiting for "the other shoe to drop," for the phone to ring with some doctor on the other end of the line with more bad news.

It was draining to live with the awareness that one minute I could be having a pretty good day and the next second learn I need to admit to the hospital with some new, potentially life-threatening problem.

The martial strife and growing tension with Michele weighed on me. I often felt my coping skills waning, in spite of my belief God was in control and ultimately would work his purposes through what I (we) were going through. All I could do was cling to that truth.

Often, I did not cling well.

More and more as the New Year approached, I felt like I was losing the battle, and I would never really be whole again on so many levels. It scared me to death to think that was how my life might play out.

The towel remained on the towel rack, not yet thrown in, but there were moments.

95

A Premonition?

Webster's Dictionary defines "Premonition" as a *"strong feeling that something is about to happen, especially something unpleasant."* In 1973 I was eleven years old and watched a movie one Saturday afternoon called "Sunshine."

It was the story of a young couple that lived in the woods with their toddler-aged daughter. The husband, a struggling musician, and his wife learned the wife had terminal cancer. Unless her leg was removed, she would die.

She decided she could not "live" without her leg, and as the cancer spread and her condition declined, she recorded her thoughts and advice for her young daughter into a cassette tape recorder so her daughter wouldn't forget she had a Mommy. Eventually, she died.

The end.

It was sad and heart wrenching. *Who thought that screenplay was worth a second look?* As I watched the movie, I had a "premonition" of sorts—a strange feeling that came over me. I had an overwhelming sense I would walk the same road as the woman in the movie. I'd only told Michele about that experience and only after my leukemia relapsed in late 2008.

It freaked me out as a young boy and still does to this day.

I can't explain the feeling that came over me. Perhaps it's beyond explanation, like trying to explain the wonders of a peanut butter and banana sandwich to someone who has never had one. I'm not sure what that deal was about, but when I was originally diagnosed in 1989, I thought about that movie, and still do from time to time. There is no way of resolving the issue in my mind. It's some of the baggage I have given over to the Lord through this ordeal.

96

2010 – Time for Some Good News

I hoped the New Year would bring some calm, some sanity, and some relief from the roller coaster that was 2009, but my January calendar quickly filled with Kaiser and Stanford appointments. There was no relief from the medical grind. It felt like 2009 had decided to extend itself, indefinitely. I thought, *Wait a minute, it's a new year. All that stuff is over and done. That was last year.*

I was ready for some good news. My prayers were answered. An eye appointment at the Stanford Eye Clinic confirmed I had merely dry eyes rather than a complication they suspected I had developed, and I was given an immune-boosting dose of IVIG as well.

The effectiveness of the Rituxan treatment was evaluated since it had been eight weeks since the final infusion. My doc felt the initial course was doing what it was supposed to, at least stabilizing the GVHD in my liver and perhaps finally managing the red blood cell problem as well. Doc decided against a second course of Rituxan, and opted to monitor my status with weekly labs.

Though some of my lab values clearly indicated my problems were not fully resolved, they were better than they had been in prior months.

There was more good news: another slight reduction in the Prednisone dose, from 40 milligrams per day to 35 milligrams. Every little bit helped! Any opportunity to reduce the amount of that bad stuff coursing through my system was a good thing.

97

Divided Road Ahead

On the home front, the chasm between Michele and I continued to widen. We were like a couple that had traveled to the Grand Canyon to check out the view. When the road split, we each went different ways. I went to the north rim, and Michele went to the south. Our views were completely different, and a mile wide valley ran between us.

Many thoughts ran through my head each day: *Were we doing any better? Were my words and actions appropriate? Did I say too much; too little?* Exhausting. I wanted to be done with it all. I felt very alone on the road to recovery. I was alone. When there was bad news, I sucked it up and didn't share much with Michele.

When I received good news at my medical appointments, I wanted to share it with her but could not or would not go there. I don't necessarily know why.

There were only a few occasions where Michele and I talked, and every now and then our exchanges were fairly positive and made me feel like forward progress was being made.

But more often than not, our home was filled with a vacuous disconnectedness. We were two individuals more than we were a couple. We were crashing and burning and I had no idea how to fix the mess.

98

Moving Day

On February 5th, 2010, Michele came home after running errands and told me she had decided to move out. I thought there had been a few occasions of good conversation, and positive times with her, and that we were making some progress in our relationship. Michele did not feel that way.

I was blown away and couldn't reconcile how we could go from seemingly doing a bit better to her deciding to take such a radical step. Michele told me she needed distance and time to sort things out.

She packed up her things pretty quickly. Lauren was already doing the same. A short while later Kristen returned from a friend's house and Michele told her to pack her stuff as well. Kris was caught completely off guard.

Michele was fed up and felt like she was at the end of her rope. After some time to pack and load the car, she and the girls drove away. I stood in our driveway, angry, bewildered, completely blown away, and strung out on my meds to boot.

It was one of the lowest points in my life. I could not understand how things had gotten so bad that my wife of twenty years felt her only option was to leave me.

That evening and the days that followed were a nightmare. I wandered through the house like a ghost of myself. The daily routine helped to keep my mind occupied: morning and evening meds, blood sugar testing, cleaning the house, cooking, grocery shopping, and keeping my appointments at Kaiser and Stanford. On the inside I felt hollowed out like a rotted oak tree, unsure of what really to do given the latest dose of reality, and without a clue as to how things would play out over time.

99

February 10, 2010 – The One-Year Anniversary of the BMT

On the morning of February 10th, I wandered around the empty house with a chip on my shoulder. It was the one-year anniversary of my bone marrow transplant. It was also the day before our twenty-first wedding anniversary.

Exactly one year ago to the day, I had been in a bed on E1 contemplating the reality of the transplant, concerned I might not survive, and bummed I would not be able to celebrate the twentieth wedding anniversary with Michele.

I remember thinking back then, *Hey by this time next year it will be a whole different story. I'll be on the road to recovery, and Michele and I will celebrate in style.*

But that's not how things played out. Instead, my wife had moved out, and taken the girls with her. There wasn't a thing I could do about it. It was what it was, but it was excruciating.

100

Blood Draws and Brownies

Because February 10th was the one-year anniversary of the transplant, it was, like reaching "Day +100" an important milestone in post-transplant recovery. In honor of the auspicious occasion, several medical events were scheduled that had me at Stanford for the better part of the day.

Blood draw and bone marrow biopsy appointments were staggered in such a way I thought I might have a window of opportunity to visit my nurses on E1.

So in an effort to do something productive with my time, I baked a big batch of brownies the night before. I figured I would take them with me, and if I couldn't get to E1, I could certainly make some other nurses happy.

I arrived at the Cancer Treatment Center around 11:15 a.m. With brownies in tow, I made my way to the ITA. On short order my name was called by one of the medical assistants.

The nurses saw the box under my arm as I walked down the corridor toward their station, just outside Infusion Room E. They got missile lock on the box and asked me what was inside. *I'm fine, thank you!*

Nurses know when yummies are close by and once they do, all bets are off. They become a ravenous band of wolves. I told them it was the one-year anniversary of my transplant, and I baked brownies for the staff on the E1 unit.

They gave me a hard time for not baking any for them.

"What are we chopped liver?" one of them asked with a big smile on her face.

"Oh man, I wanted to make you a batch, but I did not have enough mix to pull it off! But I'll make it up to you. Cool?"

They laughed and continued to poke and make wisecracks.

"Yeah, sure, whatever you say, Robert. We know you're good for it."

I did bring those gals a batch of brownies a couple weeks later, and for a second time endured a few rounds of light-hearted teasing from my nurses.

I learned an important lesson early in my relationship with Michele, when we brought pizza or doughnuts to our friend Sandi and her fellow RNs: When you feed a nurse, you make a friend for life. It's good to have a pack of wolves in your corner!

Following the appointment in the ITA, I made my way downstairs to Clinic E to meet with Dr. Robert. He had me out the door in fifteen minutes. I had just over an hour until the bone marrow biopsy. It was just enough time to implement "Operation Brownie Drop." I was amped about visiting with the gang on the transplant unit.

Because of all the time in the hospital and the meds I was taking, I had very little leg strength—little strength in most of my muscles, really. Soon after exiting the Cancer Treatment Center and beginning my walk toward the hospital entrance, I realized I had bitten off more than I could chew.

What should have been just a quick walk of eighty yards became a major chore. I lasted all of a couple minutes when I walked, then was out of gas. It was slow going, but eventually I made it to the hospital entrance and down the long corridor toward the E1 transplant unit. I didn't recall that corridor being so darn long. *Was someone messing with my mind?*

I stopped at a visiting area outside the unit and took five minutes to rest and have a drink of water. With a quick check of the time, I realized I spent twenty-five minutes just getting to that point. It would take another twenty-five to get back. I had just a few minutes to get down to the nurses station and make my delivery.

As I walked through the double doors into the E1 unit, my favorite nurse, Anne, greeted me. She was the ringleader of the Sisters of Suction. She was seated at the nurse's station at the end of the corridor. As I waved back to her from just inside the door, she got really excited.

"Oh my gosh! Robert. Is that You?"

I greeted her through my mask as I approached the reception counter. She was so excited. She got up from her chair and gave me a big hug.

"Wait right here. I'm going to go round everyone up!"

She disappeared down another corridor. A few minutes later many of the nurses who had taken care of me, along with some of the medical assistants and housekeeping staff made their way to the nurse's station.

We enjoyed several minutes of hugs and laughter. It was so great to see those wonderful folks again and under far better circumstances than a year prior.

I handed the box of brownies to Anne.

"What's this?" she asked, and held the box up to her nose.

"Oh my gosh, something smells really good in there!"

I told her I whipped up some brownies in celebration of the one-year anniversary of the transplant to thank them all for the great care they had provided. Within seconds the brownies began to disappear as the group dove in, The wolfpack was hungry.

Nurses and chocolate. It's a beautiful thing.

After only a few minutes with the group, I had to head back for the bone marrow aspiration. As I turned to leave the unit, Anne asked me if I was planning on attending the annual BMT Survivor's Picnic. It was held each July on the Stanford campus.

I told her I looked forward to it.

But as I uttered those words, I thought about my failing marriage. I wondered if I would actually attend that milestone celebration with Michele. *When that day came, would I even still want to attend, perhaps alone?*

101

Our 21st Wedding Anniversary Come and Gone

Thursday, February 11th was our 21st wedding anniversary. I wished I could crawl into a hole and pull the hole in after me. A year earlier, the transplant eclipsed any thought of a celebration. There was no dinner out with Michele, no exchange of cards, no gifts. Nothing, only the transplant, and cancer.

It wasn't a happy anniversary. It was merely another anniversary, and it came and went without a lick of fanfare, fogged over by anger, confusion, fear, and hurt.

North rim, south rim; a river ran through us.

Michele and I had been married twenty-one years. What a ride it had been to that point. I spent a lot of time thinking about our relationship, and all the horrible things we had been through when we were young and ignorant. I wished we had sought counseling back then.

More holes. More tattered edges.

Eye of the Tiger. One Day at a Time. Yeah, whatever.

But I also recalled pleasant memories of times with Michele: runs to Newport Beach and Balboa for killer deep dish pizza at BJ's, and later watching the sunset from a lifeguard tower on the beach, concerts, July 4th picnics in the park, long talks, working with the junior high group at Pasadena Covenant Church, and our travels to London and Paris.

We had good times as well after we moved to the Bay Area. Michele was so excited to finally have a garden in the backyard of our rental in Sunnyvale. We camped with the girls from the time they were very young.

We enjoyed many warm and wonderful Christmas mornings as a family. The girls loved to tear into their gifts and always freaked out over what they found under the wrapping paper.

Thoughts about the positive aspects of my life with Michele helped me get some perspective. It was a day filled with emotional ups and downs.

I felt a sense of relief when I glanced at the clock on the wall and watched the hands click past midnight and draw the day to a close. I hoped things would be different when our next anniversary came around.

102

Counseling

When our family dynamics got out of control in late 2009, we searched for a marriage and family counselor so we could get help. I found a gal just a few minutes from our place in San Jose. From the content of her web site, it seemed she was a good fit.

We met with her initially as a family, but just a few minutes into that session she asked Michele and me if we would be comfortable waiting in the outer office while she talked with our girls.

We agreed to that, and stepped out. When the counselor called us back in, she had the girls step out for the remaining few minutes of the session. She closed the door and took a seat across from us.

"Right off the bat, let me say whatever you guys are doing as parents, keep doing it." She continued. "Your girls love their family and their home. I think you two are doing a great job."

I looked at Michele. She stared at the counselor, with a surprised look on her face. In light of the struggles we had endured, I was somewhat stunned, but also encouraged. I'm not sure how Michele took her remarks, or if the significance of what the counselor said even registered with her.

That single session in early October was the only time we met with the counselor as a family. Before we left that meeting, the counselor told us she wanted to begin meeting with both of our girls for a time. We agreed and scheduled the next appointments for their sessions.

The girls met with the counselor through October and November.

Michele and I took a back seat, and waited for word from the counselor as to when and if she wanted us to attend the sessions, or meet with her as a couple. But in the closing of her email of December 7th, Michele wrote she was going to contact the counselor to set up an appointment for us to meet with her as a couple to address Michele's concerns about our relationship.

Two months later, Michele moved out.

103

Bomb's Away!

Though Michele was not living in our home, she reluctantly agreed to pick me up for our February 18th counseling appointment. The trip from our place to the counselor's office was stilted and tense. We arrived at 6:45 p.m., and awkwardly took seats in the tiny waiting room.

After what felt like an eternity, the door opened, and the counselor greeted us and gestured for us to join her. We sat across from one another. The counselor sat in a chair several feet away, creating a conversation triangle of sorts.

Michele began to share some of her frustrations. The counselor looked over at me to see how I was handling it. I sat in stunned silence. My mind went blank. I wanted to leave; just walk away.

Oh my God.

When Michele concluded her remarks, the counselor asked her to step out to the waiting room. She exited and closed the door behind her. The counselor took her seat, heaved a big sigh, and then looked my way.

"Well, Rob, what do you think of what Michele just shared?"

"I don't know how to respond."

The counselor scooted forward to the edge of her seat, leaned forward and looked me right in the eye.

"Do you think you can—are you willing to—take a look at yourself as Michele sees you? Are you willing to look at things through her 'bubble' in order to save your marriage?"

I felt like a wrecking ball had crushed me. I really couldn't even think straight. I looked back at the counselor.

"Yes. I'm willing to do what you suggest; to take a look at myself through Michele's bubble. Absolutely. I love her very much. I want to save my marriage and fix my problems, but I don't know how to proceed."

With everything else I was dealing with, I wanted to leave the building, walk into the evening commuter traffic, and become a hood ornament on someone's car. That was a new thought for me. I didn't know then if I could handle intense marital problems on top of trying to recover from the transplant.

I tried to focus. The counselor was very encouraging. She told me to take some time to think, and emphasized the importance of owning my issues and committing fully to working through them if I did indeed want to save the relationship.

We spent the remaining few minutes of the session putting together a game plan for addressing Michele's concerns. She made some suggestions for how I could proceed. "Make contact, either in person or through other means with your family and friends."

Can I just go home now, and stick my finger in a light socket?

She continued. "I would ask for feedback from them. You need to gain as much insight as possible. Their perspective may be very helpful."

When we concluded the session, I exited the counselor's office and opened the door to the waiting room. When my eyes met Michele's, she quickly looked away. I looked down at the floor. I've never found carpet more engaging than at that moment; couldn't take my eyes off it.

Michele got up fast from her chair and made her way for the door. She walked twenty feet ahead of me all the way to our car, and never said a word.

On the trip back to our house, Michele stared straight ahead, her hands at 10 and 2 on the steering wheel. I felt like I was unraveling. It was the longest ten minutes of my life. Michele pulled the truck into our driveway and waited for me to climb out. Given my physical condition, it took a little time. My legs did not like to be moved once they were comfortable. Just as soon as I closed the passenger side door, she backed out and sped off down our street.

That night I hoped I would die in my sleep.

I was sick of it all—the medical, the marital, all of it. But sleep never came. I was awake for most of the night, wrestling with thoughts about what kind of husband and father I was. I was very confused.

I thought about what the fallout would be from the email I would send to my in-laws and our friends. *Was I a total loser? How on God's green earth did my life get to this point?*

It was a rough night to say the least.

104

Owning My Issues

On Saturday, February 20th, I drafted a most difficult email message. I wrote that Michele and I were in counseling to address marital problems, and that I had chosen to fully own my contribution to our mess, and intended to get to the bottom of my issues.

God, please help me here. I'm dying inside.

I asked for feedback, and promised I would receive it in a spirit of humility and gratitude. I struggled to write those words, because at the time I didn't have a spirit of humility and gratitude, only a hope God would grant me that along the way.

I emailed the draft of the message to our counselor, and waited for her response. She replied the next day, and commented that it "sounded honest."

I sent the message out a day later to each one of my in-law family members, and several of our friends, not as a "group send" but individual messages. It did not feel good to hit the "send" button.

It was not a positive, healing step at that point in time. It was a big, steaming pot of mea culpa. Every click of the "send" button added more to the pot.

When I finished sending the messages, I walked away from the computer, and contemplated the fact I had just "unzipped" for my family and some of our closest friends, and laid it all out on the line. *What would they think of me now?* I sat for a while in a chair on our back patio and pondered the sorry state of affairs that was my marriage.

I didn't pray; just sat there like a lump. I could have prayed; should have prayed. I should have gotten as far out of my own head as possible, and drawn near to God.

His word said if I did that, he would draw near to me. I guess at that moment, I allowed my pain to cloud my convictions. The score: pity party: one, joyful in spite of circumstances: zero.

105

A Look in the Mirror

I began to receive feedback just a couple days after sending out the emails. I did not know what to expect as the recipients of my message thought about their history with Michele and me and put pen to paper. It had to be difficult for my family and friends to receive such a message, let alone respond to it in total openness and honesty.

If I had received such a message, I think it would have set me back on my heels. *You want me to what?* It's not everyday we receive an email message from a friend or relative asking for help so he can fix himself. *Hello.*

The responses were filled with encouragement, love and support. It was clear folks had taken time to craft their messages, and not merely dump a pile of thoughts on me. A couple of friends began their notes with apologies for the honesty and directness of their content.

They expressed concern their words might end our friendship. I believed it would only strengthen our bond. Real friends speak the truth, in love.

But I did feel horrible when I thought about how awkward it must have been for them. I genuinely wanted honest feedback. How else was I to gain an understanding of my problem? I was lost and needed direction.

Many years ago, my friend Gordon, his wife and their nephew came home after dinner and a movie to find the first floor of their home flooded. They found several inches of standing water, and all of their flooring, furniture, and fixtures enjoying an evening swim. It didn't stop there.

Not only was the first floor in shambles; water was wicking up the sheetrock on the walls upstairs as well. They had just finished repainting their entire house, and finished it off with new carpeting, furniture and accessories. All of that was lost.

Before they could fix the mess, they had to find the source of the problem. A pipe had broken in an upstairs bathroom, and water flowed like a river for several hours, until they arrived home.

That was my situation. My house was flooded, but where was the water coming from? I needed those I sought help from to be honest with me. I needed them to cut loose if they needed to. Tear off the sheetrock.

Help me find the broken pipe!

Many commented they had never seen anything in my relationship with Michele that caused them any concern. Others offered no commentary on the subject whatsoever. In a couple of the replies, friends referenced something I said or my attitude or the way I behaved in a certain situation that caught them off guard.

It was my way or the highway.

Reading those accounts and recalling those times had me reeling. Part of me was in shock, but another part accepted the reality, perhaps for the first time.

I spent considerable time reading and re-reading those messages, and as I did, recognized a pattern of behavior that *(thankfully)* did not define who I was in the minds of those folks, but was clearly a stumbling block, and an issue for them.

I thought I was a "glass is half full" guy. But others saw a streak in me that was very much "glass is half empty." I was taken aback by that realization.

I did not know what to do with the feedback I received, what actions to take, or what the next step was. I had never cooked Mea Culpa before and didn't have the recipe. I decided to compile each of the messages into a folder, and set them aside for a time and process what I read; give it some time to sink in.

Those dear friends were quite willing to support me in my effort to change. I sent replies to each of them, letting them know how much I loved them and reiterating my intention to fully address my issues and make things right.

106

The Floodgate Opens

On Wednesday, February 24th, I received an email from Michele that hit like a ton of bricks. It was the first time she had a chance to express in writing the full breadth of her hurt and anger toward me since moving out earlier in the month. What she shared with the counselor at our first meeting was just the tip of a very large iceberg.

More monkeys, awaking from their slumber. More "it is what it is" for me to chew on.

She shared her perceptions and impressions about our life together over the years, and our years as a family. Her words were filled with anger and desperation. I felt horrible.

I was still processing what she shared at our first appointment with the counselor, and didn't have much stomach for more grief. So, like the email feedback I received, I added Michele's message to my growing pot of Mea Culpa and just let it simmer for a while.

107

Flying Solo

In early March I began solo sessions with our counselor to begin looking at myself "through Michele's bubble." We talked about the feedback I received from the email messages I sent, and about the many dynamics in my past and present, good and bad, which I had allowed to shape my personality.

The counselor gave me homework assignments to help me dig deep on those items and gain insight into how and why those patterns of behavior came to be.

Part of me didn't want to dig deep.

I worked hard to nail down in no uncertain terms what my contribution had been over the years to bring our relationship to it's current tenuous state, and develop tools I could use to ensure I didn't fall back into old patterns. It was important to be able to show the counselor, and ultimately Michele if she ever cared to see it, I tried to address her concerns.

I learned a great deal, and very quickly, about how I had not dealt with skeletons from my past, beginning with how I was raised and the family dynamic (*or lack of it*) in our home when I was young.

It was almost as if those bones were eager to reveal themselves, like they had been waiting for me to unlock the door and release them to dance in the light of day.

Finally, Rob. What took you so long?

Probably for the first time in my life, I fully came to terms with the emotional and physical abuse both my brother and I endured from our Dad. He didn't discipline. Rather, he used anything we said or did that he didn't like as an excuse to take out his frustrations on us. He chased us through our house with a belt.

It had a name.

That didn't end for me until I was fifteen years old. I smarted off at him. That's on me. But rather than grounding me for a few days, or taking some other reasonable course of action, he came after me with that belt. His face was twisted with rage. It always was when he got angry. I stood my ground.

He swung the belt at me and I grabbed it. I yanked it out of his hand so hard it nearly dislocated his shoulder. He was stunned, and it stopped him dead in his tracks. I told him he was never going to come after me with that belt again, and if he did, we'd go one on one.

Sorry Dad. This is your wake up call.

When I wasn't dealing with direct assaults by him, he usually had a bad attitude that impacted everyone in the family. He was a worrier, unhappy with his lot in life. He let things get to him, and his attitude around the house was pretty gruff and detached most of the time.

I think that part of my history with my Dad made his spiritual awakening when I was at City of Hope so amazing. He went from being the consummate worrier and hand wringer, with a chip on his shoulder, to a man on a mission to help and encourage others.

He began to trust the Lord for the things that troubled him.

It was an amazing thing to witness.

Fully acknowledging the reality of the abuse in my past was uncharted water. I wanted to share what I was going through with Michele, but she wanted distance and time. I had to fix me on my own.

I kept working on the junk in my trunk. Beyond the baggage from my childhood, I began to realize the events surrounding the initial diagnosis and treatment of my leukemia had a profound impact on who I was and who I had become.

I didn't understand how significantly those events influenced my relationship with Michele. For years I thought we were doing okay, that we had worked through our issues and were moving on. What couple doesn't have issues from time to time?

Nice try.

The homework assignments from my counselor allowed me to see I had not fully—honestly—faced the disappointment, guilt, and anger I felt as a result of going through and "putting" others through the ordeal of my illness. Michele and I should have sought counseling at the first sign of trouble. We didn't.

Signs aren't any help to a blind man.

Without even knowing it, I had allowed those aspects of my past to negatively influence me; who I was as Michele's husband, and the kind of father I was to my girls.

When my leukemia returned, and I was thrust back into the world of cancer, chemotherapy, radiation, and ultimately the bone marrow transplant, much of that "stuff" from my past, the fears, feelings of guilt, anger, and frustration resurfaced.

I had lived much of my life looking over my shoulder, wondering when the cancer monkey would wake up. Though I thought I had moved on with my life, I hadn't on many levels.

I lived tentatively for several years following my treatment at City of Hope, and down deep where I couldn't feel it or access it I saw the cup of my life as half empty.

I was happy to be alive, but I was afraid to live.

That negativity was one of the things Michele felt she had to combat nearly every day of our marriage. It's no wonder she was so fed up with me. I would be fed up with me.

I hope I've been a good husband. I hope I've been a good Dad. Those two things are what really matter to me. I did the best I could. I suppose only time will tell. I know I blew it in the past. But waiting to learn if I was a good father to my girls could take a lifetime. I'm not sure I have that long. Painful.

I'd gladly give my left leg for a do-over.

"Don't waste my time" and "My way or the highway" became part of who I was. Over the twenty plus years of my relationship with Michele those attitudes reared their ugly heads, and wreaked havoc.

Without ever intending to do so, I was a real ass to the people I cared about most in life—my wife, family members, and our friends. I was oblivious to it. It was incredibly awkward and unnerving to learn this about myself, At times I felt like an idiot for not recognizing it until Michele, in essence, held a mirror up to my face.

Sorry Rob. This is your wake-up call!

At the same time, it was very cathartic and liberating to have that knowledge and embrace it as a reality. As painful as it was to work through those issues and the many realizations of just how *not* on top of things I was, it was far better than remaining in that old place, that old state of mind.

I began to see a change in myself. I recognized the old thought patterns and the "trigger" events that historically had caused me to overshoot my own runway. I really didn't care whether anyone else noticed the changes or not.

I tried to focus simply on fixing the things in my life I could fix. I could never change peoples' perceptions or impressions. It was completely out of my control. That was a tough pill to swallow, but it was what it was.

There were certainly days when I got fed up with all the self-examination and delving deep into my childhood and my relationship with my Dad, and how I wasn't "validated" as a unique individual, and wishing Michele and I had sought counseling back in 1991, and on and on. More "what ifs" and "if onlys" to mess with my head.

But I was inspired by the realization I could use my history to bring about positive change. God could work with me right where I was. He had no prerequisite that I be perfect before he could address my needs.

He could bring guidance, healing, and love and help me be a better man, whether or not my marriage survived. I needed to become that person.

My desire was that Michele and I would both work on our respective smoldering piles of crap, and emerge on the other end a stronger, more committed couple and a better family as well. I loved Michele and was committed to our marriage and hoped she would one day feel the same.

108

More Cellulitis, Anyone?

B esides ramping up the work with my counselor, the first part of March 2010 was filled with new challenges on the medical front.

On Monday, March 8th I had an appointment at Stanford for a follow up consultation following the bone marrow biopsy performed in mid-February.

I was always a little nervous about what they would find. But each biopsy performed post-transplant indicated 100 percent donor presence and not a trace of me to be found. All things considered, perhaps the less of me anyone could find, the better.

The line that had been in my left arm for nearly a year was removed. Doc also decided to decrease my daily dose of Prednisone to 30 milligrams. I hoped with even that slight reduction the buffalo hump on the back of my neck would get smaller, and my moon face would get a little less "moony."

I came home from the appointment with a bit of a sore left arm from what I figured was the removal of the PICC line. I was amped up and motivated to continue on the road to recovery, perhaps without having to deal with any more speed bumps along the way. It was a very positively charged day. I was actually happy.

But by Monday evening, my left forearm was painful. I felt like I had pulled a muscle, but had no recollection of doing so and figured it would pass. No big deal. The next morning I enjoyed my first real shower since Easter of 2009. There were no hoses sticking out of me, no bandages, no wounds to be concerned about.

It was… normal.

As the day progressed, the pain localized to a single spot on the top of my arm, just above my wrist. By nightfall it was slightly swollen and even more painful. By Wednesday the pain was bugging me enough that I took a painkiller to take the edge off. The swelling worsened and the area became red and warm to the touch.

Oh jeez!

I contacted the Kaiser advise nurse that evening and her counsel, in light of my history, was to head to the ER. The problem was diagnosed as Cellulitis, localized in my arm. I was sent home with a prescription for a ten-day course of oral antibiotics and instructions to follow up with Dr. Raji within twenty-four hours.

No sweat.

Doc checked out my arm, noted the persistent swelling and redness, and ordered an ultrasound to check for a blood clot or other issue. That test was unremarkable, so the diagnosis of Cellulitis seemed to be accurate. Doc had me continue with the course of antibiotics and told me to let her know if anything changed in the days ahead.

They did.

109

No Luck of the Irish Today

I was angry, and it took everything in me to keep from exploding right there in the car. Michele and I were once again, on our way to Stanford to deal with more complications. On the trip up the freeway my frustration was difficult to manage.

How much more, I thought. *How much more can we heap onto this already flaming pile of nastiness? How much more am I—are we—expected to endure? Who picked me to be on the receiving end of this twisted game of target practice?*

It was Wednesday, March 17th. St. Patrick's Day, but the luck of the Irish was nowhere to be found. The majority of that day had been relatively uneventful. Michele and the girls had not yet moved back home, but Michele happened to be at the house that afternoon.

We hung out for a while and even ended up having dinner together. In light of the tenuous nature of our relationship at that time, I really enjoyed spending some positive time with her.

When we sat down to eat, I noticed my left ankle was swollen, and there was also a moderate level of pain in my left foot. I took off my shoe and sock to have a look.

Beyond some slight swelling, there was an area on my heel where it looked like the edge of my shoe had rubbed into the skin and caused some irritation, but it wasn't the end of the world.

Because of the Prednisone, fluid retention and swelling in my legs had been a problem for months, with some days worse than others. So I didn't think much of what I found under my sock. After we finished dinner forty-five minutes later, I checked my left foot a second time just to be sure everything was cool.

It wasn't.

In one of the most frustrating and scary moments of my life, I found a deep purple, rash-like thing, once again wrapped around my heel, in between my toes, over the top of my foot, and moving up my leg.

It looked all too familiar.

Michele and I knew right away what it meant. We wasted no time contacting my doctor at Stanford to let him know what was up. I told him it had happened again—the "rash" was back. The Cellulitis had returned to my left leg.

This time around it had teeth. Just like before, it traveled up my leg in nothing flat. In just forty-five minutes it went from nothing to full-blown. It was so discouraging to think the problem I battled just a few months prior had returned.

So much for that "no-big-deal" case of Cellulitis in my arm.

Our life was already upside down and sideways; frenzied with seemingly never-ending post-transplant recovery issues and intense marital conflict to boot.

When the infection hit, it sucked the life right out of me. I was tempted to throw in the towel and declare defeat, take a walk and accidentally step into oncoming traffic.

It was just too much to deal with.

Thoughts I would never really recover from the relapse and BMT, and that my relationship with Michele would just crumble into weed infested ruins, flashed across my mind.

It was suffocating. Any notion of choosing to live joyfully in spite of my circumstances was quickly replaced by a seething anger.

110

Back Into the Fire

Michele dropped me off outside the hospital entrance and drove away to park the car. While I waited for her on a bench outside, I called our counselor to let her know I would not be able to make our scheduled appointment for that evening. Two steps forward, one, and sometimes three steps back.

I was admitted to the E1 unit within an hour or so of making the call to my doc, and hoped we caught the infection early and moved fast enough things wouldn't be so bad.

Soon after I settled into my room many of my nurses and several of the medical assistants came by with stunned looks on their faces. They couldn't believe the same problem had returned—and to the same leg. I had just visited them with brownies in hand a month prior. Four weeks later I was back on the unit with my leg going up in flames.

How quickly things can change.

Early the next morning, I was moved to surgery, and met the team of docs that would once again work their voodoo on my leg with exploratory incisions. They prepped me in the operating room and as before, knocked me senseless into la-la-land.

100… 99… ba-bye.

I woke up in the Surgical Intensive Care Unit (SICU) with my head in a fog and a nurse telling me everything went very smoothly. I learned later from Michele that statement was not entirely accurate.

My blood pressure bottomed out when I was under the knife, and I came very close to dying on the table. No one ever copped to that, and

Michele was rather vague about it as well, telling me only she was informed things "got a little dicey" during my surgery. Vague worked for me at the time. I thought I was there for a simple problem with my leg.

111

Nurses and Flight Attendants

Over my years with Michele, I learned something interesting about nurses. They share a common character trait with flight attendants. That is, the ability to remain withdrawn and distant, and spin accounts of really nasty things into palatable sound bites, turning the frightening into the innocuous.

It's a gift.

"Nurse, I noticed there is a tag on the outside of my door, reading 'cardiac risk' and I was wondering if you could tell me what that's about?"

"Oh, that just means we love you, and shouldn't get too attached, because you'll break our hearts if something goes wrong."

"Oh, really?"

"Yes. We have several notes like that one for different situations."

"Like?"

"Well, for instance, the sign that reads 'Bio-Hazard' on that door across the hall?"

"Yes, I see that."

"Well, that's a caution to the nurses to avoid prolonged conversations with that gentleman because he will share his whole life story."

"Really."

"Yes."

Flight attendants are blessed with this same special gift.

"Uh, excuse me, ma'am, I just felt a very loud 'thud' and heard what sounded like the engine here on the left side of the plane shut off. It was winding up pretty good right after takeoff, but then it just went silent. Is everything all right?"

"Oh, yes, nothing to worry about, sir. Because of noise-abatement restrictions, the Captain had to throttle back a bit on the engines until we're out over the ocean."

"Throttle back or turn them off?"

"Throttle back. Nothing to worry about."

"What about that loud 'thud'?"

"Oh, that was the door on the beverage cart closing. We'll be serving drinks shortly."

"Really?"

"Yes. You can order a drink if you like."

"No, I mean the sound. It was the beverage cart door, huh?"

"It's a very large beverage cart, sir. Care for something to drink?"

112

Fun and Games in the SICU

Sometimes I can be as dumb as a stump. I didn't immediately get the significance of waking up in the SICU. *Duh*. When the Cellulitis hit in December of 2009, I went from surgery to recovery, and straight back to my room. No sweat. No harm. No foul.

In the SICU, a nurse stayed with me 24/7. As my head cleared and I got used to my new digs, Ann, my nurse for the day, approached my bedside.

"Well now, Mr. Robert, your poor leg has been through a lot, hasn't it?"

She had a beautiful Irish accent. It just flowed out of her like a pad of butter slides off the top of a hot stack of pancakes. I talked with Ann about just how bad off my leg was.

She explained during the surgery, two large areas were found where the Cellulitis had killed off some of the tissue. It was necrotic and very deep. Deep was bad. That much I recalled from my first bout with the condition.

Tissue samples were sent to the laboratory for analysis and culturing. What remained were two big, deep incisions that would take a long time to heal. Oh, there was also the pesky little detail of whether I would be discharged from the hospital with both legs.

Did I have a big, red target on my back or what?

The surgeons were extremely concerned I might loose my left leg, more so than they ever were when the infection hit me the first time around. And they were concerned enough for my liking back then. Since the infection had "jumped the joint" and killed off tissue above my knee, the amputation would be of the entire leg, significantly limiting options for fitting a prosthetic device.

That news was way too much to handle when the surgical team addressed the issue with Michele and me. Michele focused. My head danced off into the ether and pondered the notion of possibly spending the rest of my life in a wheelchair, or at the very least, with a significant list to port.

None of the doctors that visited me on their daily rounds ever had gleaming smiles on their faces. Beyond their joking and trying to make me feel good about my really bad situation, they did not hold out much hope I would walk out of the hospital under my own power with both legs—with one exception.

Dr. Aaron, the excellent doctor who ran point on my case in December, believed with everything in him my body would respond to the antibiotics as it had before. He had seen it happen once, and thought for sure it would play out the same way.

I put my money on Dr. Aaron in this second race—to win.

At the same time, I couldn't dismiss from my mind the very real possibility that upon discharge, my middle name might change from Arthur to "Hop-a-Long."

Sobering, to say the least.

I spent several days in the SICU. It took a little time to get used to a nurse being at my bedside, hanging out with me all day. Nurse Dana and I spent a lot of time together, and we became good buddies.

She told me early on in my stay most of the patients they care for in the SICU were intubated with a breathing tube. They were usually very sick and pretty much out cold most of the time or awake, but they were unable to speak because of the tube.

"Having a patient we can talk with and who can communicate with us is a real treat," she said.

I became friends with many of my nurses. Angelica, Ann, Dana,

Mark, Mireka, Nicole; they were an incredible group of professionals for whom I have nothing but the utmost respect. We watched the Food Network on TV, commented on the recipes, and critiqued the hosts.

"If it were me, I would have substituted the Paprika for Cayenne Pepper and added some garlic into the mix as well! What do you think, Dana?"

It was great to enjoy some laughs, as there were many reality check moments, where the whole reason I was on the unit in the first place was put back in my face, often abruptly. In a second surgery, my incision sites were closed. Two of the docs making rounds on the morning following that surgery provided one of those abrupt, reality checks.

When that crew entered my room, I was peppered with questions and a few wisecracks as well. The incision above my knee on the inside of my thigh measured four inches in length, an inch wide and a half-inch deep.

The second incision, just above my ankle on the inside of my leg was just as long but twice as deep. You could have parked a car in it.

I answered the doctor's questions and discussed the plan for monitoring my leg and trying to determine the pathology of the infection.

Without any warning at all, one of those well-meaning chaps began removing the sterile gauze packed tightly into the wound during the second surgery.

The surgeons had decided to close the upper incision with sutures. The lower incision was a different story. It was close to another area of concern near my foot. So the surgeon decided to keep it open for easy access and public viewing, and pack it with the sterile gauze.

Guided tours were conducted twice daily.

One of the doctors stuck some kind of sharp object (*it's always something sharp*) into that deep, open wound, without any sort of painkiller having been administered beforehand. I think he might have been related to my ninth grade world history teacher.

The other doc prepared the new, sterile gauze and glanced up at me from time to time, I suppose to see if my eyes were rolling back in my head.

The other docs kept bantering on and on and continued with their questions. I answered them as best I could, but the pain from the old dressing being pulled out of the wound, and the other poking around by Doctors Laurel and Hardy was rather distracting.

I winced as I talked with the other docs. They had surrounded the foot of my bed to examine the wound. At one point I turned my head and looked at my nurse with what must have looked like the face of a scared puppy.

"Shouldn't we have done something about numbing the area? Shouldn't I have been knocked unconscious… with a hammer… before the prospecting began?"

She agreed and tried to get the surgeons to stop for a moment so she could run and grab a fast-acting painkiller, but the docs kind of blew that off.

"Is this painful for you?"

I had a name. Did Dr. Hardy know it or only my chart number?

"Oh yeah. I'm not happy with you guys at all right now. I had visions of us getting together for poker night, but now…"

The other docs looked at me and laughed, and gave Laurel and Hardy a bad time. They were not about to stop in mid-stream and wait for my nurse to push the pain med.

They kept working on me for several more minutes. I thought for sure my eyes were going to pop out of my skull and horns would grow out of my forehead.

I had no idea my eyebrows could travel so far across my face.

Eventually the docs had new sterile gauze packed into the wound, and did so a bit more carefully than they had extracted the old.

They slapped a square gauze pad over the top and taped it down. I peeled myself off the ceiling, and the docs went on their way.

Good times.

Fortunately, subsequent visits by the green team and the daily dressing changes happened only after I was given the dope and couldn't feel a thing.

113

Stepping Down

After several days on the antibiotics, the purple discoloration that covered my leg faded in its intensity, and the area of involvement shrank considerably. With things looking pretty positive, my doctors wrote orders to have me "stepped down" and transferred to the E1 unit for the balance of my hospitalization.

Michele came by on the day I was transferred. As we left the unit, and my gurney was rolled out of the room and down the main corridor, it seemed like the entire team of nurses wished us well.

They were so happy I was leaving with both legs still attached. It was quite a moment. Dana escorted us to E1. She was really excited about the positive outcome.

That was not routine in the SICU.

It made me realize again just how serious my situation was when I was first admitted. When we arrived back on E1, the nurses greeted our entourage warmly. They were relieved as well that things were looking better than they were several days prior.

After some time spent settling in to my room, I shared a tearful goodbye with Dana. She got really choked up. I did as well. She was such a terrific nurse and a really wonderful person. We had become very close in the short time I was on the SICU.

I spent several days on E1. The purple discoloration on my leg slowly faded away, leaving only a black outline drawn with a felt tip marker around the perimeter of the infection. It was quite a compelling visual.

The upper incision was sutured closed in the second surgery. The lower incision was a different story. Negative Pressure Wound Therapy (NPWT) was used on that wound. The dressing was like something out of a science fiction movie.

A plastic tube approximately five feet long was secured to the top of my wound with a transparent adhesive membrane. It was connected to an electric pump hung on the side of my bed. The pump created negative pressure, a vacuum seal over the surface of the incision.

The dressing drew fluid that had built up in my leg out through the incision, and also stimulated blood flow to the wound to promote new tissue growth.

The pump droned on and on 24/7. I felt like I was part of some bizarre experiment, but the dressing was very effective in accelerating the healing of the wound.

114

Conflicted

In the quiet moments during that time on E1, I tried to imagine what the day-to-day routine would be like at home after discharge. Michele and the girls were still living with her parents. Prior to the onset of the Cellulitis, Michele told me she wanted me to move out.

She said she needed distance from me, and time to heal. I understood the intensity of her hurt at that time, but struggled with the notion of moving out.

Had it really come to that? What exactly was that supposed to look like, given my stark medical realities?

I had two holes the size of cigars in my leg, little physical strength, was unable to work and support myself, couldn't drive, had no money and only had medical insurance because Michele had a job.

I couldn't bring myself to believe Michele was so cold-hearted she didn't care how I moved out or where I went.

Beyond the impracticality of her request, I wondered if such a move was morally or spiritually the right thing to do. *Would such a separation do more harm to our relationship than good? What was I as a Christian to do that honored God and also honored my wife at her point of pain?*

I was trying to do what I thought was the right thing to do. I was not a knuckle-dragging, Neanderthal, but rather, a man who was willing to take a hard look at himself, perhaps for the first time. I was willing to own my past mistakes and seek help to fix my mess.

I was conflicted.

With those thoughts in my head and a leg I knew would take a long time to heal, I was exasperated that so much of what was happening in my life was out of my control.

The work I had begun with the counselor to address my issues was the one thing I had any control over. It was the one thing I could do to honor my wife and demonstrate my commitment to her and to our marriage. That work was suddenly halted by the second onset of Cellulitis.

What message was I supposed to glean from that turn of events? Don't work on your problems because it just doesn't matter? I couldn't make my mind go there.

The notion of "it is what it is" was something I really could not stomach at that time. Far from it. Where I found myself was not where I was supposed to be. I was not supposed to be messed up with complication upon complication. I was not supposed to be having marital trouble. I was not supposed to be wondering where my life was headed!

One night I was wide-awake thinking about life and listening to tunes on my iPod. I played every James Taylor song in my collection that night. His stuff always chilled me out when things got rough in my life. The lyrics of one song in particular, *That Lonesome Road,* hit me right between the eyes.

It was like hearing that song for the first time. It was beautiful and sad, entirely "A cappela" in multi-part harmony. Slow and deliberate.

I had sung that song for years, but when I heard it that night it broke me up. It's message hit me hard: *If I had shut my mouth and listened more and seen things as they really were; if I had maintained my cool and kept a loving heart, perhaps my life and my marriage would not be as messed up as it was.*

Lord, keep working on me, please?

115

Heading Home!

By March 26th, my doctors felt the antibiotic cocktail was doing its job so they decided to set the wheels in motion for my discharge. They spent considerable time with me, discussing the post-discharge treatment plan.

Science fiction as a way of life.

I would wear a portable pump 24/7 to infuse the antibiotics. A home health nurse would be out every Monday, Wednesday and Friday to change the dressing on my leg, for at least a few months.

A few months? What happened to "weeks"?

Beyond wearing the pumps, I had to stay on top of re-ordering dressings, changing kits and collection canisters as well as gauze pads, alcohol wipes, tape, saline to flush the line in my arm, and diabetic supplies and my medications.

There would also be regular follow up appointments at Stanford so the surgeon could monitor the healing of the incisions.

Managing your health can kill you.

I was discharged on Friday, March 27th, and the fun began at home almost immediately. Not thirty minutes after Michele and I returned home from the hospital, a nurse knocked on our door for the first of what would ultimately be seventy visits.

It was good to be home, but at the same time it felt like I was living under house arrest, having to spend a majority of my time sitting with my legs elevated, wearing my two "man-purse" pumps and a plastic tube running up my leg.

And this is the way it would be for a few months? How silly am I going to look when I go outside and take my walks?

I tried to make the most of my daily routine. The days were quite busy. It seemed there were always medical supplies being delivered. We had boxes of supplies stacked up in the day room.

I'm sure I could have moved that stuff for a good price on the street. Talk about a killer yard sale!

How much do you want for the syringes and alcohol wipes?

It seemed my road to recovery was never going to be paved and smooth; more like a rutted, bumpy dirt path, like something you would see in a National Geographic special. It was one challenging problem after another with no time off for good behavior.

116

Housemates

After several weeks I had a pretty good handle on the medical part of my life. On the marital side, things were pretty rocky, with only occasional glimpses of hope. Though there was major tension and little by way of interaction, Michele and I did have some interaction.

We discussed the latest news headlines, aspects of the home improvement projects we had underway, and even details about the work I was doing with our counselor. But it was stilted and uncomfortable. We were housemates, at best.

I made some progress in changing my ways and on a couple of occasions, when I realized I blew it in exchanges with Michele I went to her and apologized.

Historically, I might not even have recognized I had screwed up. Baby steps at best, but it was a start.

Early on in my work with the counselor, I determined when situations arose or something was said that could get me fired up, I would be Switzerland—say nothing and have no opinion—for at least ten seconds. Remain neutral, as Switzerland had done during World War II.

I figured such an approach would give me a moment to consider whether my eye roll, input, opinion, or other potentially "over-the-top" energy was even necessary. More often than not, it wasn't.

There were times when my best-laid plans did not play out well at all. I over-reacted or said something stupid, swore, or otherwise royally choked.

Switzerland first. Right. Good plan. More like Nazi Germany at times. Keep trying. Or perhaps stop trying. I didn't know.

Throughout the history of our marriage, whether Michele was asleep or not, when I came to bed I always told her goodnight and that I loved her. I often told her I loved her when she was wide-awake as well.

Things deteriorated to the point where my "I love you" was not returned when I said it, or when I texted that simple message to her. So I stopped saying it.

I was tired of my words being met with a deafening silence. I struggled constantly with a growing sense that soon the other shoe was going to drop; that Michele would either announce she had had enough, did not want to continue her counseling, and wanted us to get a divorce or some other big "thing."

In light of how things had gone since December of 2009, I didn't trust her much at all. I had a very uneasy feeling something was up, and I had no idea what that even meant. But in my gut I felt like it was just a matter of time before she dropped another bombshell.

To my surprise, Michele told me she was ready to move back home when I was discharged following the second battle with Cellulitis. My counselor made it clear to me in light of history I needed to double check with Michele on matters of any significance. She needed to know she was given an opportunity to express her thoughts and see that I listened to what she said.

When Michele told me she was ready to move back home, I asked her specifically if she was coming home because she was ready to come home or because she knew I needed help. Managing the pumps and the antibiotics and everything else would be a lot to handle.

She told me that was not the case. She was ready to come home following her time away from me. I took her words at face value.

But within a few weeks, our relationship went into a downward spiral. Our communication ceased, and I felt very much on my own to forge ahead along the seemingly never-ending road to recovery, wherever it was leading. Michele was fed up with every aspect of our life together. There were days when it was just too much, and I wanted to throw in the towel. Perhaps Michele had those same thoughts.

For the first month following discharge, I had incredibly painful neuropathy in both feet, and I could not get out and walk as I had hoped. I spent a majority of my time in my recliner with my legs elevated to reduce the swelling.

The road to recovery was a slow grind. I did not meet face-to-face with the counselor during those months because I was not going to have sessions with her when I was wearing my two pumps, buzzing and spitting in the background.

I really did not feel that great, but with plenty of time spent sitting around, I did continue work on the homework assignments she had given me prior to the second Cellulitis onset.

I was happy I could keep that ball rolling forward on at least a minimal level and looked forward to a time when I could reconnect with her for face-to-face sessions.

As the months passed, I got stronger, and each day the wounds in my leg healed a little bit more. Given the medical realities I faced, I did my best to honor Michele's request for distance and time by making myself as small, invisible and non-existent as possible. At six foot three inches tall and 225 pounds, that was not an easy task.

I spent considerable time in the day room, even when I didn't have to, so Michele could "feel free to move about the cabin" and avoid awkward encounters with me. I also spent several nights each week at local coffee houses and libraries to pour my energy into this memoir and several other projects.

I was still deep into a very hectic period of medical treatment and recuperation but began to feel pretty darn good. The level of fatigue I felt each day was nothing close to what it was when I came home following the transplant.

Thoughts that I might be able to return to work at some point in the not so distant future crossed my mind from time to time. I updated several versions of my resume, searched the job listings, and networked to reconnect with friends, former clients, and vendors.

I began to test drive my capacity for logging work hours by spending time in my office in our backyard, working on the book, doing homework from my counselor, and completing several freebie graphic design projects for friends as well.

I pushed as much as I could and paid close attention to how I held up over the course of the day.

By the end of July I was able to work a few hours a day in my office for a couple days each week. After three or four hours, I was whipped and needed to take a break, as the fatigue hit pretty hard.

But a half-day's work was a far cry from lying in a hospital bed or being parked in my recliner without the strength to even stand up.

At the same time, I was unsure about how best to move forward on that front. One of the big issues for Michele was that my self-employment was not a "stable" job with the "predictable" income.

Her memories of the years prior to my relapse in 2008 were only of the lean times. Yes, things were tight for us at times. Living in this part of the country, it was difficult to find a situation where life was a smooth, easy ride. Is that possible anywhere?

I felt bad about the pressure and strain Michele said she felt over the years, but as I looked back at the big picture, the positives and the things we achieved I saw God's provision and blessing on our lives.

We were able to buy a home in one of the most beautiful parts of the country—Michele's "home turf." She was near her family and friends.

We lived a modest but comfortable lifestyle, and our daughters had both their parents around for most of their waking hours, for virtually all of their formative years.

Our girls had very frequent contact with both sets of grandparents and their aunts, uncles, and cousins as well. We made many capital improvements on our property, always made our mortgage payment, purchased vehicles, paid off our unsecured debt, and maintained outstanding credit scores. Not bad.

Though I spent the majority of my professional career working for myself, I did hold several full-time jobs. But I also worked freelance projects on the side, and often the income from the side work matched or exceeded what I brought home from the fulltime gigs.

Even with that supplemental income, times were tough every now and then. I guess that's life, especially in the Bay Area.

But God always provided for our needs, and beyond that, blessed us immeasurably. I was frustrated that Michele seemed unable at that time to see how our lives had been blessed, in spite of the road not being as smooth as we would have liked.

117

Mr. Smith Goes to Utah

One evening in late July, I ran across the phone number of Ron Smith, my good friend and former colleague from Focus on the Family. It had been a long time since we last spoke. Had to be close to ten years.

I dialed the number, not knowing if it was still his, but to my surprise, he answered. I heard his familiar gravely voice.

"Hello?"

"Ron, it's Rob. How are you buddy?"

"Rob! Hey, it's been a while. I'm good. How about you."

It was so good to make contact with him. We had history.

We talked for a long while. I filled him in on the events of the previous couple of years. He was shocked by the news. He brought me up to date on how his family was doing. We compared notes about our kids, and quickly found common ground, relating stories of the highs and lows of parenting.

I asked him about his Dad, Ron Sr., who I had become good friends with when we met at City of Hope. I knew his plan was to move to Utah and ride horses until the day he died.

"Whatever happened to Ron Sr.?" I asked.

"He passed away several years ago, but he lived his life to the fullest right to the very end."

"He told me he was going to move to Utah and ride horses."

"He did. He lasted seven years. You beat him by a few years, huh?"

"Was he in pretty good health during those years?" I asked.

"Actually he was. He made it to seventy years old, and on his birthday, went and had a big 70 tattooed on the side of his neck."

We both cracked up. Ron couldn't stop laughing. That's how his Dad was, a crazy man with a wacky sense of humor. I used to love our conversations, because I never knew what to expect from him. He always had some wild thought up his sleeve.

Suddenly I missed Ron Sr., but was so glad to learn he lived the final years of his life on his terms. He went out, quite literally, with his boots on. He was never cured, but he rode off into the sunset after all. After hanging up with Ron Jr., I realized one of those holes in my life had been filled in.

118

The Other Shoe Drops

I wrestled with the strange dynamic at home for several months while trying to focus on the daily medical tasks. At times, it was all-consuming. On Sunday, August 1st, Michele and I had a brief conversation about "the way we were."

At one point she told me she "did not love me right now," wanted us to separate "either legally or agreeably," and *(once again)* told me she wanted me to move out.

It was the first time she ever said she did not love me. Those words caught me completely off guard. In all honesty, I had zero feelings of love for her. But I still loved Michele very much, in that I was committed to her and to addressing my issues, fixing my part of our mess, and restoring our marriage.

Feelings of love come and go over time, but in my mind and heart, love was more than just those feelings—that emotional layer so easily manipulated and tossed, like desert sand.

It had to mean more than that. It had to be grounded in commitment, regardless of circumstances.

I wish I had been a better husband to Michele, but that was history. It was what it was. There was nothing I could do except look forward and focus on becoming a better person, first, and then a better husband and father, if that was possible. With God's grace, I hoped to restore my relationship with Michele and enjoy a bright future with her.

119

Back to Church

On Sunday, August 15th, I went to church for the first time in nearly eighteen months. Michele and Lauren, and a friend of our family and her daughter were away for the weekend, riding horses at a ranch in northern California. Kristen decided not to go on that trip, so she could hang out with her friends. I made a solo trip to church that morning.

With the relapse, three hospitalizations to get into and stay in remission, the bone marrow transplant and complications following discharge, there was never a time in the previous year and a half where I was able to attend a single morning service. My world was very small. I felt so frustrated.

As much as I wanted to get back to church, I was either too wiped out from chemo treatments, had an immune system that was tanked, and required me to wear my mask in public, had to avoid crowds altogether, or I was stuck in the hospital with complications, or just homebound.

Even though Michele and other family members and friends came to visit me when I was in the hospital, and pastors from our church stopped by our home to pray with me, I battled feelings of loneliness all the time.

When a BMA had to be performed, I went through it alone. When I had a spinal tap, I was the one laying on the treatment table. When I was "cognitively impaired," I had an MRI of my brain at 1:00 a.m. in the basement of Stanford Hospital, and I was alone, sandwiched between the two giant metal plates, with a steel cage over my face.

At home, while everyone else I knew was working for a living, I sat alone in my chair and watched TV, waiting to feel better. I felt completely detached from everything that had been a part of my life prior to the relapse.

There was this "other" life to live, and I had no idea how long I would have to live it.

When I was an undergraduate at Azusa Pacific University, chapel was held three times each week. With few exceptions (read: Nursing students), the entire study body was required to attend. I was a Religion major. What was my excuse?

I'm sorry I couldn't make any of the chapel services this week. I was exhausted from working so hard for God.

With the course load I was carrying, it was often difficult to make it to every chapel service. There was a limit to how many could be missed without consequences. I did my best to attend as many of them as I could.

When I graduated and began the next chapter of my life, I missed those chapel services immensely, and wished I had made it to more of them over my years as at APU.

It was a special gift to have access to those gatherings throughout the week. It helped keep me grounded. I took it for granted. *Get a clue, Rob.*

Not being able to make it to church for that long period felt the same way. I wanted so much to get back there, to be part of the congregation. I needed to reconnect with my friends and other folks that had kept my family in their prayers, visited me in the hospital, and sent amazing notes of encouragement.

I had faith, but I needed community. I think the two are meant to go hand in hand. I needed to be part of the community of believers, but I couldn't.

I will always cherish the memory of walking back into church on that Sunday in mid-August. I sat down in the pew and drank in the sights and sounds as folks from the earlier service visited, and then departed, while others arrived and took their seats for the second service.

When the service got under way, we stood to sing several songs and I got really busted up, but I did my best to contain myself. I didn't want to make a scene, but it was difficult to keep it all bundled up. Part of me wanted to shout out loud.

"It feels so GREAT to be here this morning!"

When I was young and ignorant, I heard plenty of visiting pastors and guest speakers tell the church congregation how "glad they were to be with us," and I used to think, *Yeah, right. Of course you are.* But now that I'm older *(perhaps just as ignorant)*, I realize the sincerity of their words.

Perhaps when we are deprived access to certain things—things previously unappreciated—only then do we fully realize the precious gift those things are in our life; caring, comfort, fellowship, friendship, worship. That is certainly the case in my life. I shouted on the inside that morning in church.

I try now to shout on the inside each day.

About the time the first song ended, some good friends came in, sat down next to me, and greeted me with hugs and smiles. Those friends were recipients of my email in late February when I asked for help to understand and fix my mess.

They provided some very helpful feedback, along with a ton of encouragement and love. It was an important reconnection with them, made my whole morning. There was an amazing spirit of forgiveness, love, and solidarity in the sanctuary that morning.

I think that is how it is supposed to work.

120

No Longer Hosed

On Tuesday, August 24th, I was back to Stanford for an appointment with my surgeon, for an assessment of the incision wound on my lower leg. At our previous encounters, he spent just a few minutes in the exam room. He would come in, greet me, glove up, pull off the vacuum dressing, and stare at the wound for a moment. Our interaction was about the same each time.

"Well Rob, how's the leg?"

"Oh, I think doing well. My home health nurse is really happy with how it's looking. How about you?"

"Looks pretty good. Is the vacuum dressing driving you nuts yet?"

"Yes, but I'd rather ride it out than go under the knife for a skin graft."

"You bet. If you can put up with the dressing, do it. I can understand how you wouldn't want to spend any more time in the hospital than you already have."

"I'll ride the pump for as long as it takes."

"Okay, then lets see you in a month."

That was how it usually went. It had gone that way since early April. But at the August 24th appointment, doc broke the mold. In light of how great the incision looked, he decided it was time to terminate the vacuum pump and transition to a simple, absorbent foam dressing. No more plastic hose sticking out of my leg. No more pump whining and snorting 24/7, like a water buffalo with sleep apnea. No more man purse!

121

Counselor Tag

In early September of 2010, I began work with a new counselor. He was a great guy. He was an alumnus of Azusa Pacific University, having graduated just before I began my studies there. We got off to a good start.

He was very warm and welcoming. He asked me to give him a snapshot of where I was in life and what was going on, and why I felt I needed counseling. I gave him the nickel tour of all that Michele and I had been through over the previous twenty years, including Michele's revelations of anger and frustration.

The counselor didn't ask many questions, just had me run off at the mouth for forty minutes. He nodded a lot, and shook his head, seemingly in disbelief over what he was hearing. When I concluded, I asked him what he thought.

"I'm speechless," he said, and raised his hand to his cheek in stunned disbelief.

"Pretty wild, huh, doc?"

"Wild? I can't believe what you and your wife have endured. I just can't get over it. The trials and tribulations of your illness alone would be enough to destroy a marriage."

I wondered if my account was a little too much for our first, "Hi, how are you?" Doc rolled with it. Without much hesitation, he asked me if I thought Michele would be willing to come in and talk with him, so he could get her take on things. I was impressed he wanted to get Michele's side of the story, to allow her to fully express herself, and share what she was feeling. I told him I thought she would be open to that, and I broached the subject with her later that day.

Much to my relief, Michele agreed to attend the next appointment. We met at the counselor's office. She was clearly tense and felt awkward, and was a bit freaked out that I was also present.

I offered to wait in the lobby to ease the tension. The counselor gave me a nod as I left his office. He and Michele spent the bulk of the session talking.

I have no idea what she shared or how open she was. I don't want to know. Her take on things was just that—her take. I was just thankful she was open to coming in, and so glad my counselor would at least have a fundamental understanding of our situation from "both sides of the street" as we began our work together.

Throughout September and October, I was more frustrated than focused. Though I was finished playing counselor tag and seemed to be off to the races with my new guy, I wished we could just be done with all the marital problems.

I thought, *Can't we just grow up and deal with this like adults?* I was tired of living like a ghost and trying to be invisible.

Several positive exchanges with Michele had me chomping at the bit to wrap it all up and move on with our life. Other times, the cold, curt, and distant Michele surfaced, and I was reminded we were still very deep in the woods.

No sunlight filtered through the canopy of trees in our forest. We were in the thick of it, enveloped in darkness.

122

Cloud Nine

Dr. Robert entered the examination room. "Man, you look great!" It was the most positive and uplifting thing a doctor had said to me for as long as I could remember. What a great way to kick off my Monday.

"Thanks doc. I feel like a million bucks."

It was October 25th, two months since my last appointment, and time for another evaluation. I was upstairs in the ITA first thing for lab draws, and while I was there, I dropped off some pre-Halloween brownies for my nurses.

The next stop was downstairs in Clinic E, where Dr. Robert made my morning with his enthusiastic greeting. He was rather animated that day. "You actually look as good as your labs say you're doing."

"How do they say I'm doing?"

"Things look really good. Some of your liver panels are still slightly elevated, but they seem to be trending down a bit."

I had decent white cell, red cell, and platelet counts, and my Hematocrit value was hanging tough in the mid 30s. No complaints. I was on cloud nine. Before long I was out the door and headed home.

I felt so positive about life on the drive south. There was plenty of commuter traffic, and at times we sat at a dead stop, for no reason other than sheer volume. But I really didn't care.

I used those moments to think about my exchange with Dr. Robert and enjoyed feeling fantastic for the first time in a long while.

My road had been so rocky, so filled with potholes that slowed my progress. At times, any happiness I felt in the midst of the struggle was easily eclipsed by an overwhelming sense the wheels were coming off the cart.

Not on October 25, 2010. It was my day to rise above it all. If that "cloud nine" feeling only lasted twenty-four hours, it would have been worth every second. Nobody could take that away.

123

Thanksgiving and the Language of Love

I was on the road by 8:00 a.m. sharp Thanksgiving Day. The trip north to my buddy Lou's place in Cottonwood would take four hours. Michele wanted distance and time. *Got it.* I wasn't about to sit around my house over the holiday weekend. Lou and his wife Penny invited me to join them for Thanksgiving if I felt like things were going to be uncomfortable at home.

I knew they would be.

A week or so before the holiday, I let Michele know I would be out of town and needed the truck. Before I could even finish my sentence, she cut me off with an abrupt "Okay."

As I made my way north, I thought about the way Michele and I had been living—nearly a year in separate bedrooms with only minimal communication.

I wondered if the day would ever come when we could sit down and talk about our problems and all that we had been through. I was happy to get away for a few days.

The day before I left, I met with one of the pastors from my church. He was a great guy, a sounding board and a tremendous help as I began the hard work of personal growth.

He was one of the two pastors that visited me when I was a patient at Kaiser Hospital. We began meeting on a fairly regular basis once I recovered a bit from the second Cellulitis infection.

Over a steaming mocha, I shared that I wanted to write Michele some kind of note before I left, urging her to consider the notion of us sitting down and beginning to talk about our problems. I thought she could read it and ponder the contents for a few days without me being around.

But Pastor had a totally different take on the matter. What he shared caused me to completely rethink my plan.

"You are good with words, Rob. There's no question about that. But right now, your words would mean nothing to Michele. She won't even hear you."

"What?"

"Are you familiar with the concept of love languages?"

"Yes. I've never read anything about them, but I'm familiar with the concept."

"You need to figure out what love language Michele speaks and communicate with her in that fashion. Do you know what love language she speaks—what language you speak?"

I had to think about that question for a few moments. Pastor mentioned five types of love languages: words of affirmation, quality time, receiving gifts, acts of service, and physical touch.

"Historically I have given Michele purple Iris flowers, sometimes for special occasions but at times just for the fun of it. She has always appreciated them. So I'm thinking the 'receiving gifts' language is one that we both speak."

"Okay. That's a good place to start," he said.

"Beyond flowers and really good chocolate, I know Michele appreciates coming home to a kitchen sink free of dirty dishes. I've tried to take care of that type of thing as much as possible. So 'acts of service' might be a language she speaks."

"She may just need more time. The important thing is to keep speaking the right language. You might be speaking English, but right now Michele can only understand Portuguese."

A letter was pointless.

My pastor's counsel that morning went a long way in steering me onto a better course. At one point in our conversation, he grabbed his umbrella and set it on the table in front of me.

"There. That's what you should do for Michele. Do something, and don't say a word. Find something you know she would appreciate and simply give it to her. This way you can send the message you were thinking about her before you left for your trip."

"Okay. That works for me. I can do that."

"Good. And don't forget your girls. They will need to know you were thinking of them as well, and not abandoning them during the holiday weekend."

Wise counsel. I took it to heart.

When we wrapped up our meeting, I went to a shop and bought Michele a big bouquet of purple Iris. At another store, I found little snowman Christmas ornaments with the girl's names imprinted on them. I brought those goodies back to my office and packed for the trip.

On Thanksgiving morning, I was up early to pack the last of my gear. Kristen was still asleep. Michele was awake, reading a book in bed.

The last thing I did before leaving was place the vase full of flowers for Michele and the two small boxes containing the ornaments for the girls on the kitchen counter. I stopped by Michele's room and wished her a Happy Thanksgiving, then I headed out the door.

A couple hours later, I stopped in Vacaville off Interstate 80 for a cup of coffee and a stretch of the legs. It was my "halfway point" in the trip. When I checked my phone, there was a new message from Kristen.

"I love you Dad. The ornament is so cool. Have a great Thanksgiving. Love you."

It made my day.

With Lauren living up the peninsula with her grandparents, I'm not sure when she received her ornament, but we exchanged a Happy Thanksgiving text message later in the day.

The drive north on Interstate 5 during the latter part of the year was beautiful. East of the Bay Area, and extending north to the Oregon border, the California landscape is quite rural, part of the state's agricultural heartland. Though the outside air temperature hovered in the mid-forties, a warm morning sun cast long shadows across fruit and nut orchards and open farmland as far as my eye could see.

As I drew closer to Cottonwood, I had a beautiful view due north of Mt. Shasta, a 14,411-foot high volcanic mountain. It sat at the southern end of the Cascade Range that extended from northern California, through Oregon and into Washington State.

Shasta was crusted with snow and lit up in vivid sunlight, like a bride on her wedding day.

To the east, Mt. Lassen, another volcanic peak in the Cascade Range, rose to 10,457 feet. The foothills at the lower elevations were dusted with fresh snow, as were the peaks of the Trinity Range to the west.

Breathtaking.

It didn't take long for the concerns swirling around in my head to vanish, replaced by a simple appreciation for the natural beauty of my surroundings.

I pulled into Lou's driveway at 12:00 noon sharp. There was hardly any traffic on the road, so even with my stop for coffee I made the trip in four hours flat. Lou greeted me with a big smile and a hug.

It was good to be with my friend and fellow traveler on the path of faith. Lou was like a brother to me. Our friendship had a twenty-five year history, back to a time when both of us had hair.

Lou's house was filled with the delightful smells of the season; a "Turducken" (a chicken stuffed inside a duck, stuffed inside a turkey) was cooking in the oven. Sweet potatoes, cole slaw, green beans, mashed potatoes and gravy, and hot rolls were staged on a serving table. It felt like Thanksgiving.

The gathering around the table that afternoon included Lou and his wife Penny, their daughter, and a wonderful couple, long time friends of Lou and Penny from their days living in southern California, who made the trip north for the weekend, as I had.

It didn't take long before we were all carrying on like old friends.

The laughter and conversation came easily, as did meaningful conversations about what we were thankful for, the challenges of marital relationships, faith, and how we had faced various medical challenges in our lives.

Powerful stuff. I felt like God was sitting there with us. My hope is he had a big grin on his face as he listened to our conversations. I could hear him cheering us on.

"There you go gang. Now you are chewing on the 'stuff' of life. Keep working it out. I have you in my grip."

124

The Rockets Red Glare

Model rocketry was a childhood hobby I rediscovered in 2005. I began building kits, but I also created custom designs. Lou and I had launched rockets on a couple occasions prior to my relapse. We were both looking forward to the day we could get back to that fun.

We always came home following a launch with our clothes musty and smelling like rotten eggs from the burnt potassium nitrate, carbon, and sulfur that burned when the engines were ignited.

We launched our rockets at a Middle school just a mile or so from his place in Cottonwood. There was a gigantic field that allowed us to launch to fairly respectable altitudes and still recover the rockets (relatively) unscathed.

I designed several new rockets during my long period of recovery. On days when I felt pretty good, I refined the designs and created the templates and patterns needed for construction.

Eventually I had the designs fleshed out and wasted no time in building the prototypes and getting them flight-ready. They sat quietly in my office, waiting for their first launch.

For several weeks prior to Thanksgiving, Lou and I talked about when we might be able to launch. It had been more than two years since we were last out on the field on a beautiful day in May of 2008. We called it "SpringBlast." Five months after we sent those birds aloft, I was diagnosed with the relapse. From that point on, my favorite hobby and the life I knew were put on hold.

As the Thanksgiving holiday drew near, I finalized plans with Lou. We were amped over the possibility of catching a favorable weather window for launching the rockets on the Friday following Thanksgiving. Cold, cloudy conditions with rain were forecast for the majority of the weekend.

Friday was supposed to be a glorious day, with temperatures in the mid-fifties, zero wind, and high clouds—perfect launch conditions. I packed my rockets and range box along with my personal gear and crossed my fingers.

Following our Thanksgiving Day gathering, we were indeed blessed with a perfect day. "TurkeyBlast 2010" was a GO! We donned our coats, packed the camp chairs, and a couple folding tables into Lou's truck, and caravanned down the road to the school.

Seeing those rockets thunder skyward gave me a lot of joy. Amidst Lou's cheering and the laughter and enthusiasm from the rest of our group, I thought about all that had transpired in my life since that day in May two years prior.

Back then, Lou and I shot off our birds and yelled like giddy school kids with Michele and Penny looking on. I hadn't laughed like that in a long time.

There was something very powerful about the way the rockets blasted into the sky. The custom designs provided a special thrill—especially since they flew straight and true as intended!

But even if they hadn't, and things went very wrong (read: ballistic re-entry without parachute deployment and subsequent grass fire), it still would have been a fantastic day.

TurkeyBlast 2010 was a big success. It was a beautiful day in God's country, laughing and carrying on with dear friends, some of whom had never seen a model rocket before that day. I reveled in a simple childhood pleasure. On my big list of "Best Days Ever," that day definitely holds a spot in the top ten.

From that point on, I made a conscious decision to LIVE, to get out of my four walls, go and do, and see and be. I fought so hard to get well, to get back on my feet, and amongst the living. Every day was sacred and not to be wasted.

125

Message from God

I had been home from Lou's for several days. It was such fun to be with my friends up north, celebrating the goodness of God and actually smiling and laughing, having real conversations about the stuff of life. Returning to the Bay Area, to our home, with the marital discord and tensions and hurt, brought me back to a reality I dreaded.

I was in a bad mood, sad more than angry, wondering if I had been a good father to my girls, and how bad a husband I had been. In general I was spiraling down and feeling lost and unanchored.

My youngest daughter Kristen had to write a speech for her Speech class. The assignment was to present a narrative, essentially telling a story about someone.

When she finished drafting it, she knocked on the door to the day room and asked me if I wanted to read it. I read the first couple of lines and was intrigued. "'The only real disability in life is a bad attitude.' Those words were uttered by Olympic Gold Medal Figure Skater, Scott Hamilton." I had no idea what was coming next. Her words blew me out of the water:

> "It is better to have a positive outlook on life, than waste the time you have with a negative attitude. In other words, live life optimistically. Live with the hope of having a better day each day, and do not let the sorrow of one day bring you down.

In 1989, six months after my parents had gotten married, my dad was diagnosed with Leukemia. He battled the cancer and was pronounced in remission in 1992.

One day in October of my freshman year, my dad came to me with tears in his eyes. He told me the cancer had come back, and he would be going in to start treatment the next day.

What my dad also told me was that he was going to fight this cancer till the end, because he had everything to live for.

For nearly two years now my dad has been in and out of the hospital, coming home each time not only with a big hug for each of us, but also with a look in his eyes that said everything, in time, will get better.

Between radiation treatments, surgeries, a ton of different pills to take, and one very big bone marrow transplant, my dad is finally home now, with only minor delays here and there that bring him back to the hospital.

My dad's disability doesn't stop him from enjoying Christmas or birthdays or Father's day, but rather makes him realize how thankful he is for all the small things in life we seem to overlook everyday.

Throughout these past two years my dad has kept his head up the whole way, even when things seemed like they couldn't get any worse. These days I seem to hear him encouraging me to do more stuff and enjoy life as much as I can.

His most common response to me when I ask to do something is, "Oh sure, you only live once!" Before, I would've seen this as a sarcastic or cliché thing for my dad to say, but now I see it as someone who knows from experience, telling me that you never know what's going to be around the next bend, so take a risk, do something with your life, have fun.

What I've learned from watching my dad go through this experience is to never let any setback, big or small, affect the way you live your life. Life is full of surprises. My dad never expected to get cancer, just as my parents never expected to have children after all the treatment.

Have the past couple of years been difficult? Difficult, to say the least. But have they made us all take a step back and realize what's really important? It doesn't matter how many gifts you get on Christmas. It doesn't matter if you have your own car, or the best version of a cell phone.

What really matters is that we accept life for what it brings us, and we keep a good attitude even when it brings us something we didn't want. My dad has been the best dad and the best role model for me to look up to, and I'm extremely thankful for him.

'The only real disability in life is a bad attitude.' —Scott Hamilton."

The words Kris put to paper were much more than an assignment for her speech class. They were a message from the lips of God. God knew I needed to read those words and have that message burned into my heart.

126

Distance, Time, and Drano

I spent much of Saturday, December 11th restless and frustrated. The sink in the bathroom off our "master" bedroom, if a 10 x 12 foot room could be called that, developed some type of clog. It had been slow to drain for a couple weeks. We poured bleach down the pipe and flushed with hot tap water, spent lots of money on Drano and other products, but nothing cleared the blockage.

When I left the house on Thanksgiving morning, I left the sink full of water, draining slowly. I figured I would just deal with it once and for all after the holiday. While I was away, Michele poured more Drano and hot water down the drain and cleared the clog.

After using the sink a couple times when I returned home, it stopped up once again. I gave the Drano a few more tries. No joy. We needed to snake the line, or call a plumber or sacrifice a chicken, or something.

Staring at the standing water in the sink, I realized Michele and I had spent more time talking, and invested more time and energy into unclogging the stupid drain than we had ever spent talking about our crumbling relationship.

The drain? Priority one. But it had been a year and four days since Michele sent me the email, stating she wanted to "open a dialogue" about our relationship. A year and four days.

I wondered how long were we supposed to keep living under these conditions? *Couldn't we sit down and begin to talk about our situation?*

127

Massive Retch

I had hoped by the time Christmas rolled around, things would be better; my health would be better and my marriage as well. I suppose one out of two ain't bad. I felt like a million bucks physically, but I was really down over how the Christmas holiday was playing out.

Michele and the girls, and the rest of her family would be leaving Christmas Day for a cabin in the Gold Country to enjoy a few days in the snow. I would fly solo at home.

I wanted to take my girls out for lunch on Christmas Eve. Lauren was down with a bad cold and couldn't make it, but Kris was up for the lunch run, and we enjoyed a really good time at one of our favorite spots.

Early in the evening, Michele and Kristen left to meet the rest of the family for a Christmas Eve service at a church up the peninsula. My hopes sank. I felt like the coming year would bring only more of the same brokenness and dysfunction.

I went out to my office. I was hacked off and thought writing a bit might help me clear my head. I'm a big fan of anagrams, words or phrases created by rearranging the letters in other words or phrases.

Often I find myself running different words and phrases through on-line anagram generators to see what bubbles to the surface. Sometimes the results were very intriguing, and often the catalyst for a good laugh or unique story content.

In my mind, it was looking like Christmas was going to stink. In a moment of pathetic, lonely frustration, I typed "Christmas Eve" into one such anagram generator and slowly scrolled through the long list of results. One phrase jumped right off the screen.

"Massive Retch."

How interesting. Really, the antithesis of what Christmas Eve was supposed to be. If there was ever a time each year when our stomachs shouldn't be in knots over the things in this life that torment us, it was Christmas Eve. But that is how I felt.

In all honesty, that was a choice I made. I could have directed my mind and my spirit towards the positive, the hopeful, but I allowed my frustrations to get the best of me.

Christmas Eve, up to that point, was a massive retch. I planned on attending the candlelight service at our church later that night, but I had a chip on my shoulder the size of Cleveland. I felt sorry for myself, and I was mad at Michele. Merry Christmas!

Christmas was not supposed to stink. It was not supposed to be a massive retch.

I wanted the Norman Rockwell painting. I got Picasso instead.

I was done trying to be joyful in spite of circumstances, done living with every aspect of my life in constant flux, done watching our family fall apart and our traditions crumble away. I yelled at God from the confines of my backyard office.

Can I just have my life back, please? Can we just be DONE with all the marital strife? Can Michele and I just be friends like we used to be? Can we get past the hurt, past the pain, past the long list of grievances and work through them like two grownups? Can you not work a miracle in our lives? God help me keep my sanity. It's about gone.

Massive Retch!

Curious about what other truths my query may have revealed, I scrolled to the bottom of the list. God spoke.

"Save Me Christ."

Yes. Save me, Christ.

128

Stunning Detachment

I had a very painful conversation with Michele on the evening of January 6th. She told me she believed her hurts were too deep and too big to face, and she didn't see us ever restoring our relationship. Case closed.

"You need to move out," she stated firmly. I told her God was doing a major work in me, and I continued to work on my issues, that I was committed to becoming the person he wanted me to be and if it was his will, to restoring our marriage.

Michele told me she had "total peace" about her current take on our situation and her present stance. I told her I had peace as well. I wanted to fix my messes, whether our marriage survived or not.

I believed that separation and divorce would only bring about more problems than it resolved. I never used the word "divorce" in the history of our relationship. I didn't see it as a solution, but rather, a symptom of a much greater problem.

Before I concluded my conversation with her, I once again reiterated my commitment to becoming the man God wanted me to be, that I loved her deeply and was committed to working through our issues and coming out on the other end a stronger couple. That was all I could say. Nothing really mattered beyond that.

Before I could finish saying those things to her, she cut me off, reiterating her belief the hurts were too deep and had been there for too long. I ached for us, and what had been our life together. I ached for Michele.

Crushing.

It was a most difficult evening. I wanted to crawl out of my skin. I wanted lightning bolts to strike, for the voice of God to speak and proclaim his profound love and his power to help us overcome even the deepest hurts and pain. He was teaching me that lesson every single day of my life.

Michele had seen the power of God sustain us through the roughest days of my illness: the initial onset back in 1989, the relapse, the bone marrow transplant, and the many complications following my discharge.

But for whatever reason, she believed her pain and struggles were too big to overcome. I couldn't make sense of it.

Another gaping hole. Another tattered edge.

129

Game Over

The next day, I was really down. I tried to process the mindset and mentality that seemed to be driving Michele to the edge. I asked myself over and over if our situation was really that bad. *Was I some kind of beast, yet to discover the full extent of my depravity? Was I missing something painfully obvious to everyone else?*

That wasn't the feedback I received, when I first reached out for help. I really had no answers, no way to stop the constant stream of thoughts, second-guessing and wondering.

All I knew for sure was God had me in his grip. I had to keep the faith.

I was fallen and imperfect, a broken clay pot in need of his grace. I was willing to take a long, hard look at myself and engage in the difficult process of change, and allow the Lord to bring healing and restoration to my life.

I was committed to walking that path. I believed with every bone in my body God could help me work through my issues. I believed he could do the same for my marriage.

On that horrible Friday, I guess I realized for the first time I no longer knew my wife. The Michele I knew, the incredible woman I fell in love with, with the easy smile and wonderful laugh, was gone. She had checked out, and it felt as though she had already begun her new life without me.

Like so many other instances in my past—all of our pasts, I

suppose—there wasn't a darn thing I could do about it but put it all in God's hands. I had to trust that his plan for my life, for Michele's life, and for the lives of my two incredible daughters was perfect.

He would guide all of us through the present darkness and keep us on his path. But I was devastated, felt almost paralyzed, and unsure how to proceed.

An insightful pilot once said, "You can only tie the record for low-level flight."

We had tied that record.

We were at the bottom, the wreckage of our marriage and our family plowed deep into life's runway. There was only a smoldering pile of twisted metal with four occupants trapped inside, and at that moment, no fire trucks, no ambulance; no sign that help was on the way; no sense that we would all be okay.

As those cold January days passed, there were plenty of periods where I was angry and didn't know what to do with myself. Michele didn't utter a word to me unless she had to.

If I'm honest with myself, I will admit I was angry with God. *Why couldn't he just intervene in dramatic fashion? Why couldn't he just save our marriage? Come on, God! Do you really want this to end in a train wreck?*

130

Distracted

With the interpersonal struggles reaching a peak with Michele, and with my mind working overtime to make sense of it all, an important milestone crept up on me. I had been dreading February 11, which would mark our 22nd wedding anniversary.

In my mind, I had already written that day off, knowing full well, given the lay of the marital land, that there was no way on God's green earth Michele and I would be celebrating.

Part of me was okay with that, resigned to the fact things were what they were. I really didn't spend too much time wishing they were any different because after that exercise in futility, I would find myself in the same place, in the midst of the same smoldering ashes.

Why waste the mental and emotional energy? Perhaps I was finally getting a clue. I hoped that was the case.

On February 9th, I was out in my office, scheduling project deadlines and client meetings in my calendar, and also confirming the time for the appointment I had at Stanford the next day. It was time for another bone marrow biopsy.

A gal from Clinic E contacted me a couple weeks prior to set up the appointment. When she called, the significance of the timing really didn't click in my head.

I can be really thick sometimes. I had a major "duh!" moment that morning when I realized I had another year of life post-transplant in the books. It dawned on me that the very next day would mark the two-year anniversary of my bone marrow transplant. My head was slogging through a moment of mental gymnastics over the coming wedding anniversary, and then February 10th flashed across my mind in vivid color.

Two years post-transplant! Awesome. Two years… *Wait a minute,* I thought. *I can attempt contact with my donor. Oh, my gosh.* I had reached the two-year mark. *Where was my head?* I got a big, dopey smile on my face when I realized the mandatory waiting period had passed. I could finally attempt contact with the man who saved my life.

That afternoon, I contacted Melanie at Stanford Hospital. She worked in the office that coordinated donor-recipient contact *(they have an office for that)*.

"Melanie, this is Rob Henslin. How are you?"

"I'm fine, Robert. I haven't heard from you in a long while."

"You bet. I'm calling today because tomorrow will mark the two year anniversary of my transplant."

"Wow, that's great news. How are you doing?"

"I feel like a million bucks now, and I'm flying higher than a kite even more because I realized the two-year waiting period has passed."

"You're right. Oh, how exciting! Do you want to attempt contact?"

"Absolutely. I've been waiting for this day for two years. Can you hook me up?"

"Sure thing. I can fax you the necessary paperwork for you to complete."

I told Melanie I would be at Stanford's ITA Clinic E on the 10th. She faxed the paperwork to the nurse's station, and when I was finished with the bone marrow aspiration, the paperwork was waiting for me.

I returned home from the appointment with a bandage on my backside and the donor contact authorization paperwork in hand. That evening, I read through the seven-page document. Melanie's handwritten note on the fax cover page spelled out my instructions.

"Fill-in and return the second page to me at the fax number below."

Page two of that stack of paperwork was a disclosure form. *How much personal information was I willing to disclose? My first and last name, sure. My address. Yes. My phone number and email address? You bet.*

I filled in the form and put a check in all the "Yes" boxes. It felt great. It felt like the right thing to do. And then I was struck with the full weight of what I was about to do.

Through Stanford, and the National Marrow Donor Program, I was giving up all of my personal contact information to someone I didn't know, and I was choosing to do that.

All I knew about this man was that he agreed to be a donor, and he saved my life, He chose to do so in a manner that was personally taxing on him—having his bone marrow harvested rather than his peripheral stem cells.

What an amazing act of love. What an amazing sacrifice.

The latter procedure was much like donating blood; it was fairly low key. The former, a marrow harvest, was more intense for the donor, and would have left my donor feeling a little punky for a week or so.

Imagine multiple bone marrow aspirations, lots of them. They were typically performed by two doctors, working on each side of the donor's backside.

My guy went through a rather cumbersome procedure. He didn't just recline in a lounge chair while they skimmed a few cells from his blood.

Beyond that, I didn't know him. He didn't know me. I wondered if he would want to know me. I had been warned by Melanie and others at Stanford that in some cases donors are not interested in making contact with their recipients.

I hoped with all my heart that my donor would be willing to engage in some level of communication. I would have been happy with an email exchange.

I wanted to thank the man for saving my life.

I faxed the completed paperwork to Melanie. If it worked out that my donor was open to establishing contact with me, it would be the ultimate blessing. If the story was not meant to play out that way, that was fine as well. It was what it was.

Perhaps for the first time, I was completely content with that reality. But I really hoped it would work out.

It was in God's hands. Maybe that was the more important lesson I needed to learn. After sending off that fax to Melanie, I had a realization—the "big takeaway" I should treasure—my whole life was in God's hands.

With few exceptions, just about every aspect of my life: my marriage, striving to become a better human being, and my long-term health prognosis, were all quite literally up in the air.

There was nothing I could do on my own to "force" a wonderful resolution of any of those open items, those holes and annoying tattered edges. The holes were deep—a mile deep—and the tattered edges worn thin. I realized how utterly powerless I was to change that which was out of my control.

At the same time, I was filled with a sense of joy that in the midst of my mess (*and life was a mess*) incredible blessings were bestowed along the way; the simple realization of reaching (*living!*) two years post-transplant was one such blessing.

Had life been easy in that two-year timeframe? No way. Far from it. Those were the darkest days of my life. But they were in the past, and I was still alive and kicking. That's what mattered.

Michele's revelations of hurt and pain, was another blessing. That's not easy to admit, but if I'm honest with myself and God, I must acknowledge it as the truth.

Addressing her points of pain, and seeking to become a better man had me on a path of renewal and growth. I was a different man; I believe a better man, by God's grace, but I had a long way to go.

131

"Ever Been to Germany?"

Thirty days past, and I didn't hear a word from Melanie. She told me the process of notification and exchange of donor and recipient contact information could take as long as a month, perhaps longer. I tried to focus on my project deadlines. The business was showing signs of growth, so I worked as hard as I could, but couldn't work like I needed to due to fatigue.

The days passed, one by one, until Wednesday, March 23, 2011. On that day, I received a phone call that changed my life.

"Hello?"

"Hi Rob. This is Melanie. Ever been to Germany?"

"No way! Should I make plans?"

I sensed her excitement over the phone line.

"Your donor lives in Germany. He's twenty-two years old. His name is Michael."

When Melanie spoke those words to me, I lost it. I had waited two years, wondering who he was, knowing only his blood type. Suddenly, 771 days post-transplant, he became real. He had a name.

Michael was the man who saved my life.

Melanie and I talked for several minutes. I fought back the tears. The happiness in Melanie's voice was infectious. She asked how I had been doing since my transplant. I shared with her some of the challenges I had faced with complications and the difficult road I had traveled before finally feeling good enough to return to some level of work.

"I'm so excited to be able to pass on this good news to you Robert. Michael authorized the release of his full name, the town in which he lives, his email address, and his phone number."

"I just can't believe I will be able to connect with him, Melanie. This is the best day of my life. And, by the way, you have the coolest job on the planet."

"I love my job," she said, and with that we concluded our amazing conversation. I hung up the phone, leaned back in my chair, and sat quietly in the stillness of my office. I had turned down the radio when the phone rang. There was only the low hum of my computer systems in the background.

I stared at the notes I had taken as Melanie rattled off Michael's contact information. I just stared at them in disbelief. *How inspiring,* I thought, *that a young man in a small town in Germany would end up saving the life of another man, living 9200 kilometers away, on the other side of the planet.*

What a miracle. What a humbling miracle.

What would I say to this young man, who so selflessly gave of himself that I might live? I really didn't know what to do with that thought. Part of me wanted to call him right away. I glanced at the clock on the wall—3:15 p.m.. Michael was ten hours ahead of me—1:15 am Thursday morning in Germany. Had to wait. *What do I do now,* I wondered.

I grabbed the phone and called Lou. He flipped out when I told him the news.

"Are you going to call him? Call him! Write him! Oh my gosh," he exclaimed.

"Well, I don't think I can right now. It's the middle of the night over there."

I decided to just think about things and let Michael get a good night's sleep. But on Thursday, I wrote my first email to him, sending him greetings from California, and letting him know how excited I was to learn his identity, and how much I looked forward to calling him my friend.

I thanked him for saving my life.

I spent the balance of Thursday on cloud nine. The realization that a new, very positive chapter of life post-transplant was being written right before my eyes was the highest of highs. I felt so blessed to have made it that far—far enough to say thank you to my bone marrow donor. How many nights did I lay in my bed on the E1 unit, hoping I would make it; hoping I would live to see that day come?

And then it came. And it changed me forever.

132

Someone's at the Door for You

Friday morning dawned, and I was eager to check my email in hopes of finding a reply message from Michael. I wondered how my message would be received. There were plenty of emails in my Inbox: advertisements for cut-rate Canadian pharmaceuticals, miracle diet plans, newsletters from companies I'm sure I've never done business with.

There was also a notification from a dignitary from some foreign land alerting me that I had been selected to receive more than $2,000,000,000 dollars in investment windfall but nothing from Michael.

I was a bit bummed, but there was plenty of work to do, and several project deadlines breathing down my neck, so I set my mind to taking care of business. Around the middle of the afternoon, my office door opened and my youngest daughter Kristen entered.

I was on the phone with a client and gestured to her to write me a note. I thought she was leaving and would write, "Bye, Dad. I'm heading to so-and-so's house. Love you!" like she had done so many times in the past. But this time, her message was different.

"Someones at the door to see you," her note read.

I gestured back to her that if it was a sales guy, tell him to scram.

Kristen whispered, "He has an envelope for you and said he needed to hand deliver it to you."

I wasn't expecting any packages. *Uh oh...*

Fifteen minutes passed before I concluded the phone call with my client. I got up from my chair, concerned that the chap at my door had to wait so long. I had a creepy feeling come over me as I realized what that "envelope" probably contained.

I met the fellow at the door, and he asked, "Are you Robert Henslin?"

I nodded in the affirmative. "Yes I'm Robert."

"Robert, I hate to be the one to deliver this to you."

"I know, man. I appreciate that. Do you need me to sign anything?" I asked.

"Nope. I just need to hand this to you."

"Okay. Thanks for keeping it low key around my daughter."

"No problem. I didn't want to upset her," he said. "I didn't know how much she knew."

"She knows, but this might have been pretty upsetting to her."

"Alright then, best of luck to you. Maybe things will work out."

I replied. "Yes, maybe they will. It could happen. We'll have to see."

With that, the process server departed my property, and I stood on my front porch in stunned silence. Michele had filed for divorce, and the packet of documents delivered to me, was official notification that her petition had been recorded with the court.

It is what it is, I thought.

In just forty-eight hours, life had gone from the highest of highs, when I learned of my donor's identity, to the lowest of lows. My wife of twenty-two years had officially filed for divorce.

One hole filled; one new gash opened deep in my heart.

133

Time to Get Out of Dodge

I returned to my office out back, envelope in hand, closed the door behind me, sat down in my chair, and just stared at the floor for a few moments. *Okay, what's my next move? Where is my head right now?* It wasn't where I usually find it, right there with me. It had already left for the day.

I decided to wrap things up as quickly as possible, make sure my clients had all the files they needed to close out the week, and then I decided it would be best if I got out of Dodge.

I did not want to spend the weekend at home, not speaking a word to Michele and her doing the same in return. I couldn't stand the painful thought of being home when she arrived having just received official confirmation from her that our life together would be coming to a painful, bitter train wreck of an end.

No, I figured a different place hours or even days away from my home—which had suddenly become a house of pain—would be a better place to be for at least the weekend, and perhaps longer. *Hmm... where to go?* I picked up the phone, and almost without thinking, I dialed Lou's number. The phone rang a couple times, and then Lou answered.

"Hello?"

"I just got served," I said.

He replied, "Oh, buddy. I'm so sorry."

I got choked up and couldn't get too many words out.

"Come up here for the weekend, or for as long as you like," He offered.

"Okay. Will you be up?"

"Oh, you bet."

I told him I had some work to wrap up, but then I would probably hit the road. We talked for a few minutes then concluded the call so I could get back to closing out the day. An hour later, I was done.

I threw a load of laundry into the washer, packed my gear in a Duffel bag, and within a couple hours was heading out of the Bay Area for Cottonwood.

Michele had been gone all morning, I'm sure because she knew the documents would be delivered sometime that day. Even late in the day, when I pulled out of our driveway, she still wasn't around. Probably best.

I wasn't going to say a word to her, as I figured under the circumstances, something stupid might spew forth from my lips, and I would probably end up regretting it.

Eye of the Tiger? Oh yeah, I had that. I had the eyes, the fangs, and the claws.

One Day at a Time? Um, how 'bout we try fifteen minute increments for now?

I hit the road for Cottonwood, stopped halfway and parked in a Denny's parking lot *(how fitting, right?)* and called a good friend to let her know what had happened.

She listened quietly as I rambled on about the events of the day. I so appreciated her being there for me. She didn't try to solve my problem but instead encouraged me to focus on the future—the positives that at the time lay on the distant horizon—and not beat myself up about the past.

She was an amazing friend, and a very wise woman.

After about an hour, I got back on the freeway and continued my journey north. I rolled into Lou's place around midnight. He greeted me with open arms, a warm smile, and a big hug. We spent several hours that night talking about my marriage and relationships and my marrow donor, Michael.

On one level, I was flying higher than a kite over being able to make contact with him, and realize the fulfillment of a wish that had been on my heart for two years. On another level, I was at rock bottom, unsure of what the days and months ahead held in store.

That night, and through the weekend, I was hit with realizations that my life with Michele, our marriage, our family, our home, our garden, my livelihood—everything—was toast.

The thought I would need to contact an attorney to represent me in divorce proceedings just about broke me in half. Divorce is what other people did. Not me. I didn't want a divorce. I loved Michele and was committed to working my program and renewing our relationship. She was not. That was the sad, unfortunate reality.

It is what it is, Rob. Yeah, I know. But that doesn't take the pain away.

Saturday morning came early, very early. I logged a few hours of good sleep, then found myself wide awake, listening to rain pound the roof of Lou's house.

After a while, I rolled out of bed and fired up the laptop to check emails. My thoughts were all over the place, clear-headed one minute, in a fog the next.

"Message from Michael, Your Bone Marrow Donor."

The subject line jumped out at me as I scrolled through the new messages in my Inbox. Lou had stumbled out of his room and wiped the sleep from his eyes. I called out to him. He came running.

I opened the message. We laughed and cried together, as Michael became real, right before our eyes. The following is the content of his message, with some editing:

Hi Robert! First, greetings back from Germany! I am so glad to hear that all went fine for you! I don't know where to begin to write. Let's start with something about me and my family.

I'm twenty-two and live in a small village in Germany with about 5000 residents. I have a younger sister who turned eighteen last December. We live a normal family life here with my parents, who are in their mid-40s. All is fine here, and we were all waiting eagerly for a reply from you when we read the note that you wanted to get in contact with me. We had a project in our school where we could register as a bone marrow donor to help out a teacher from a nearby school who got leukemia. My classmates didn't think for too long and decided to do this to help. I was just eighteen at the time, and it didn't take long, about half a year, and I received a letter that I might be a fit person to help someone.

When I first read the letter many things were running through my head. What do I need to do now? What can happen to me? Can I die? For me, there were tons of unknowns. Than the most important thing came through my head: I can save a Life! Why am I still thinking about what can happen to me?

Then it all was clear for me, and I made the call to get more instructions. After a lot of pre-examines to see if my body was healthy, and all was fit and fine, I received a date for the transplantation. It was a nice service and went fast. 500km by car was the worst part of this :). In the evening, I had a nice meal. The next morning, the operation took only twenty-five to thirty minutes, and the next day I returned home.

Now after two years of waiting, I finally know what it was: You are fine and I am more than glad and the feeling is indescribable.

I added you right away in Facebook after I wrote the message to you. Hope we will stay in contact and all the best for you and your family. I hope you will have a long life :)

Sincerely,
Michael out of the far Germany ;)

And as a last note: Hope my English is readable and understandable for you.

I couldn't believe what I read. Michael was presented with an opportunity to save a man's life, "realized the most important thing," and set his own concerns aside in order to help me, to save me.

Selfless love.

Reading Michael's words that morning went a long way in shifting my focus to the positives in my life. There were moments where my mind wandered back to my relationship with Michele and the cloud of uncertainty that hung over my life.

But for much of my time over that long weekend, I considered the incredible gift Michael had given me, the gift of life. Is any gift more precious? Is anything more worthy of thoughtful consideration?

What an incredible guy! I wanted to thank his parents for raising such an awesome son!

Being Switzerland, remaining neutral, surrounded by good friends, and not spending a great deal of mental or emotional energy pondering my current state of affairs was good medicine. Leaving for the weekend was one of the best decisions I've ever made.

Who knew Switzerland was just four hours from home?

134

Back to The House of Pain

I returned to the Bay Area on Monday. The drive south took about six hours as I hit civilization about the time everyone decided to leave work for that day. But the hours still seemed to fly by, as my mind considered what life would look like "post-petition for divorce."

I dreaded the thought of any type of encounter with Michele, unsure as to what either one of us might blurt out of our mouths. About an hour into my drive south, I made the decision to say nothing to her upon my return.

What was there to say?

She spoke volumes when the process-server knocked on my door and handed me the short stack of officially recorded documents. It was what it was. The notion of any type of conversation between the two of us at that point was laughable.

Laughable—and tragic.

On the upside, Michael and I began to cultivate our new friendship. The donor and his recipient quickly became two friends, bonded together by blood and sharp objects. We exchanged emails, instant messages through Facebook and had video chats using Skype.

We learned we both loved to cook and favored Mexican food. Michael told me he could make a pretty decent burrito. We both loved a wide variety of music. Michael played the guitar. I used to be a drummer when I was young and had hair. We found a lot of common ground and really hit it off.

Often our conversations migrated to the weightier matters of life: his career path, relationships, his former girlfriend and his wishing they were still together, and how he hoped to find a wife someday and raise a family. We talked about how we might meet face-to-face. He offered his home in Germany to me and my family.

"We have plenty of room here," he wrote. "You will have your own little house to stay in when you come. My family is eager to learn more about you, and they can't wait to meet you."

I was honored he would extend that invitation.

I replied to Michael with the same offer.

"What if I fly you out to California? We could go tear up San Francisco, Pier 39, ride the cable cars, the whole ball of wax. Then we'll head to Disneyland!"

The microphone on Michael's computer wasn't working just then, but I watched a big smile come over his face as he read my message. He shook his head "yes" and quickly fired off a reply.

"I'm a little hesitant about flying, but heck yes, I would come to California!"

We're working on our plan. I'm not sure how it will play out, but we'll get it done. When we do, meeting Michael will be one of the best days of my life.

A blessing, beyond measure.

135

Four Hats

When Michele filed for divorce, "Husband and Wife" became "Petitioner and Respondent." I had thirty days to file my response—thirty days to find a good lawyer. I heard they could be found everywhere, but they were never on sale. I would have to pay retail, and there was no refund if I decided the one I bought didn't fit so well, or shrunk after washing.

It was time to don the "Respondent" hat. I had no idea what it would look like or how it would fit. I liked wearing the "Husband and Father" hats. They seemed to fit well. The "Patient" hat was not that comfortable, far from it. I owned two of them, and both of them left a mark.

Prior to wearing the "Recipient" hat, I couldn't really grasp what it would look like. I'd heard descriptions of it from others who had worn it, but I had no clue how it would feel and if it would be the right kind of hat for me. It was awkward and took well over a month to get used to it. It was probably the most difficult hat to wear.

But the "Respondent" hat was like nothing I had ever seen. The styling was completely foreign to me, as was the material from which it was made. The first time I laid eyes on it, I knew it was going to cost me a fortune, even though I would only wear it for a short period of time.

136

A Message from the Heart

Several days after receiving the divorce papers, I began work on a note I wanted to send to Michele. I wanted to make one last attempt to reaffirm my love for her and my commitment to becoming a better husband to her and father to our daughters. I acknowledged my past failings in both those roles and expressed my knowledge that God had forgiven me for all the mistakes of my past, by his grace.

I wrote that if she chose to re-engage and work on our marriage, I would be right there by her side to work with her. If she chose to continue on the path to divorce, I would not pursue her further and play the cards dealt me.

But my deepest wish and perhaps the most earnest prayer I've ever prayed, was that God would reach into Michele's heart and soften it, and she would choose us.

I worked on several drafts of that note, each time getting a little closer to what I thought I really wanted to say, but it was a struggle. A good friend challenged me to whittle my words down to what was really on my heart and nothing more.

After living like I had for the past year plus, I was about tapped out on "feelings" and "from the heart." It felt like all of that had been sucked out of me, and I was sputtering along on vapors with my tank empty.

I did love Michele, and I was committed to the vows I took twenty-two years prior. I felt sadness over how far our relationship had spun out of control. I was sad that the investment of our blood, sweat, and tears to build a life together was about to be discarded like old clothes donated to charity or thrown into the trashcan.

I sent my note to Michele late on a Tuesday night. After I hit the "Send" button on my laptop, I was overcome, struck with the full knowledge that was my last-ditch effort to save our marriage.

I felt like I was drifting at sea, and I had just fired the last flare from my flare gun into the starry blackness of the night sky. I had no idea if Michele would see it, let alone turn about and set her course in my direction.

I wrote from the heart, or what was left of it at the time, and hoped with everything in me she would see the flare and decide our sinking ship was worth saving.

137

Spank You Very Much

Several days passed without a reply from Michele. I wondered if she would be able to "hear" me in the few words I wrote. I wondered if the painstaking process of writing and rewriting the draft of that note several times over would pay off.

Four days after I fired the flare gun, I received her reply. It was everything I hoped it wouldn't be. I was saddened by the attitude and agenda that was painfully evident in her words.

"I will stay on the course I have set," she wrote. It was a done deal. I had to play the cards dealt me. I decided at that moment, for my own sanity, I had to close the book hard and fast on what was, because it was no more. "What was" at that time, was daunting, and it required considerable time and energy.

I had to find an attorney and out of thin air come up with monstrous amounts of cash for legal fees. I was trying to rebuild my business from the ground up after two years of non-operation, and trying to fully recover from the previous two years of battling cancer again.

Has anyone seen my life? It was just here a couple years ago.

I knew if I allowed myself to get consumed by the pain over the undoing of my marriage, I wouldn't accomplish a thing. But I did have my moments where I felt overwhelmed by all the problems. The previous two years had been such a struggle, to the point where there were days I didn't care if I lived or died.

I thought a great deal about what I had experienced during the relapse and bone marrow transplant and all the complications and ups and downs during that time. In the midst of those storms, I recalled the rather frank words, spoken by Dr. Robert at Kaiser on that morning in late October of 2008: "It is what it is."

It was pointless to bang my head against the wall and gnash my teeth over what should have been. My leukemia had relapsed. It was what it was.

The same held true for my relationship with Michele. In spite of my best efforts to address her concerns, to begin to make positive changes in my life, to accommodate as best I could her request for distance and time, she chose divorce as the solution.

It was what it was.

Getting that through my thick head was almost a daily chore. It may take a lifetime to learn that lesson. I catch myself all the time, looking back over my shoulder; looking for the life I was supposed to lead.

I see the monkeys, wide-awake, and in some cases, wreaking havoc and seemingly having their way. Perhaps there are more of them out there, still deep in slumber. I'm sure there are.

So far, in spite of my weaknesses and human failings, they haven't gotten the best of me, by God's grace. They've come close. Real close.

But I can't live my life looking over my shoulder at the monkeys and the fading images of my past, the holes and tattered edges, too numerous to recall.

Lord, grant me the *Eye of the Tiger* to face life's challenges, and help me keep looking forward. Help me to live one day at a time, hopeful for better days to come.

Epilogue

With this memoir completed, I thought back two and one half years to the day in June of 2009 when I began writing. At the time, I wanted to write a journal of the events occurring in my life; something I could give to my girls. But it became more than that. Many friends urged me to tell my story so others could be helped, perhaps even inspired by what they read. This memoir is the result of those promptings.

As my recovery from cancer continues even today, many aspects of my life remain very much up in the air and unresolved. In spite of all that, I'm driven by a new vision. That is, to do all I can to help folks dealing with cancer. I want to make a difference in the lives of people facing the challenges of bone marrow transplantation, and anyone touched by the devastation and heartache cancer brings.

With that as my focus, I volunteer time to support the efforts of the *Be The Match Marrow Registry* and the *National Marrow Donor Program* (www.marrow.org), working at donor drive events and speaking on behalf of the organization as well. I am eager to share my story, my journey with cancer, and the miracle of my bone marrow transplant. I love to tell the story about connecting with the young man in Germany who donated his marrow and saved my life. We're now the best of friends, bonded by blood.

I pray each day that God would grant me the strength and the opportunities to continue to tell my story. I want to pay forward the tremendous encouragement, love, and support I received from so many when I was fighting for my life.

Rob
San Jose, California
November 2011

Resources

Cancer Information/Education

American Cancer Society
(800) 227-2345
www.cancer.org

Leukemia and Lymphoma Society
1311 Mamaroneck Avenue, Suite 300
White Plains, NY 10605
(800) 955-4572
www.lls.org

National Cancer Institute at The National Institutes of Health
NCI Office of Communications and Education
Public Inquiries Office
6116 Executive Boulevard, Suite 300
Bethesda, MD 20892-8322
(800) 4 CANCER (422-6237)
www.cancer.gov

Patient Support Web Sites

Care Pages.com
Care Pages, Inc.
345 Hudson Street, 16th Floor
New York, NY 10014
(646) 728-9500
www.carepages.com

CaringBridge.org
1715 Yankee Doodle Road, Suite 301
Eagan, MN 55121
(651) 452-7940
www.caringbridge.org

Cancer Treatment Facilities

Cancer Treatment Centers of America
1336 Basswood Road
Schaumburg, IL 60173
(800) 641-9710
www.cancercenter.com

City of Hope National Medical Center
1500 East Duarte Road
Duarte, CA 91010
(626) 256-HOPE (4673)
www.cityofhope.org

Stanford Hospital and Clinics
300 Pasteur Drive
Stanford, CA 94305
(650) 723-4000
www.stanfordhospital.org

Be The Match Foundation / National Marrow Donor Program
3001 Broadway Street N.E.
Suite 601
Minneapolis, MN 55413-1753
(800) 507-5427
www.marrow.org